P9-APW-160

H.D.

Collected
Poems
1912~1944

Also by H.D.

End to Torment
The Gift
The Hedgehog
Helen in Egypt
hermetic Definition
HERmione
Kora and Ka
Nights
Selected Poems
Tribute to Freud
Trilogy

H.D.

Collected Poems 1912~1944

Edited by Louis L. Martz

A New Directions Book

Copyright 1925 by Hilda Doolittle
Copyright © 1944, 1945, 1957, 1958, 1959, 1961, 1969 by Norman Holmes Pearson
Copyright © 1957 by the Estate of Norman Holmes Pearson
Copyright © 1950, 1971, 1972, 1975, 1981, 1982, 1983 by Perdita Schaffner
Copyright © 1982 by the Estate of Hilda Doolittle
Copyright © 1983 by Louis L. Martz

All rights reserved. Except for brief passages quoted in a newspaper, magazine, radio, or television review, no part of this book may be reproduced in any form or by any means, electronic or mechanical, including photocopying and recording, or by any information storage or retrieval system, without permission in writing from the Publisher.

Grateful acknowledgment is made to magazines and small presses that in recent years first published much of the material gathered here as "Uncollected and Unpublished Poems (1912-1944)": *Antaeus*, Ārif Press, *Contemporary Literature*, Copper Canyon Press, *Feminist Studies*, Five Trees Press, *Iowa Review*, *Southern Review*, *The Yale Review*.

Manufactured in the United States of America
New Directions books are printed on acid-free paper.
First published clothbound in 1983 and as New Directions Paperbook 611 in 1986
Published simultaneously in Canada by Penguin Books Canada Limited

Library of Congress Cataloging in Publication Data
H.D. (Hilda Doolittle), 1886-1961.
    Collected poems, 1912-1944.
    (A New Directions Book)
    Includes index.
    I. Martz, Louis Lohr. II. Title.
PS3507.0726A6 1983   811'.52   83-6380
ISBN 0-8112-0876-1
ISBN 0-8112-0971-7 pbk.

New Directions Books are published for James Laughlin
by New Directions Publishing Corporation
80 Eighth Avenue, New York 10011

SEVENTH PRINTING

Contents

Preface   ix
Introduction, by Louis L. Martz   xi
Collected Poems (1925)   1
    Sea Garden (1916)   3
    The God (1913–1917)   43
    Translations (1915–1920)   69
    Hymen (1921)   99
    Heliodora (1924)   145
Red Roses for Bronze (1931)   209
Uncollected and Unpublished Poems (1912–1944)   307
Trilogy   505
    The Walls Do Not Fall   507
    Tribute to the Angels   545
    The Flowering of the Rod   575
Notes   613
Index of Titles   625
Index of First Lines   627

To the memory of
Norman Holmes Pearson

Preface

Our aim has been to bring together here the poems that H.D. wrote, from the time when Pound read her poems in London in 1912, up through the completion of her wartime trilogy in December of 1944. Her earlier volumes have long been out of print, and a large and important body of her poetry, mostly written during the 1930s, has remained unpublished or scattered about in magazines. To keep this volume within a manageable size we have not included H.D.'s two long dramatic pieces, the verse drama *Hippolytus Temporizes* (1927) and her translation of the *Ion* of Euripides (1937); and we have not included the poems scattered through her prose works, *Palimpsest* (1926) and *Hedylus* (1928), since these poems are best read in their prose context. We wish to express our gratitude to Perdita Schaffner, H.D.'s daughter, for permission to publish her mother's writings, and to the Beinecke Rare Book and Manuscript Library of Yale University for permission to study and publish materials from the valuable collection of manuscripts and letters by and associated with H.D., the legacy of Norman Holmes Pearson, whose belief in H.D.'s poetry led to the formation of this archive. The editor wishes to thank the staff of the Beinecke Library for many favors and courtesies performed in connection with this volume; Louis Silverstein, cataloguer of the H.D. archive, for his constant interest and advice; Peter Glassgold and James Laughlin for their constant encouragement of the project; and Claire Preston for her intelligent and indispensable help in the gathering of materials for this edition.

L.L.M.

Introduction

"I believe in women doing what they like," says Mrs. Carter in H.D.'s *Bid Me to Live.* "I believe in the modern woman." But then the author adds: "In 1913, the 'modern woman' had no special place on the map, and to be 'modern' in Mrs. Carter's sense, after 1914, required some very specific handling. 'I believe in intelligent women having experience' was then a very, very thin line to toe, a very, very frail wire to do a tight-rope act on."[1] For Hilda Doolittle, born in Bethlehem, Pennsylvania, in 1886 and reared in her mother's strict Moravian tradition, the move to London in 1911 and life in the circles of Ezra Pound, Richard Aldington, and D.H. Lawrence offered her the modern experience, along that very thin line, that very frail wire.

Her situation, as it developed, became very close to the role of Astrid that she played in the movie *Borderline*, made by Kenneth Macpherson in 1930. As H.D. explains in a pamphlet that she wrote about the movie, Astrid and her lover Thorne have come to a "borderline town of some indefinite mid-European mountain district . . . because of some specific nerve-problem, perhaps to rest, perhaps to recuperate, perhaps to economise, perhaps simply in hope of some emotional convalescence. They live as such people do the world over, in just such little social borderline rooms as just such couples seek in Devonshire, in Cornwall . . ." —places that H.D. knows well. "They are borderline social cases, not out of life, not in life . . . Astrid, the white-cerebral is and is not outcast, is and is not a social alien, is and is not a normal human being, she is borderline."[2]

Her poetry and her prose, like her own psyche, live at the seething junction of opposite forces. Whoever conceived the original jacket design for *Bid Me to Live* realized the central truth about her work; for the jacket displays the active, shifting scene where land and ocean meet. This junction is the setting for many of her earliest poems: "Sea Rose," "Sea Poppies," "Sea Violet," "Sea Gods," "Sea Iris"—these poems scattered throughout her first book, *Sea Garden* (1916), are only the most obvious examples of the basic theme of the entire volume: the "beauty" that results from the fierce clashing of natural forces, as in "Sea Poppies":

your stalk has caught root
among wet pebbles
and drift flung by the sea
and grated shells
and split conch-shells.

She cannot abide the "Sheltered Garden":

For this beauty,
beauty without strength,
chokes out life.
I want wind to break,
scatter these pink-stalks,
snap off their spiced heads,
fling them about with dead leaves . . .

O to blot out this garden
to forget, to find a new beauty
in some terrible
wind-tortured place.

Even this early volume shows the inadequacy of the term
"Imagist" when applied to this poet. For "Imagism" may
suggest a crystalline formation, static, brief, a quick moment
of apprehension, as in Pound's classic "In a Station of the
Metro" or in Lawrence's "Green"—

The dawn was apple-green,
    The sky was green wine held up in the sun,
The moon was a golden petal between.

She opened her eyes, and green
    They shone, clear like flowers undone
For the first time, now for the first time seen.

But even the poems of H.D. that Pound read in 1912 will not
fit so limited a view of Imagism. "Hermes of the Ways" was
one of these, and the crossroads that this god inhabits is
again the junction of sea and shore:

Dubious,
facing three ways,
welcoming wayfarers,

he whom the sea-orchard
shelters from the west,
from the east
weathers sea-wind;
fronts the great dunes.

Wind rushes
over the dunes,
and the coarse, salt-crusted grass
answers.

Heu,
it whips round my ankles!

It is true that her poems in *Sea Garden* tend to meet the
principles set forth by Pound, H.D., and Aldington in 1912:
she gives "direct treatment of the 'thing' whether subjective
or objective"; she tries "to use absolutely no word that does
not contribute to the presentation"—though sometimes her
exclamations overrun the mark; and as for rhythm, she
certainly composes "in the sequence of the musical phrase."
Most of the poems too will meet Pound's definition of the
"Image" as "that which presents an intellectual and emo-
tional complex in an instant of time," if we allow the
"complex" to hold the psychological overtones that Pound
intends and if the complex is created by the interaction of
many images within an "instant" of considerable duration.[3]
What is important is that the doctrines of Imagism pro-
vided H.D. with a discipline that enabled her to control the
surges that arose from the depths of her violently responsive
nature. William Carlos Williams gives us a glimpse of this
in his *Autobiography*, when he tells of a walk that he took
with H.D. through the countryside near her home outside
Philadelphia, where Ezra Pound and he (especially Ezra)
used to visit often during their student days. A thunderstorm
arose, and Williams looked for shelter. "We were at the
brink of a grassy pasture facing west, quite in the open, and
the wind preceding the storm was in our faces. . . . Instead
of running or even walking toward a tree Hilda sat down in
the grass at the edge of the hill and let it come. 'Come,
beautiful rain,' she said, holding out her arms. 'Beautiful
rain, welcome.'"[4]

Her ecstatic response to the forces of nature is characteristic: it is the union of self with nature that she creates in her famous "Oread" (1914), where the spirit of the Greek mountain-nymph comprehends the waves of the ocean as the pines of her own shore, in one dynamic and unified complex:

Whirl up, sea—
whirl your pointed pines,
splash your great pines
on our rocks,
hurl your green over us,
cover us with your pools of fir.

To live constantly at the juncture of such forces, inner and outer, to inhabit constantly the borderline—this was to be the life that lay ahead for H.D., as person and as poet.

For a time, as in "Oread" or "Hermes of the Ways," the combination of Imagist principles with Greek myths and themes served to focus her responses; Greek myths in particular served as dramatic masks and channels. But by 1916–17 the infidelities of Richard Aldington (whom she had married in 1913, after her close friendship with Pound had faltered) created a sense of betrayal that became too strong for these modes of mythic or poetic control. The story is told in a triad of poems, "Amaranth," "Eros," and "Envy," preserved in a carefully bound typescript containing only these poems and bearing on the flyleaf the inscription in H.D.'s hand: "Corfe Castle – Dorset – summer 1917 – from poems of *The Islands* series –" The date should probably be 1916, for that was the summer she spent at Corfe Castle, while Richard Aldington was beginning his military training nearby. "The Islands" was published in 1920, but it is significant that H.D. could not bring herself to publish the trio of poems, in any form, until 1924, when portions of them appeared in *Heliodora*, dispersed among other poems, and masked as expansions of fragments of Sappho. The association with the years 1916–17, with Aldington, and with "The Islands" (a poem that evokes the legend of Ariadne) gives us the necessary clues to the trio, for these are all poems that enact the anguish of a deserted woman.

The situation within the three poems is basically the same as that presented in *Bid Me to Live*, where the husband of Julia (counterpart of H.D.) has flagrantly betrayed her with a woman who, in Julia's eyes, has merely physical attractions—and earlier, there was another woman. The betrayal has arisen in large part from Julia's own frigidity, caused by the death of her stillborn child and the subsequent warning of the nurse that she must not have another child until the war had ended. The speaker of "Amaranth" refers to her apparent coolness and her failure to respond:

> I was not indifferent when I strayed aside
> or loitered as we three went,
> or seemed to turn a moment from the path
> for that same amaranth.
>
> I was not dull and dead when I fell
> back on our couch at night.
> I was not indifferent though I turned
> and lay quiet.
> I was not dead in my sleep.

She makes a valiant effort toward a generous gesture, giving her praise to Aphrodite for the love that her lover bears "for his mistress":

> Let him go forth radiant,
> let life rise in his young breast,
> life is radiant,
> life is made for beautiful love
> and strange ecstasy,
> strait, searing body and limbs,
> tearing limbs and body from life;
> life is his if he ask,
> life is his if he take it,
> then let him take beauty
> as his right.

But she cannot make that gift so easily. In the final section the effort recoils upon itself and she turns to denounce her faithless lover:

> how I hate you for this,
> how I despise and hate,
> was my beauty so slight a gift,
> so soon, so soon forgot?

And then in desperation she cries out:

> Turn, for I love you yet,
> though you are not worthy my love,
> though you are not equal to it.

"Turn back," she cries again, "before death strike, / for the goddess speaks." And what the goddess says to the man is this: the two are both poets of Aphrodite, and they belong together:

> *Turn if you will from her path*
> *for one moment seek*
> *a lesser beauty*
> *and a lesser grace,*
> *but you will find*
> *no peace in the end*
> *save in her presence.*

The first three sections of "Amaranth" (out of five) appear in *Heliodora* under the title "Fragment Forty-one / . . . *thou flittest to Andromeda.* / Sappho." The rest of the fragment is important: "So you hate me now, Atthis, and / Turn towards Andromeda."[5] For the title was not merely an afterthought: this fragment by Sappho underlies the original version of the poem, where, instead of the words "Aphrodite, shameless and radiant," the first section reads: "Andromeda, shameless and radiant," while the second section adds the other name:

> Nay, O my lover, Atthis:
> shameless and still radiant
> I tell you this . . .

Thus the attributes of the goddess are carried over subtly to describe the three mortals involved. H.D. has performed a bitterly clever adaptation: Atthis was a woman in Sappho's poetry, but the male fertility god Attis was a counterpart of Adonis—who provided the title and theme for another poem of these years.

The poem "Eros" follows directly from the cry "Turn back" at the close of "Amaranth." Now the speaker calls to the love-god in agony: "Where is he taking us / now that he has turned back?" And the "fever" of her passion leads to the most intimate account of physical love to be found in H.D.'s early poetry. But the passion cannot be kept: the lover is drifting away, again:

> Is it bitter to give back
> love to your lover if he wish it
> for a new favourite,
> who can say,
> or is it sweet?

Yet there is poetic compensation: "to sing love, / love must first shatter us."

In 1924 the last five sections of "Eros" (out of seven) appeared in *Heliodora* under the title "Fragment Forty / Love . . . bitter-sweet. / Sappho." But the first two sections were omitted; they were too personal, too intimate, for public presentation. The Greek mask had to cover the personal cry: "Once again limb-loosening Love [Eros] makes me tremble, the bitter-sweet, irresistible creature."[6]

"Envy" is directly related to the wartime threat of death to the lover: "I envy you your chance of death, / how I envy you this."

> what can death loose in me
> after your embrace?
> your touch,
> your limbs are more terrible
> to do me hurt.
>
> What can death mar in me
> that you have not?

And in this fearful context she remembers a gentle gift of violets that he had brought to her, perhaps in that nursing home in 1915 after the death of their child—an incident recorded in her unpublished "Autobiographical Notes": "R. brings huge bunch of violets."

> You gathered violets,
> You spoke:
> "your hair is not less black
> nor less fragrant,

nor in your eyes is less light . . ."
why were those slight words
and the violets you gathered
of such worth?

But the poem ends with a death wish, conceding victory to
the goddess of "Amaranth":

crushed under the goddess' hate,
though I fall beaten at last,
so high have I thrust my glance
up into her presence.

Do not pity me, spare that,
but how I envy you
your chance of death.

In 1924 three sections out of the four appeared in *Heliodora*
under the title: "Fragment Sixty-eight / . . . *even in the
house of Hades*. / Sappho." Again, the missing third section
would have revealed too much:

Could I have known
you were more male than the sun-god,
more hot, more intense,
could I have known?
for your glance all-enfolding,
sympathetic, was selfless
as a girl's glance.

In all the revisions of these poems the evidence that the
faithless lover is male has been removed; for this would not
belong to the mask of Sappho. And yet, if indeed the rest of
this last Sappho fragment was recalled by these two poet-
lovers, what a bitter sting is implied, for Sappho there
denies poetic immortality to the person addressed: "But
when you die you will lie there, and afterwards there will
never be any recollection of you or any longing for you since
you have no share in the roses of Pieria; unseen in the house
of Hades also, flown from our midst, you will go to and fro
among the shadowy corpses."[7]
It is clear, from the original version of these three poems,
that by 1916–17 H.D. was beginning to create a strongly

personal voice, breaking out of the Imagist confines, breaking through the Greek mask. One suspects that this tendency toward greater openness was encouraged by her friendship with D.H. Lawrence, which began in 1914 and ended abruptly about 1918, after they had exchanged poems and letters for several years. We shall probably never know the whole truth about this relationship, since Lawrence's letters to H.D. were destroyed by Aldington (as part of a more general destruction of letters). But from "Advent" (the extracts from her journal of Freud's treatment), from her unpublished letters, and especially from *Bid Me to Live*, we can grasp the essentials and realize how deeply Lawrence influenced her life and poetry.

Normally, of course, it would be risky to trust a work cast in the form of a novel for autobiographical facts—and with many of H.D.'s prose writings a great deal of caution should be used, since she tended to fictionize and fantasize. But *Bid Me to Live* constitutes a special case, for it was written under advice from Freud himself that she should write *history*. "I have been soaking in D.H.L. letters," she writes to her friend Bryher (Winifred Ellerman) on May 15, 1933, "not too good for me, but Freud seems to agree with me for once. Evidently I blocked the whole of the 'period' and if I can skeleton-in a vol. about it, it will break the clutch." She says that she has "the counters sorted out," but then she adds the crucial point: "the 'cure' will be, I fear me, writing that damn vol. straight, as history, no frills as in Narthex, Palimp.,[8] and so on, just a straight narrative, then later, changing names and so on." And again, after she has been reading Middleton Murry's book on Lawrence, *Son of Woman*, she writes to Bryher (May 18, 1933): "papa [Freud] seems to believe explicitly that it would be best for me to make this vol. of mine about 1913–1920 explicit." Freud, she says, thinks that her dreams show that a "bridge" has now been made in her unconscious, and that the whole psychoanalysis "now is more or less 'over' (in the primitive sense) but it will need a lot of 'guts,' (my word) my end, to get the thing down in a stern manner and not leap goat-like on the top of things in a dope-y stream of consciousness like Narthex."

Freud's advice, then, explains why *Bid Me to Live* has a style so different in its tautness, terseness, and directness, when compared with the "goat-like" style of some of her other prose works. The essential point to note here is that *Bid Me to Live* makes it plain that there was never any physical relationship with Lawrence.[9] Their relationship was, I believe, very much like Lawrence's relations with half a dozen other women—spiritual, poetical, emotional, erotic in part, but not carnal: exactly as Lawrence describes it in the letter to Cecil Gray where Lawrence includes "Hilda Aldington" among his "women," as Gray has evidently called them. For Lawrence these women represent "the threshold of a new world, or underworld, of knowledge and being. . . . my 'women' want an ecstatic subtly-intellectual underworld, like the Greeks—Orphicism—like Magdalene at her feet-washing—"[10]

Bid Me to Live also provides some glimpses of what Lawrence thought of H.D.'s poetry. Speaking of Rico (Lawrence) she writes: "You jeered at my making abstractions of people—graven images, you called them. You are right. Rafe [Aldington] is not the Marble Faun, not even a second-rate Dionysus. I wrote that cyclamen poem for him in Dorset, at Corfe Castle, where I wrote your Orpheus. But you are right. He is not Dionysus, you are not Orpheus. You are human people, Englishmen, madmen." (p. 164). Lawrence would have liked that outburst: it shows the kind of anger that he admired. The "cyclamen poem" is "The God" (1917), where the male lover is treated as a Dionysus descended to earth, flooding the speaker with the "cyclamen-purple" of passion: "cyclamen-red, colour of the last grapes." And yet there is a touch of foreboding, a sense that the poem is already an elegy: "I thought I would be the last / you would want . . ." "Your Orpheus" is apparently the poem "Eurydice" (1917), though its published form may not be the original version. Here the female speaker bitterly laments the backward glance of the Orpheus-figure who, "for your arrogance / and your ruthlessness," has defeated her return to the flowers and the light of the upper world toward which he seemed to be leading her. Now through his failure she is condemned to this place "where dead lichens drip / dead cinders upon moss of ash." Nevertheless at the close she accepts her plight with a firm reliance upon her inward strength:

> At least I have the flowers of myself,
> and my thoughts, no god
> can take that;

I have the fervour of myself for a presence
and my own spirit for light . . .

Still, if we trust *Bid Me to Live*, she has not yet grasped
what Lawrence has been trying to tell her:

> He had written about love, about her frozen altars; "Kick
> over your tiresome house of life," he had said, he had
> jeered, "frozen lily of virtue," he had said, "our languid
> lily of virtue nods perilously near the pit," he had
> written, "come away where the angels come down to
> earth"; "crucible" he had called her, "burning slightly
> blue of flame"; "love-adept" he had written, "you are a
> living spirit in a living spirit city." (pp. 138–39)

"What did he mean?" she asks. What sort of invitation is
implied? But the pre-Raphaelite imagery, with the allusion
to Rossetti's "House of Life," seems to indicate that he is
talking mainly about her poetry, about the attitudes toward
life in her poetry: it is frozen, dividing the spirit from the
earth. He seems to be urging her to strike out on her own, be
free and human, as he himself was attempting to be in his
own poetry at this time: the poems of *Look! We Have Come
Through!*—of which, Lawrence reports, "Hilda Aldington
says they won't do at all: they are not *eternal*, not sublimated:
too much body and emotions."[11]
But in 1918, or thereabouts, after she had gone off with
Cecil Gray to Cornwall, the friendship ended. Rico-Law-
rence had warned her: "Do you realize," he said, "what you
are doing?" (p. 138) What she was doing was breaking the
image, shattering the role that Lawrence had conceived for
her: the disciple, the believer, the Tree of Life that she
played for Lawrence in that charade of *Bid Me to Live*. All
this she was destroying. "'I hope never to see you again,' he
wrote in that last letter," she records in "Advent."[12] The
effect was disastrous: Pound, Aldington, Lawrence—all her
best-loved men had left her.
Then Bryher saved her, in the depths of illness and despair,
after the birth of her daughter in the spring of 1919; and the
voyage to Greece in 1920 brought back her health and her
poetry—but with another tension and still under the masks
of Greece. That painfully open poem, "I Said," written in
the winter of 1919 and dedicated to "W.B.," remained un-

published until 1982, while the borderline problems of her psyche reveal themselves guardedly in the volume *Hymen* (1921). Here the opening masque of "Hymen" seems to celebrate a bridal of the past, with manifold allusions to music that suggest a relation with someone deeply musical —and Cecil Gray was a composer. Then in the same volume we find the poem headed "Not Honey"—later given the full title: "Fragment 113 / "*Neither honey nor bee for me.*" /— Sappho."—where the speaker with reluctant memory seems to renounce male love and accept the Sapphic lyre. It is the same ambivalence that marks the much more painful "Fragment Thirty-six / *I know not what to do:* / *my mind is divided.* /—Sappho," published in *Poetry* in 1921, where the state of mind is expressed in her favorite imagery of the wave-crest:

> I know not what to do:
> strain upon strain,
> sound surging upon sound
> makes my brain blind;
> as a wave-line may wait to fall
> yet (waiting for its falling)
> still the wind may take
> from off its crest,
> white flake on flake of foam,
> that rises,
> seeming to dart and pulse
> and rend the light,
> so my mind hesitates
> above the passion
> quivering yet to break,
> so my mind hesitates
> above my mind,
> listening to song's delight.

Here is the deep center of her poetry, but it can only be dealt with through a mask; it cannot be directly explored, as it was in "Amaranth." Here is the borderline state: between old values and new, between old loves and new, between physical passion and poetical dedication.

The result, for a time, is fine poetry. But the strain was too great. She could not find the confidence to open out, as Lawrence had urged. *Heliodora* (1924) is a good volume, but much of it derives from the previous decade, as far back as 1913. Now, in the later 1920s, she tries many modes of writing: the three-act verse drama *Hippolytus Temporizes* (1927), successful only in its lyric parts; prose fiction; translations from the Greek. But her volume of 1931, *Red Roses for Bronze*, shows no development: the Greek mask is still holding, even more tightly, and, despite some excellent sequences (such as "Let Zeus Record") the struggle for expression is almost desperate in places, as in the tendency to heap up repetitions that cry out after emotion, but do not create it:

> I live,
> I live,
> I live,
> you give me that;
> this gift of ecstasy
> is rarer,
> dearer
> than any monstrous pearl
> from tropic water;
> I live,
> I live,
> I live . . .

This is pitiful, grasping for a response the words cannot command. H.D. seems to realize that she has come to the end of a road, and so, near the close of this volume, she places her "Epitaph":

> So I may say,
> "I died of living,
> having lived one hour";
>
> so they may say,
> "she died soliciting
> illicit fervour";
>
> so you may say,
> "Greek flower; Greek ecstasy
> reclaims for ever
>
> one who died
> following
> intricate songs' lost measure."

Realizing her condition, H.D. sought psychiatric help, first in London, and then in Vienna, where she consulted with Freud himself for three months in 1933 and for five weeks in 1934. The story of that treatment and its success is best told by H.D. herself in the two parts of her *Tribute to Freud*—in many ways the best introduction to H.D.'s life and writings that we possess.[13] Here all one needs to say is that Freud restored her confidence in herself as a gifted woman and renewed the ability to create a personal voice that she had begun to develop in "Amaranth," "Eros," and "Envy," so many years before.

Between 1931 and 1944 H.D. published no volumes of poetry, except for her version of the *Ion* of Euripides in 1937. To the outer world, despite a few poems that kept on appearing in periodicals, it must have seemed that she had fallen fallow. In fact she was writing a great deal, in a personal voice, and it was very good—but she was not ready to publish much of it. It all lay too close to the inmost self that she had now discovered, or recovered. When, for example, Robert Herring was pressing her hard to publish both "The Master," her poem about Freud, and "The Poet," her poem (I think) about Lawrence, she resisted violently, as she tells Bryher in a letter of November 1, 1935:

> We talked of poems and we compromised on Poet, as I said I would have none at all, and he argued, as for you, for Master and I screamed and said I will not, NOT, NOT have my analysis spoiled again . . . and that is about Freud and I will never write again . . . etc. So in the end we compromised on Poet, though I think it is too much and I don't and didn't want to be printed this time.

Much later, during the winter of 1948–49, in Lausanne, in response to the sensitive advice of Norman Holmes Pearson, she read over and sorted out "some of the hay-stack of notes and loose leaves and old MSS that Bryher brought out here," as she writes to him on January 10, 1949. And she promises, "I will do my best bravely to un-earth old poems and you do what seems indicated with them—or shelve them on the shelf. It is a good thing I know, to tidy-up and your interest is a spur and inspiration." Then on March 16, 1949, she writes to Pearson with the good news:

But now I have had typed, a series of poems, I do not "place" them, except as mile-stones on my own way. They follow, as a matter of fact, after Chatto and Windus, *Red Roses for Bronze*. They seem to follow *after* and yet are better technically, in many ways than the 1931 Chatto. Some of the poems or sections from the long-poems were published. I have noted that in the MS. I call this series, *A Dead Priestess Speaks*. That is the title of the first poem and rather describes my own feelings. I do not want to publish this, nor in a way, many of the other things I have sent. Yes – some day, I want to see my Rossetti book and some day my other Delia Alton. [The nom-de-plume she had adopted for some of her prose writings.] But I am in no rush. But I do not want to feel that I have neglected these papers—any of them. You will file or place them on that famous "shelf," and someday, we can talk about their sequence and value. I have the carbon of each of these things I have sent you, and will keep them all together. I go over them in a way I have never done with my work. I can see, taken all in all, that there is a sequence, it is my *Commedia*.

Her "sequence" seems to include both the prose and the poetry that she had sent to him, but the word also applies well to the selection and arrangement of her projected volume *A Dead Priestess Speaks*, which we present here in H.D.'s own ordering. The arrangement is not chronological. It begins with the speech of the Dead Priestess, Delia of Miletus, whose voice has come alive in the form of a personal confession. The Greek mask here is quite transparent: the prophetess is a modern woman speaking modern thoughts about herself and her psychic resurrection—presumably after the consultation with Freud (whom, she says in "The Master," she spoke with in "Miletus"—and "Delia" [Alton] was her favorite nom-de-plume). Then follows a long group of pieces dealing with Greek themes in her older mode; since parts of these were published in 1932 and early in 1933, most or all of these may have been written before the journey to "Miletus." After these follow the short lyrics of the "Sigil" series—begun with seven short and successful poems in *Red Roses for Bronze*, and now completed with a powerful sequence of twelve more "seals," each poem a demonstration of personal voice speaking of love with great conviction, subtlety, and strength. Then comes the longest and most openly personal poem of the book: "Priest," cast in the form of a frank conversation with a lover of long ago—a poem based upon her fifteen-year fixation upon Peter Rodeck (Peter Van Eck of "Advent"), whose relation to her she describes in a letter to George Plank (May 1, 1935) that provides a helpful background for the poem. She says she met Rodeck on the boat that she and Bryher took to Greece in the spring of 1920:

> He was just ten years older, an architect, ex-officer, on his way to a job in India . . . He became a symbol of everything I had not had, the perfect balance in my life, and the support and the father for Perdita. We parted very abruptly in Athens—because I hadn't any strength, had been too battered. I have held to his image all these years . . . I found out, by accident, that he had married later in India—and I never saw him till seven years after. He was the same, but then seemed ill and his wife was an invalid. She died about four years ago.
>
> He had some kind of break-down or crise and went into the church. I see him now occasionally, in fact, he seems to be filling out—you know how it is—bits in the waste-land of the pattern.[14]

Then the proposed volume concludes with "Magician"—a long and subtle evocation of the spirit of Jesus as evidenced in his effect upon his followers and audiences. This poem, however, does not derive from her Freudian sessions: it was published earlier, in January of 1933 (her sessions began in March), and the strength of the poem shows what Freud himself appears quickly to have understood: that H.D. needed chiefly the counsel that would bring forth in her the poems of the future. Since she was determined not to publish her poem on Freud, "The Master," she transferred this title to "Magician" in her later typescript, perhaps in this way indicating to herself the service of healing that the later Master had performed in Vienna. *A Dead Priestess Speaks* conveys its sense of resurrection by moving from Greek masks toward a personal voice, in a volume that moves at the same time from Greek to Christian themes.

Her typescripts show that, earlier, H.D. had experimented with another arrangement of her uncollected and unpublished poems, in at least four groupings. Most significant of all is her suggestion for "Part IV": "The Priest," "The Master," "The Dancer," and "The Poet"—all four highly personal poems and all speaking in an open voice about another human being for whom the speaker feels a strong attachment. "Priest," we may say, has exorcised the ghost of Peter Rodeck. In the typescripts the three remaining poems are grouped together under the heading "Three Poems," apparently in this order: "The Dancer," "The Master," and "The Poet." This order seems best. For "The Dancer," with its tribute to the achievement and perfection of the female artist, prepares the way for an allusion to this poem in the middle of "The Master," recognizing by implication that the knowledge of herself brought about by Freud had made possible that intrepid assertion of feminine integrity.

"The Master" reveals, with an intimacy and anguish beyond anything in her prose *Tribute*, how Freud taught her to accept and understand the ambivalent responses of her nature as a part of God's creation:

I did not know how to differentiate
between volcanic desire,
anemones like embers
and purple fire
of violets
like red heat,
and the cold
silver
of her feet:

I had two loves separate;
God who loves all mountains,
alone knew why
and understood
and told the old man
to explain

the impossible,

which he did.

But she had trouble in grasping what he taught, for she was made intensely angry by "his talk of the man-strength," and by his apparently casual and inadequate explanation, "You are a poet." Gradually, the implication is, she came to realize that to have "two loves separate" was the lot of many a creative artist (one thinks of Lawrence and of Shakespeare, in the Sonnets). "You are a poet," then, becomes the ultimate answer, the definition of her created and creative condition, and with this understanding, she says, "it was he himself, he who set me free / to prophesy." Her prophecy here is her passionate assertion of woman's integrity and independence and creative power, as represented in her erotic evocation of the Dancer:

> O God, what is it,
> this flower
> that in itself had power over the whole earth?
> for she needs no man,
> herself
> is that dart and pulse of the male,
> hands, feet, thighs,
> herself perfect.

One is bound to wonder who this dancer might be who has aroused so strong a response. Perhaps she is a composite figure, but one component in that figure may be the young singer-dancer-actress Anny Ahlers, whose performance in the operetta *The Dubarry* stirred H.D. to write a whole page of admiration in a letter of 1932.[15] But the exact identification is not so significant here as it is with the other three poems in this kind, for the Dancer is observed only in performance; the symbolism arises from her role on the stage, not from any personal relationship.

What seems more certain is that H.D. in "The Poet" has paid a calm and measured tribute to the memory of D. H. Lawrence. Many of the details in this poem are private and obscure, but enough emerges to make the identification of the male poet fairly clear. "There is death / and the dead past:" she writes, "but you were not living at all / and I was half-living"—alluding apparently to the years immediately after Lawrence's death (in 1930) when her creative powers were blocked. "I don't grasp his philosophy, / and I don't understand," she says,

but I put out a hand, touch a cold door,
(we have both come from so far;)
I touch something imperishable;
I think,
why should he stay there?
why should he guard a shrine so alone,
so apart,
on a path that leads nowhere?

She is speaking in imagination before "your small coptic temple" which

is left inland,
in spite of wind,
not yet buried
in sand-storm . . .

everyone has heard of the small coptic temple,
but who knows you,
who dwell there?

Is this a reference to the "shrine" in New Mexico, the little building at the top of a steep ascent where Frieda had placed Lawrence's ashes in April, 1935?

he couldn't live alone in the desert,
without vision to comfort him,
there must be voices somewhere.

And so she sends her voice in a final reconciliation:

I am almost afraid to speak,
certainly won't cry out, "hail,"
or "farewell" or the things people do shout:

I am almost afraid to think to myself,
why,
he is there.

It is a beautiful and significant triad, the healing Master in the center, with the flaming tribute to the female artist on the one side, and the sad, deeply affectionate memorial to the male artist on the other. "I had two loves separate." Now

Freud has set her free to prophesy. Her powers are restored and prepared to face the challenge of another borderline—the London bombing of the second war, where a whole civilization stands on the edge of destruction, where millions of ordinary people live nightly on the edge of death—and the poet shares it all.

The uncollected poems beginning with "Body and Soul" up through "Christmas 1944," with their careful dating in the wartime era, prepare the way for the climax of her career, the trilogy written in 1942-44. The first part, *The Walls Do Not Fall*, represents a series of experiments in responding to the danger and the bravery of the scene, a sequence firmly grounded at beginning and end in the actual experience of the bombing:

> pressure on heart, lungs, the brain
> about to burst its brittle case . . .
>
> under us, the earth sway, dip of a floor,
> slope of a pavement
>
> where men roll, drunk
> with a new bewilderment,
> sorcery, bedevilment:
>
> the bone-frame was made for
> no such shock knit within terror,
> yet the skeleton stood up to it . . .

But the question remains: "we passed the flame: we wonder / what saved us? what for?"

Already the opening section has begun its tacit answer to that question, as, in accord with the dedication, "for Karnack 1923 / from London 1942," the poem equates the opening of an Egyptian tomb with the "opening" of churches and other buildings by the bombs:

> there, as here, ruin opens
> the tomb, the temple; enter,
> there as here, there are no doors:
>
> the shrine lies open to the sky . . .

xxx

So too an opening happens in the mind, under the impact
of disaster:

> ruin everywhere, yet as the fallen roof
> leaves the sealed room
> open to the air,
>
> so, through our desolation,
> thoughts stir, inspiration stalks us
> through gloom:
>
> unaware, Spirit announces the Presence . . .

The fourth section presents this opening in yet another way:
reverting to her old Imagist technique, she picks up the
image of "that craftsman, / the shell-fish," and makes it
represent the tough integrity of the artist, saying, "I sense
my own limit"—and yet know "the pull / of the tide."

> be firm in your own small, static, limited
>
> orbit and the shark-jaws
> of outer circumstance
>
> will spit you forth:
> be indigestible, hard, ungiving,
>
> so that, living within,
> you beget, self-out-of-self,
>
> selfless,
>
> that pearl-of-great-price.

This is only a beginning. From here she moves out to
explore "the valley of a leaf," to remember the meaning of
"Mercury, Hermes, Thoth," inventors and patrons of the
Word. And then, "when the shingles hissed / in the rain of
incendiary," a Voice speaks louder than the "whirr and roar
in the high air," and she has her vision and dream where
"Ra, Osiris, *Amen* appeared / in a spacious, bare meeting-
house"—in Philadelphia or in Bethlehem, Pennsylvania:

yet he was not out of place
but perfectly at home

in that eighteenth-century
simplicity and grace . . .

As in Freud's study, all religions are blending into one in
her mind, though critics, she knows, will complain that
"Depth of the sub-conscious spews forth / too many incon-
gruent monsters." Nevertheless, through word-play and all
her other poetic devices, like them or not, her aim is to

recover the secret of Isis,
which is: there was One

in the beginning, Creator,
Fosterer, Begetter, the Same-forever

in the papyrus-swamp
in the Judean meadow.

This is all preliminary: the secret is not yet found. It is
discovered in the second part, *Tribute to the Angels*, a
sequence wholly unified and sustained, moving forward
confidently under the guidance of Hermes Trismegistus,
inventor of language, father of alchemy, founder of Egyp-
tian culture; and with the support of the book of Revelation,
in which she boldly and wittily finds her role as prophet
justified:

I John saw. I testify;
if any man shall add

God shall add unto him the plagues,
but he that sat upon the throne said,

I make all things new.

H.D. is remembering how the author of the book of Revela-
tion emerges in his own voice at the very end: "For I
testify unto every man that heareth the words of the proph-
ecy of this book, If any man shall add unto these things,
God shall add unto him the plagues that are written in this
book"—thus denying future prophets any function. But the

poet prefers to take her stand upon the words of Jesus himself, earlier in the book: "And he that sat upon the throne said, Behold, I make all things new. And he said unto me, Write: for these words are true and faithful." (21:5)

She writes because she has been privileged to witness an apocalyptic scene of war in the heavens such as no earlier generation had seen, and more than this, she has watched with all the others who

> with unbowed head, watched
> and though unaware, worshipped
>
> and knew not that they worshipped
> and that they were
>
> that which they worshipped . . .

that is, the very spirit "of strength, endurance, anger / in their hearts." Out of all this her visions appear: "where the red-death fell / . . . the lane is empty but the levelled wall / is purple as with purple spread / upon an altar"—but this is not the sacrifice of blood: "this is the flowering of the rood, / this is the flowering of the reed." Thus in her word-play the rod of Aaron and the cross of Christ are merged; the reed that struck Christ merges with the reed of the Nile earlier mentioned, with overtones of music and of poetry. Now the poetry shows an alchemical change, as "a word most bitter, *marah*," changes into "mer, mere, mère, mater, Maia, Mary, / Star of the Sea, / Mother," and this star changes into "Venus, Aphrodite, Astarte, / star of the east, / star of the west," as the crucible of the mind creates a jewel

> green-white, opalescent,
>
> with under-layer of changing blue,
> with rose-vein; a white agate
>
> with a pulse uncooled that beats yet,
> faint blue-violet;
>
> it lives, it breathes,
> it gives off—fragrance?

It is an image that suggests a concentration of creative power in a mind prepared to realize the miracle happening

xxxiii

in the outer world, which now in May (Maia) is re-creating
itself in the same subtle hues:

> tell me, in what other place

> will you find the may flowering
> mulberry and rose-purple?

> tell me, in what other city
> will you find the may-tree

> so delicate, green-white, opalescent
> like our jewel in the crucible? . . .

> the outer precincts and the squares
> are fragrant . . .

Thus inner world and outer world share in this power of re-
creation.

In this spirit of discovery the first half of the sequence
reaches a climax as she crosses a "charred portico," enters "a
house through a wall," and then sees "the tree flowering; /
it was an ordinary tree / in an old garden-square"—a tree
"burnt and stricken to the heart," yet flowering. This was
actual, "it was not a dream / yet it was vision, / it was a
sign"—

> a half-burnt-out apple-tree
> blossoming;

> this is the flowering of the rood,
> this is the flowering of the wood

> where, Annael, we pause to give
> thanks that we rise again from death and live.

But now the dream follows, to create a higher climax,
out of a dream interpreted in ways that she had learned from
Freud to trust. Instead of one of the seven angels of the
poem, "the Lady herself" has appeared. But who was this
Lady? Was she the Virgin Mary, as painted in the Renais-
sance with all her grace and glory and "damask and figured
brocade"? No, she was none of these, though she had
something of the pagan and "gracious friendliness / of the

marble sea-maids in Venice / who climb the altar-stair / at *Santa Maria dei Miracoli*." This joyous, teasing mood is something rare in H.D., and it continues in its tantalizing way. Her "veils were *white as snow*," to use the language of Christ's transfiguration, but in fact she bore "none of her usual attributes; / the Child was not with her." So then it was not Mary. But who then?

> she must have been pleased with us,
> for she looked so kindly at us
>
> under her drift of veils,
> and she carried a book.

This is a trap for the academic interpreter, whom she now proceeds to parody:

> Ah (you say), this is Holy Wisdom,
> *Santa Sophia*, the SS of the *Sanctus Spiritus* . . .
>
> she brings the Book of Life, obviously.

And so on and so on. But now the poet intervenes:

> she carries a book but it is not
> the tome of the ancient wisdom,
>
> the pages, I imagine, are the blank pages
> of the unwritten volume of the new . . .
>
> she is Psyche, the butterfly,
> out of the cocoon.

It is the spirit of the poet, reborn, reaching out toward the future, predicting its redemption, exulting in the victory of life over death.

The third part, *The Flowering of the Rod*, is more relaxed, even diffuse in places, though never out of control. Continuing her happy mood, the poet here creates a new myth of redemption by her story of how Mary Magdalen gained from Kaspar, one of the Magi, the alabaster jar from which she anointed the feet of Christ. It is a tale that reaches out now to cover all the "smouldering cities" of Europe— not only London, but other "broken" cities that need re-

demption, in other lands. It is a universal myth of for-
giveness and healing, a parable like that of the grain of
mustard-seed:

> *the least of all seeds*
> that grows branches
>
> where the birds rest;
> it is that flowering balm,
>
> it is heal-all,
> everlasting;
>
> *it is the greatest among herbs*
> *and becometh a tree.*

It is told in a manner that in places resembles a children's
story—but then one remembers that it is a Christmas tale, as
the date at the end reminds us: "December 18–31, 1944."

LOUIS L. MARTZ

COLLECTED POEMS
1925

Sea Garden
1916

Sea Rose

Rose, harsh rose,
marred and with stint of petals,
meagre flower, thin,
sparse of leaf,

more precious
than a wet rose
single on a stem—
you are caught in the drift.

Stunted, with small leaf,
you are flung on the sand,
you are lifted.
in the crisp sand
that drives in the wind.

Can the spice-rose
drip such acrid fragrance
hardened in a leaf?

The Helmsman

O be swift—
we have always known you wanted us.

We fled inland with our flocks,
we pastured them in hollows,
cut off from the wind
and the salt track of the marsh.

We worshipped inland—
we stepped past wood-flowers,
we forgot your tang,
we brushed wood-grass.

We wandered from pine-hills
through oak and scrub-oak tangles,
we broke hyssop and bramble,
we caught flower and new bramble-fruit
in our hair: we laughed
as each branch whipped back,
we tore our feet in half buried rocks
and knotted roots and acorn-cups.

We forgot—we worshipped,
we parted green from green,
we sought further thickets,
we dipped our ankles
through leaf-mould and earth,
and wood and wood-bank enchanted us—

and the feel of the clefts in the bark,
and the slope between tree and tree—
and a slender path strung field to field
and wood to wood
and hill to hill
and the forest after it.

We forgot—for a moment
tree-resin, tree-bark,
sweat of a torn branch
were sweet to the taste.

We were enchanted with the fields,
the tufts of coarse grass
in the shorter grass—
we loved all this.

But now, our boat climbs—hesitates—drops—
climbs—hesitates—crawls back—
climbs—hesitates—
O be swift—
we have always known you wanted us.

The Shrine

("She watches over the sea")

I

Are your rocks shelter for ships—
have you sent galleys from your beach,
are you graded—a safe crescent—
where the tide lifts them back to port—
are you full and sweet,
tempting the quiet
to depart in their trading ships?

Nay, you are great, fierce, evil—
you are the land-blight—
you have tempted men
but they perished on your cliffs.

Your lights are but dank shoals,
slate and pebble and wet shells
and seaweed fastened to the rocks.

It was evil—evil
when they found you,
when the quiet men looked at you—
they sought a headland
shaded with ledge of cliff
from the wind-blast.

7

But you—you are unsheltered,
cut with the weight of wind—
you shudder when it strikes,
then lift, swelled with the blast—
you sink as the tide sinks,
you shrill under hail, and sound
thunder when thunder sounds.

You are useless—
when the tides swirl
your boulders cut and wreck
the staggering ships.

II

You are useless,
O grave, O beautiful,
the landsmen tell it—I have heard—
you are useless.

And the wind sounds with this
and the sea
where rollers shot with blue
cut under deeper blue.

O but stay tender, enchanted
where wave-lengths cut you
apart from all the rest—
for we have found you,
we watch the splendour of you,
we thread throat on throat of freesia
for your shelf.

You are not forgot,
O plunder of lilies,
honey is not more sweet
than the salt stretch of your beach.

III

Stay—stay—
but terror has caught us now,
we passed the men in ships,
we dared deeper than the fisher-folk
and you strike us with terror
O bright shaft.

Flame passes under us
and sparks that unknot the flesh,
sorrow, splitting bone from bone,
splendour athwart our eyes
and rifts in the splendour,
sparks and scattered light.

Many warned of this,
men said:
there are wrecks on the fore-beach,
wind will beat your ship,
there is no shelter in that headland,
it is useless waste, that edge,
that front of rock—
sea-gulls clang beyond the breakers,
none venture to that spot.

IV

But hail—
as the tide slackens,
as the wind beats out,
we hail this shore—
we sing to you,
spirit between the headlands
and the further rocks.

Though oak-beams split,
though boats and sea-men flounder,
and the strait grind sand with sand
and cut boulders to sand and drift—

your eyes have pardoned our faults,
your hands have touched us—
you have leaned forward a little
and the waves can never thrust us back
from the splendour of your ragged coast.

Mid-day

The light beats upon me.
I am startled—
a split leaf crackles on the paved floor—
I am anguished—defeated.

A slight wind shakes the seed-pods—
my thoughts are spent
as the black seeds.
My thoughts tear me,
I dread their fever.
I am scattered in its whirl.
I am scattered like
the hot shrivelled seeds.

The shrivelled seeds
are split on the path—
the grass bends with dust,
the grape slips
under its crackled leaf:
yet far beyond the spent seed-pods,
and the blackened stalks of mint,
the poplar is bright on the hill,
the poplar spreads out,
deep-rooted among trees.

O poplar, you are great
among the hill-stones,
while I perish on the path
among the crevices of the rocks.

Pursuit

What do I care
that the stream is trampled,
the sand on the stream-bank
still holds the print of your foot:
the heel is cut deep.
I see another mark
on the grass ridge of the bank—
it points toward the wood-path.
I have lost the third
in the packed earth.

But here
a wild-hyacinth stalk is snapped:
the purple buds—half ripe—
show deep purple
where your heel pressed.

A patch of flowering grass,
low, trailing—
you brushed this:
the green stems show yellow-green
where you lifted—turned the earth-side
to the light:
this and a dead leaf-spine,
split across,
show where you passed.

You were swift, swift!
here the forest ledge slopes—
rain has furrowed the roots.
Your hand caught at this;
the root snapped under your weight.

I can almost follow the note
where it touched this slender tree
and the next answered—
and the next.

And you climbed yet further!
you stopped by the dwarf-cornel—
whirled on your heels,
doubled on your track.

This is clear—
you fell on the downward slope,
you dragged a bruised thigh—you limped—
you clutched this larch.

Did your head, bent back,
search further—
clear through the green leaf-moss
of the larch branches?

Did you clutch,
stammer with short breath and gasp:
wood-daemons grant life—
give life—I am almost lost.

For some wood-daemon
has lightened your steps.
I can find no trace of you
in the larch-cones and the underbrush.

The Contest

I

Your stature is modelled
with straight tool-edge:
you are chiselled like rocks
that are eaten into by the sea.

With the turn and grasp of your wrist
and the chords' stretch,
there is a glint like worn brass.

The ridge of your breast is taut,
and under each the shadow is sharp,
and between the clenched muscles
of your slender hips.

From the circle of your cropped hair
there is light,
and about your male torso
and the foot-arch and the straight ankle.

II

You stand rigid and mighty—
granite and the ore in rocks;
a great band clasps your forehead
and its heavy twists of gold.

You are white—a limb of cypress
bent under a weight of snow.

You are splendid,
your arms are fire;
you have entered the hill-straits—
a sea treads upon the hill-slopes.

III

Myrtle is about your head,
you have bent and caught the spray:
each leaf is sharp
against the lift and furrow
of your bound hair.

The narcissus has copied the arch
of your slight breast:
your feet are citron-flowers,
your knees, cut from white-ash,
your thighs are rock-cistus.

Your chin lifts straight
from the hollow of your curved throat.
your shoulders are level—
they have melted rare silver
for their breadth.

Sea Lily

Reed,
slashed and torn
but doubly rich—
such great heads as yours
drift upon temple-steps,
but you are shattered
in the wind.

Myrtle-bark
is flecked from you,
scales are dashed
from your stem,
sand cuts your petal,
furrows it with hard edge,
like flint
on a bright stone.

Yet though the whole wind
slash at your bark,
you are lifted up,
aye—though it hiss
to cover you with froth.

The Wind Sleepers

Whiter
than the crust
left by the tide,
we are stung by the hurled sand
and the broken shells.

We no longer sleep
in the wind—
we awoke and fled
through the city gate.

Tear—
tear us an altar,
tug at the cliff-boulders,
pile them with the rough stones—
we no longer
sleep in the wind,
propitiate us.

Chant in a wail
that never halts,
pace a circle and pay tribute
with a song.

When the roar of a dropped wave
breaks into it,
pour meted words
of sea-hawks and gulls
and sea-birds that cry
discords.

The Gift

Instead of pearls—a wrought clasp—
a bracelet—will you accept this?

You know the script—
you will start, wonder:
what is left, what phrase
after last night? This:

The world is yet unspoiled for you,
you wait, expectant—
you are like the children
who haunt your own steps
for chance bits—a comb
that may have slipped,
a gold tassel, unravelled,
plucked from your scarf,
twirled by your slight fingers
into the street—
a flower dropped.

Do not think me unaware,
I who have snatched at you
as the street-child clutched
at the seed-pearls you spilt
that hot day
when your necklace snapped.

Do not dream that I speak
as one defrauded of delight,
sick, shaken by each heart-beat
or paralyzed, stretched at length,
who gasps:
these ripe pears
are bitter to the taste,
this spiced wine, poison, corrupt.
I cannot walk—
who would walk?
Life is a scavenger's pit—I escape—
I only, rejecting it,
lying here on this couch.

Your garden sloped to the beach,
myrtle overran the paths,
honey and amber flecked each leaf,
the citron-lily head—
one among many—
weighed there, over-sweet.

The myrrh-hyacinth
spread across low slopes,
violets streaked black ridges
through the grass.

The house, too, was like this,
over painted, over lovely—
the world is like this.

Sleepless nights,
I remember the initiates,
their gesture, their calm glance.
I have heard how in rapt thought,
in vision, they speak
with another race,
more beautiful, more intense than this.
I could laugh—
more beautiful, more intense?

Perhaps that other life
is contrast always to this.
I reason:
I have lived as they
in their inmost rites—
they endure the tense nerves
through the moment of ritual.
I endure from moment to moment—
days pass all alike,
tortured, intense.

This I forgot last night:
you must not be blamed,
it is not your fault;

as a child, a flower—any flower
tore my breast—
meadow-chicory, a common grass-tip,
a leaf shadow, a flower tint
unexpected on a winter-branch.

I reason:
another life holds what this lacks,
a sea, unmoving, quiet—
not forcing our strength
to rise to it, beat on beat—
a stretch of sand,
no garden beyond, strangling
with its myrrh-lilies—
a hill, not set with black violets
but stones, stones, bare rocks,
dwarf-trees, twisted, no beauty
to distract—to crowd
madness upon madness.

Only a still place
and perhaps some outer horror
some hideousness to stamp beauty,
a mark—no changing it now—
on our hearts.

I send no string of pearls,
no bracelet—accept this.

Evening

The light passes
from ridge to ridge,
from flower to flower—
the hepaticas, wide-spread
under the light
grow faint—

18

the petals reach inward,
the blue tips bend
toward the bluer heart
and the flowers are lost.

The cornel-buds are still white,
but shadows dart
from the cornel-roots—
black creeps from root to root,
each leaf
cuts another leaf on the grass,
shadow seeks shadow,
then both leaf
and leaf-shadow are lost.

Sheltered Garden

I have had enough.
I gasp for breath.

Every way ends, every road,
every foot-path leads at last
to the hill-crest—
then you retrace your steps,
or find the same slope on the other side,
precipitate.

I have had enough—
border-pinks, clove-pinks, wax-lilies,
herbs, sweet-cress.

O for some sharp swish of a branch—
there is no scent of resin
in this place,
no taste of bark, of coarse weeds,
aromatic, astringent—
only border on border of scented pinks.

19

Have you seen fruit under cover
that wanted light—
pears wadded in cloth,
protected from the frost,
melons, almost ripe,
smothered in straw?

Why not let the pears cling
to the empty branch?
All your coaxing will only make
a bitter fruit—
let them cling, ripen of themselves,
test their own worth,
nipped, shrivelled by the frost,
to fall at last but fair
with a russet coat.

Or the melon—
let it bleach yellow
in the winter light,
even tart to the taste—
it is better to taste of frost—
the exquisite frost—
than of wadding and of dead grass.

For this beauty,
beauty without strength,
chokes out life.
I want wind to break,
scatter these pink-stalks,
snap off their spiced heads,
fling them about with dead leaves—
spread the paths with twigs,
limbs broken off,
trail great pine branches,
hurled from some far wood
right across the melon-patch,
break pear and quince—
leave half-trees, torn, twisted
but showing the fight was valiant.

O to blot out this garden
to forget, to find a new beauty
in some terrible
wind-tortured place.

Sea Poppies

Amber husk
fluted with gold,
fruit on the sand
marked with a rich grain,

treasure
spilled near the shrub-pines
to bleach on the boulders:

your stalk has caught root
among wet pebbles
and drift flung by the sea
and grated shells
and split conch-shells.

Beautiful, wide-spread,
fire upon leaf,
what meadow yields
so fragrant a leaf
as your bright leaf?

Loss

The sea called—
you faced the estuary,
you were drowned as the tide passed.—
I am glad of this—
at least you have escaped.

The heavy sea-mist stifles me.
I choke with each breath—
a curious peril, this—
the gods have invented
curious torture for us.

One of us, pierced in the flank,
dragged himself across the marsh,
he tore at the bay-roots,
lost hold on the crumbling bank—

Another crawled—too late—
for shelter under the cliffs.

I am glad the tide swept you out,
O beloved,
you of all this ghastly host
alone untouched,
your white flesh covered with salt
as with myrrh and burnt iris.

We were hemmed in this place,
so few of us, so few of us to fight
their sure lances,
the straight thrust—effortless
with slight lift of muscle and shoulder.

So straight—only we were left,
the four of us—somehow shut off.
And the marsh dragged one back,
and another perished under the cliff,
and the tide swept you out.

Your feet cut steel on the paths,
I followed for the strength
of life and grasp.
I have seen beautiful feet
but never beauty welded with strength.
I marvelled at your height.

22

You stood almost level
with the lance-bearers
and so slight.

And I wondered as you clasped
your shoulder-strap
at the strength of your wrist
and the turn of your young fingers,
and the lift of your shorn locks,
and the bronze
of your sun-burnt neck.

All of this,
and the curious knee-cap,
fitted above the wrought greaves,
and the sharp muscles of your back
which the tunic could not cover—
the outline
no garment could deface.

I wonder if you knew how I watched,
how I crowded before the spearsmen—
but the gods wanted you,
the gods wanted you back.

Huntress

Come, blunt your spear with us,
our pace is hot
and our bare heels
in the heel-prints—
we stand tense—do you see—
are you already beaten
by the chase?

We lead the pace
for the wind on the hills,
the low hill is spattered
with loose earth—
our feet cut into the crust
as with spears.

We climbed the ploughed land,
dragged the seed from the clefts,
broke the clods with our heels,
whirled with a parched cry
into the woods:

Can you come,
can you come,
can you follow the hound trail,
can you trample the hot froth?

Spring up—sway forward—
follow the quickest one,
aye, though you leave the trail
and drop exhausted at our feet.

Garden

I

You are clear
O rose, cut in rock,
hard as the descent of hail.

I could scrape the colour
from the petals
like spilt dye from a rock.

If I could break you
I could break a tree.

24

If I could stir
I could break a tree—
I could break you.

II

O wind, rend open the heat,
cut apart the heat,
rend it to tatters.

Fruit cannot drop
through this thick air—
fruit cannot fall into heat
that presses up and blunts
the points of pears
and rounds the grapes.

Cut the heat—
plough through it,
turning it on either side
of your path.

Sea Violet

The white violet
is scented on its stalk,
the sea-violet
fragile as agate,
lies fronting all the wind
among the torn shells
on the sand-bank.

The greater blue violets
flutter on the hill,
but who would change for these
who would change for these
one root of the white sort?

Violet
your grasp is frail
on the edge of the sand-hill,
but you catch the light—
frost, a star edges with its fire.

The Cliff Temple

I

Great, bright portal,
shelf of rock,
rocks fitted in long ledges,
rocks fitted to dark, to silver granite,
to lighter rock—
clean cut, white against white.

High—high—and no hill-goat
tramples—no mountain-sheep
has set foot on your fine grass;
you lift, you are the world-edge,
pillar for the sky-arch.

The world heaved—
we are next to the sky:
over us, sea-hawks shout,
gulls sweep past—
the terrible breakers are silent
from this place.

Below us, on the rock-edge,
where earth is caught in the fissures
of the jagged cliff,
a small tree stiffens in the gale,
it bends—but its white flowers
are fragrant at this height.

And under and under,
the wind booms:
it whistles, it thunders,
it growls—it presses the grass
beneath its great feet.

II

I said:
for ever and for ever, must I follow you
through the stones?
I catch at you—you lurch:
you are quicker than my hand-grasp.

I wondered at you.
I shouted—dear—mysterious—beautiful—
white myrtle-flesh.

I was splintered and torn:
the hill-path mounted
swifter than my feet.

Could a daemon avenge this hurt,
I would cry to him—could a ghost,
I would shout—O evil,
follow this god,
taunt him with his evil and his vice.

III

Shall I hurl myself from here,
shall I leap and be nearer you?
Shall I drop, beloved, beloved,
ankle against ankle?
Would you pity me, O white breast?

If I woke, would you pity me,
would our eyes meet?

27

Have you heard,
do you know how I climbed this rock?
My breath caught, I lurched forward—
I stumbled in the ground-myrtle.

Have you heard, O god seated on the cliff,
how far toward the ledges of your house,
how far I had to walk?

IV

Over me the wind swirls.
I have stood on your portal
and I know—
you are further than this,
still further on another cliff.

Orchard

I saw the first pear
as it fell—
the honey-seeking, golden-banded,
the yellow swarm
was not more fleet than I,
(spare us from loveliness)
and I fell prostrate
crying:
you have flayed us
with your blossoms,
spare us the beauty
of fruit-trees.

The honey-seeking
paused not,
the air thundered their song,
and I alone was prostrate.

O rough-hewn
god of the orchard,
I bring you an offering—
do you, alone unbeautiful,
son of the god,
spare us from loveliness:

these fallen hazel-nuts,
stripped late of their green sheaths,
grapes, red-purple,
their berries
dripping with wine,
pomegranates already broken,
and shrunken figs
and quinces untouched,
I bring you as offering.

Sea Gods

I

They say there is no hope—
sand—drift—rocks—rubble of the sea—
the broken hulk of a ship,
hung with shreds of rope,
pallid under the cracked pitch.

They say there is no hope
to conjure you—
no whip of the tongue to anger you—
no hate of words
you must rise to refute.

They say you are twisted by the sea,
you are cut apart
by wave-break upon wave-break,
that you are misshapen by the sharp rocks,
broken by the rasp and after-rasp.

That you are cut, torn, mangled,
torn by the stress and beat,
no stronger than the strips of sand
along your ragged beach.

II

But we bring violets,
great masses—single, sweet,
wood-violets, stream-violets,
violets from a wet marsh.

Violets in clumps from hills,
tufts with earth at the roots,
violets tugged from rocks,
blue violets, moss, cliff, river-violets.

Yellow violets' gold,
burnt with a rare tint—
violets like red ash
among tufts of grass.

We bring deep-purple
bird-foot violets.

We bring the hyacinth-violet,
sweet, bare, chill to the touch—
and violets whiter than the in-rush
of your own white surf.

III

For you will come,
you will yet haunt men in ships,
you will trail across the fringe of strait
and circle the jagged rocks.

You will trail across the rocks
and wash them with your salt,
you will curl between sand-hills—

you will thunder along the cliff—
break—retreat—get fresh strength—
gather and pour weight upon the beach.

You will draw back,
and the ripple on the sand-shelf
will be witness of your track.
O privet-white, you will paint
the lintel of wet sand with froth.

You will bring myrrh-bark
and drift laurel-wood from hot coasts!
when you hurl high—high—
we will answer with a shout.

For you will come,
you will come,
you will answer our taut hearts,
you will break the lie of men's thoughts,
and cherish and shelter us.

Acon

I

Bear me to Dictaeus,
and to the steep slopes;
to the river Erymanthus.

I choose spray of dittany,
cyperum, frail of flower,
buds of myrrh,
all-healing herbs,
close pressed in calathes.

For she lies panting,
drawing sharp breath,
broken with harsh sobs,
she, Hyella,
whom no god pities.

II

Dryads
haunting the groves,
nereids
who dwell in wet caves,
for all the white leaves of olive-branch,
and early roses,
and ivy wreaths, woven gold berries,
which she once brought to your altars,
bear now ripe fruits from Arcadia,
and Assyrian wine
to shatter her fever.

The light of her face falls from its flower,
as a hyacinth,
hidden in a far valley,
perishes upon burnt grass.

Pales,
bring gifts,
bring your Phoenician stuffs,
and do you, fleet-footed nymphs,
bring offerings,
Illyrian iris,
and a branch of shrub,
and frail-headed poppies.

Night

The night has cut
each from each
and curled the petals
back from the stalk
and under it in crisp rows;

under at an unfaltering pace,
under till the rinds break,
back till each bent leaf
is parted from its stalk;

under at a grave pace,
under till the leaves
are bent back
till they drop upon the earth,
back till they are all broken.

O night,
you take the petals
of the roses in your hand,
but leave the stark core
of the rose
to perish on the branch.

Prisoners

It is strange that I should want
this sight of your face—
we have had so much:
at any moment now I may pass,
stand near the gate,
do not speak—
only reach if you can, your face
half-fronting the passage
toward the light.

Fate—God sends this as a mark,
a last token that we are not forgot,
lost in this turmoil,
about to be crushed out,
burned or stamped out
at best with sudden death.

The spearsman who brings this
will ask for the gold clasp
you wear under your coat.
I gave all I had left.

Press close to the portal,
my gate will soon clang
and your fellow wretches
will crowd to the entrance—
be first at the gate.

Ah beloved, do not speak.
I write this in great haste—
do not speak,
you may yet be released.

I am glad enough to depart
though I have never tasted life
as in these last weeks.

It is a strange life,
patterned in fire and letters
on the prison pavement.
If I glance up
it is written on the walls,
it is cut on the floor,
it is patterned across
the slope of the roof.

I am weak—weak—
last night if the guard
had left the gate unlocked
I could not have ventured to escape,
but one thought serves me now
with strength.

As I pass down the corridor
past desperate faces at each cell,
your eyes and my eyes may meet.

You will be dark, unkempt,
but I pray for one glimpse of your face—
why do I want this?
I who have seen you at the banquet
each flower of your hyacinth-circlet
white against your hair.

Why do I want this,
when even last night
you startled me from sleep?
You stood against the dark rock,
you grasped an elder staff.

So many nights
you have distracted me from terror.
Once you lifted a spear-flower.
I remember how you stooped
to gather it—
and it flamed, the leaf and shoot
and the threads, yellow, yellow—
sheer till they burnt
to red-purple in the cup.

As I pass your cell-door
do not speak.

I was first on the list—
they may forget you tried to shield me
as the horsemen passed.

Storm

You crash over the trees,
you crack the live branch—
the branch is white,
the green crushed,
each leaf is rent like split wood.

You burden the trees
with black drops,
you swirl and crash—
you have broken off a weighted leaf
in the wind,
it is hurled out,
whirls up and sinks,
a green stone.

Sea Iris

I

Weed, moss-weed,
root tangled in sand,
sea-iris, brittle flower,
one petal like a shell
is broken,
and you print a shadow
like a thin twig.

Fortunate one,
scented and stinging,
rigid myrrh-bud,
camphor-flower,
sweet and salt—you are wind
in our nostrils.

Do the murex-fishers
drench you as they pass?
Do your roots drag up colour
from the sand?
Have they slipped gold under you—
rivets of gold?

Band of iris-flowers
above the waves,
you are painted blue,
painted like a fresh prow
stained among the salt weeds.

Hermes of the Ways

The hard sand breaks,
and the grains of it
are clear as wine.

Far off over the leagues of it,
the wind,
playing on the wide shore,
piles little ridges,
and the great waves
break over it.

But more than the many-foamed ways
of the sea,
I know him
of the triple path-ways,
Hermes,
who awaits.

Dubious,
facing three ways,
welcoming wayfarers,
he whom the sea-orchard
shelters from the west,
from the east
weathers sea-wind;
fronts the great dunes.

Wind rushes
over the dunes,
and the coarse, salt-crusted grass
answers.

Heu,
it whips round my ankles!

II

Small is
this white stream,
flowing below ground
from the poplar-shaded hill,
but the water is sweet.

Apples on the small trees
are hard,
too small,
too late ripened
by a desperate sun
that struggles through sea-mist.

The boughs of the trees
are twisted
by many bafflings;
twisted are
the small-leafed boughs.

But the shadow of them
is not the shadow of the mast head
nor of the torn sails.

Hermes, Hermes,
the great sea foamed,
gnashed its teeth about me;
but you have waited,
where sea-grass tangles with
shore-grass.

Pear Tree

Silver dust
lifted from the earth,
higher than my arms reach,
you have mounted,
O silver,
higher than my arms reach
you front us with great mass;

no flower ever opened
so staunch a white leaf,
no flower ever parted silver
from such rare silver;

O white pear,
your flower-tufts
thick on the branch
bring summer and ripe fruits
in their purple hearts.

Cities

Can we believe—by an effort
comfort our hearts:
it is not waste all this,
not placed here in disgust,

39

street after street,
each patterned alike,
no grace to lighten
a single house of the hundred
crowded into one garden-space.

Crowded—can we believe,
not in utter disgust,
in ironical play—
but the maker of cities grew faint
with the beauty of temple
and space before temple,
arch upon perfect arch,
of pillars and corridors that led out
to strange court-yards and porches
where sun-light stamped
hyacinth-shadows
black on the pavement.

That the maker of cities grew faint
with the splendour of palaces,
paused while the incense-flowers
from the incense-trees
dropped on the marble-walk,
thought anew, fashioned this—
street after street alike.

For alas,
he had crowded the city so full
that men could not grasp beauty,
beauty was over them,
through them, about them,
no crevice unpacked with the honey,
rare, measureless.

So he built a new city,
ah can we believe, not ironically
but for new splendour
constructed new people
to lift through slow growth
to a beauty unrivalled yet—

and created new cells,
hideous first, hideous now—
spread larvae across them,
not honey but seething life.

And in these dark cells,
packed street after street,
souls live, hideous yet—
O disfigured, defaced,
with no trace of the beauty
men once held so light.

Can we think a few old cells
were left—we are left—
grains of honey,
old dust of stray pollen
dull on our torn wings,
we are left to recall the old streets?

Is our task the less sweet
that the larvae still sleep in their cells?
Or crawl out to attack our frail strength:
You are useless. We live.
We await great events.
We are spread through this earth.
We protect our strong race.
You are useless.
Your cell takes the place
of our young future strength.

Though they sleep or wake to torment
and wish to displace our old cells—
thin rare gold—
that their larvae grow fat—
is our task the less sweet?

Though we wander about,
find no honey of flowers in this waste,
is our task the less sweet—
who recall the old splendour,
await the new beauty of cities?

The city is peopled
with spirits, not ghosts, O my love:

Though they crowded between
and usurped the kiss of my mouth
their breath was your gift,
their beauty, your life.

The God
1913-1917

The God

I

I asked of your face:
is it dark,
set beneath heavy locks,
circled with stiff ivy-fruit,
clear,
cut with great hammer-stroke,
brow, nose and mouth,
mysterious and far distant
from my sense.

I asked:
can he from his portals of ebony
carved with grapes,
turn toward the earth?

I even spoke this blasphemy
in my thoughts:
the earth is evil,
given over to evil,
we are lost.

II

And in a moment
you have altered this;

beneath my feet, the rocks
have no weight
against the rush of cyclamen,
fire-tipped, ivory-pointed,
white;

beneath my feet the flat rocks
have no strength
against the deep purple flower-embers,
cyclamen, wine spilled.

III

As I stood among the bare rocks
where salt lay,
peeled and flaked
in its white drift,

I thought I would be the last
you would want,
I thought I would but scatter salt
on the ripe grapes.

I thought the vine-leaves
would curl under,
leaf and leaf-point
at my touch,

the yellow and green grapes
would have dropped,
my very glance must shatter
the purple fruit.

I had drawn away into the salt,
myself, a shell
emptied of life.

IV

I pluck the cyclamen,
red by wine-red,
and place the petals'
stiff ivory and bright fire
against my flesh;

now I am powerless
to draw back
for the sea is cyclamen-purple,
cyclamen-red, colour of the last grapes,
colour of the purple of the flowers,
cyclamen-coloured and dark.

Adonis

I

Each of us like you
has died once,
each of us like you
has passed through drift of wood-leaves,
cracked and bent
and tortured and unbent
in the winter frost,
then burnt into gold points,
lighted afresh,
crisp amber, scales of gold-leaf,
gold turned and re-welded
in the sun-heat;

each of us like you
has died once,
each of us has crossed an old wood-path
and found the winter leaves
so golden in the sun-fire
that even the live wood-flowers
were dark.

II

Not the gold on the temple-front
where you stand,
is as gold as this,
not the gold that fastens your sandal,
nor the gold reft
through your chiselled locks
is as gold as this last year's leaf,
not all the gold hammered and wrought
and beaten
on your lover's face,
brow and bare breast
is as golden as this:

each of us like you
has died once,
each of us like you
stands apart, like you
fit to be worshipped.

Pygmalion

I

Shall I let myself be caught
in my own light?
shall I let myself be broken
in my own heat?
or shall I cleft the rock as of old
and break my own fire
with its surface?

does this fire thwart me
and my craft,
or does my work cloud this light?
which is the god,
which is the stone
the god takes for his use?

II

Which am I,
the stone or the power
that lifts the rock from the earth?
am I the master of this fire,
is this fire my own strength?

am I master of this
swirl upon swirl of light?
have I made it as in old times
I made the gods from the rock?

have I made this fire from myself?
or is this arrogance?
is this fire a god
that seeks me in the dark?

III

I made image upon image for my use,
I made image upon image, for the grace
of Pallas was my flint
and my help was Hephaestos.

I made god upon god
step from the cold rock,
I made the gods less than men
for I was a man and they my work;

and now what is it that has come to pass?
for fire has shaken my hand,
my strivings are dust.

IV

Now what is it that has come to pass?
over my head, fire stands,
my marbles are alert:

each of the gods, perfect,
cries out from a perfect throat:
you are useless,
no marble can bind me,
no stone suggest.

V

They have melted into the light
and I am desolate;
they have melted;
each from his plinth,
each one departs;

they have gone;
what agony can express my grief?

each from his marble base
has stepped into the light
and my work is for naught.

VI

Now am I the power
that has made this fire
as of old I made the gods
start from the rocks?
am I the god?
or does this fire carve me
for its use?

Eurydice

I

So you have swept me back,
I who could have walked with the live souls
above the earth,
I who could have slept among the live flowers
at last;

so for your arrogance
and your ruthlessness
I am swept back
where dead lichens drip
dead cinders upon moss of ash;

so for your arrogance
I am broken at last,
I who had lived unconscious,
who was almost forgot;

if you had let me wait
I had grown from listlessness
into peace,
if you had let me rest with the dead,
I had forgot you
and the past.

II

Here only flame upon flame
and black among the red sparks,
streaks of black and light
grown colourless;

why did you turn back,
that hell should be reinhabited
of myself thus
swept into nothingness?

why did you turn?
why did you glance back?
why did you hesitate for that moment?
why did you bend your face
caught with the flame of the upper earth,
above my face?

what was it that crossed my face
with the light from yours
and your glance?
what was it you saw in my face?
the light of your own face,
the fire of your own presence?

What had my face to offer
but reflex of the earth,
hyacinth colour
caught from the raw fissure in the rock
where the light struck,
and the colour of azure crocuses
and the bright surface of gold crocuses
and of the wind-flower,
swift in its veins as lightning
and as white.

III

Saffron from the fringe of the earth,
wild saffron that has bent
over the sharp edge of earth,
all the flowers that cut through the earth,
all, all the flowers are lost;

everything is lost,
everything is crossed with black,
black upon black
and worse than black,
this colourless light.

IV

Fringe upon fringe
of blue crocuses,
crocuses, walled against blue of themselves,
blue of that upper earth,
blue of the depth upon depth of flowers,
lost;

flowers,
if I could have taken once my breath of them,
enough of them,
more than earth,
even than of the upper earth,
had passed with me
beneath the earth;

if I could have caught up from the earth,
the whole of the flowers of the earth,
if once I could have breathed into myself
the very golden crocuses
and the red,
and the very golden hearts of the first saffron,
the whole of the golden mass,
the whole of the great fragrance,
I could have dared the loss.

V

So for your arrogance
and your ruthlessness
I have lost the earth
and the flowers of the earth,
and the live souls above the earth,
and you who passed across the light
and reached
ruthless;

you who have your own light,
who are to yourself a presence,
who need no presence;

yet for all your arrogance
and your glance,
I tell you this:

such loss is no loss,
such terror, such coils and strands and pitfalls
of blackness,
such terror
is no loss;

hell is no worse than your earth
above the earth,
hell is no worse,
no, nor your flowers
nor your veins of light
nor your presence,
a loss;

my hell is no worse than yours
though you pass among the flowers and speak
with the spirits above earth.

VI

Against the black
I have more fervour
than you in all the splendour of that place,
against the blackness
and the stark grey
I have more light;

and the flowers,
if I should tell you,
you would turn from your own fit paths
toward hell,
turn again and glance back

and I would sink into a place
even more terrible than this.

VII

At least I have the flowers of myself,
and my thoughts, no god
can take that;
I have the fervour of myself for a presence
and my own spirit for light;

and my spirit with its loss
knows this;
though small against the black,
small against the formless rocks,
hell must break before I am lost;

before I am lost,
hell must open like a red rose
for the dead to pass.

Oread

Whirl up, sea—
whirl your pointed pines,
splash your great pines
on our rocks,
hurl your green over us,
cover us with your pools of fir.

The Pool

Are you alive?
I touch you.
You quiver like a sea-fish.
I cover you with my net.
What are you—banded one?

Moonrise

Will you glimmer on the sea?
will you fling your spear-head
on the shore?
what note shall we pitch?
we have a song,
on the bank we share our arrows;
the loosed string tells our note:

O flight,
bring her swiftly to our song.
She is great,
we measure her by the pine trees.

Orion Dead

(Artemis speaks.)

The cornel-trees
uplift from the furrows;
the roots at their bases
strike lower through the barley-sprays.

So arise and face me.
I am poisoned with rage of song.

I once pierced the flesh
of the wild deer,
now I am afraid to touch
the blue and the gold-veined hyacinths.

I will tear the full flowers
and the little heads
of the grape-hyacinths;
I will strip the life from the bulb
until the ivory layers
lie like narcissus petals
on the black earth.

Arise,
lest I bend an ash-tree
into a taut bow,
and slay—and tear
all the roots from the earth.

The cornel-wood blazes
and strikes through the barley-sprays
but I have lost heart for this.

I break a staff.
I break the tough branch.
I know no light in the woods.
I have lost pace with the wind.

Hermonax

Gods of the sea;
Ino,
leaving warm meads
for the green, grey-green fastnesses
of the great deeps;
and Palemon,
bright seeker of sea-shaft,
hear me.

Let all whom the sea loves
come to its altar front,
and I
who can offer no other sacrifice to thee
bring this.

Broken by great waves,
the wavelets flung it here,
this sea-gliding creature,
this strange creature like a weed,
covered with salt foam,
torn from the hillocks of rock.

I, Hermonax,
caster of nets,
risking chance,
plying the sea craft,
came on it.

Thus to sea god,
gift of sea wrack;
I, Hermonax, offer it
to thee, Ino,
and to Palemon.

Sitalkas

Thou art come at length
more beautiful
than any cool god
in a chamber under
Lycia's far coast,
than any high god
who touches us not
here in the seeded grass,
aye, than Argestes
scattering the broken leaves.

The Tribute

1

Squalor spreads its hideous length
through the carts and the asses' feet,
squalor coils and reopens
and creeps under barrow
and heap of refuse
and the broken sherds
of the market-place—
it lengthens and coils
and uncoils and draws back
and recoils
through the crooked streets.

Squalor blights and makes hideous
our lives—it has smothered
the beat of our songs,
and our hearts are spread out,
flowers—opened but to receive
the wheel of the cart,
the hoof of the ox,
to be trod of the sheep.

Squalor spreads its hideous length
through the carts and the asses' feet—
squalor has entered and taken our songs
and we haggle and cheat,
praise fabrics worn threadbare,
ring false coin for silver,
offer refuse for meat.

2

While we shouted our wares
with the swindler and beggar,
our cheap stuffs for the best,
while we cheated and haggled and bettered
each low trick
and railed with the rest—

In a trice squalor failed,
even squalor to cheat
for a voice
caught the sky in one sudden note,
spread grass at the horses' feet,
spread a carpet of scented thyme
and meadow-sweet
till the asses lifted their heads
to the air
with the stifled cattle and sheep.

Ah, squalor was cheated at last
for a bright head flung back,
caught the ash-tree fringe
of the foot-hill,
the violet slope of the hill,
one bright head flung back
stilled the haggling,
one throat bared
and the shouting was still.

Clear, clear—
till our heart's shell was reft
with the shrill notes,
our old hatreds were healed.

Squalor spreads its hideous length
through the carts and the asses' feet,
squalor coils and draws back
and recoils
with no voice to rebuke—
for the boys have gone out of the city,
the songs withered black on their lips.

3

And we turn from the market,
the haggling, the beggar, the cheat,
to cry to the gods of the city
in the open space
of the temple—

we enter the temple-space
to cry to the gods and forget
the clamour, the filth.

We turn to the old gods of the city,
of the city once blessed
with daemon and spirit of blitheness
and spirit of mirth,
we cry;
what god with shy laughter,
or with slender winged ankles is left?

What god, what bright spirit for us,
what daemon is left
of the many that crowded the porches
that haunted the streets,
what fair god
with bright sandal and belt?

Though we tried the old turns of the city
and searched the old streets,
though we cried to the gods of the city:
O spirits, turn back,
re-enter the gates of our city—
we met
but one god,
one tall god with a spear-shaft,
one bright god with a lance.

4

They have sent the old gods from the city:
on the temple step,
the people gather to cry for revenge,
to chant their hymns and to praise
the god of the lance.

They have banished the gods
and the half-gods
from the city streets,
they have turned from the god
of the cross roads,
the god of the hearth,
the god of the sunken well
and the fountain source,
they have chosen one,
to him only
they offer paean and chant.

Though but one god is left in the city,
shall we turn to his treacherous feet,
though but one god is left in the city,
can he lure us
with his clamour and shout,
can he snare our hearts in his net,
can he blind us
with the light of his lance?

Could he snare our spirit and flesh,
he would cast it in irons to lie
and rot in the sodden grass,
and we know his glamour is dross,
we know him a blackened light,
and his beauty withered and spent
beside one young life that is lost.

5

Though not one of the city turned,
not one girl but to glance
with contempt toward us
that our hearts were so faint
with despair and doubt,
contempt for us that our lips
could not sing to the god of the lance—

Though not one of the city turned
as we searched through the city streets,
though the maidens gathered their veils
and the women their robes
as we passed:—

Though not one of the city turned
as we paused at the city gate,
a few old men rose up
with eyes no fear or contempt
could harden—with lips worn frail
with no words of hate.

A few old men rose up
with a few sad women to greet and to hail us,
a few lads crept to welcome
and comfort us, their white brows
set with hope
as light circles an olive-branch.

6

With these we will cry to another,
with these we will stand apart
to lure some god to our city,
to hail him:
return from your brake,
your copse or your forest haunt.

O spirit still left to our city,
we call to your wooded haunt,
we cry:
O daemon of grasses,
O spirit of simples and roots,
O gods of the plants of the earth—

O god of the simples and grasses,
we cry to you now from our hearts,
O heal us—bring balm for our sickness,
return and soothe us with bark
and hemlock and feverwort.

O god of the power to strike out
memory of terror past,
bring branch of heal-all and tufts,
of the sweet and the bitter grass,
bring shaft and flower of the reeds
and cresses and meadow plants.

Return—look again on our city,
though the people cry through the streets,
though they hail another,
have pity—return to our gates,
with a love as great as theirs,
we entreat you
for our city's sake.

7

As we lift the bright heads
of the wild flowers,
compare leaf to leaf,
as we touch the hemlock and poppy,
may our spirits released,
forget this despair and torture,
this terror and doubt.

As we lift the bright heads
of the wild flowers,
may we know that our spirits are kept
as they are, folded and wrapped
apart in a sheltering leaf.

We are veiled as the bud of the poppy
in the poppy-sheath,
and our hearts will break from their bondage
and spread as the poppy-leaf—
leaf by leaf, radiant and perfect
at last in the summer heat.

May we know that our spirits at last
will be cleansed of all bitterness—
that no one god may trample the earth,
but the others still dwell apart
in a high place
with our dead and our lost.

8

That the boys our city has lost
and the gods still dwell apart
in a city set fairer than this
with column and porch.

That the boys still dwell apart
and laugh in their gladness and shout
their challenges each to each
for the foot race or the wrestling match—

They stand in a circle and laugh
and challenge each other to meet
with jest that no shield or shape
of banner or helmet or dress—

That no banner or shield or shape
or colour of tunic or vest
can divide now or rend their hearts
as they leap toward the wrestling match,
as they strip for the race—

That the boys of the cities keep
with the gods apart,
for our world was too base
for their youth,
our city too dark,
our thoughts were too dull for their thoughts,
our heart for their hearts.

We will choose for each lad of the city,
a flower or a spray of grass—

For the lads who drew apart,
the scholar and poet we place
wind-flower or lily or wreath
of ivy and crocus shaft,
and the lads who went to slay
with passion and thirst,
we give roses and flowers of bay.

That the lads in that city apart
may know of our love and keep
remembrance and speak of us—
may lift their hands that the gods
revisit earth.

That the lads of the cities
may yet remember us,
we spread shaft of privet and sweet
lily from meadow and forest,
and the wild white lily,
and the wood-lily,
and the red shaft from the mountain-side.

10

And this we will say for remembrance,
speak this with their names:

Could beauty be done to death,
they had struck her dead
in ages and ages past,
could beauty be withered from earth,
they had cast her forth,
root and stalk
scattered and flailed—

They had trod her to death with sneers,
they had bartered her
for a piece of thin money tossed up
to fall half alloy,
they had stripped her and sent her forth.

Could beauty be caught and hurt,
could beauty be rent with a thought,
for a thrust of a sword,
for a piece of thin money tossed up
then beauty were dead.

Long, long before we came to earth,
long, long before we rent our hearts
with this worship, this fear
and this dread.

11

Could beauty be done to death—
though the swirl of the thousands cross
and eddy and fall away,

though the crowd of the millions meet
to shout and slay,

though the host of the people pass
and famish in bitterness,
state by state, people by people,
and perish—we cry:

Could beauty be caught and hurt,
could beauty be rent with a thought,
could beauty be beaten out,
O gold, stray but alive
on the dead ash of our hearth—

Could beauty be caught and hurt
they had done her to death with their sneers
in ages and ages past,
could beauty be sacrificed
for a thrust of a sword,
for a piece of thin money
tossed up to fall half alloy—
then beauty were dead
long, long before we saw her face.

Could beauty be beaten out,—
O youth the cities have sent
to strike at each other's strength,
it is you who have kept her alight.

Translations
1915–1920

From the *Iphigeneia in Aulis* of Euripides

I

Chorus of the Women of Chalkis

1

I crossed sand-hills.
I stand among the sea-drift before Aulis.
I crossed Euripos' strait—
Foam hissed after my boat.

I left Chalkis,
My city and the rock-ledges.
Arethusa twists among the boulders,
Increases—cuts into the surf.

I come to see the battle-line
And the ships rowed here
By these spirits—
The Greeks are but half-man.

Golden Menelaus
And Agamemnon of proud birth
Direct the thousand ships.
They have cut pine-trees
For their oars.
They have gathered the ships for one purpose:
Helen shall return.

There are clumps of marsh-reed
And spear-grass about the strait.

Paris the herdsman passsed through them
When he took Helen—Aphrodite's gift.

For he had judged the goddess
More beautiful than Hera.
Pallas was no longer radiant
As the three stood
Among the fresh-shallows of the strait.

2

I crept through the woods
Between the altars:
Artemis haunts the place.
Shame, scarlet, fresh-opened—a flower,
Strikes across my face.
And sudden—light upon shields,
Low huts—the armed Greeks,
Circles of horses.

I have longed for this.
I have seen Ajax.
I have known Protesilaos
And that other Ajax—Salamis' light
They counted ivory-discs.
They moved them—they laughed.
They were seated together
On the sand-ridges.

I have seen Palamed,
Child of Poseidon's child:
Diomed, radiant discobolus:
Divine Merion, a war-god,
Startling to men:
Island Odysseus from the sea-rocks:

And Nireos, most beautiful
Of beautiful Greeks.

3

A flash—
Achilles passed across the beach.
(He is the sea-woman's child
Chiron instructed.)

Achilles had strapped the wind
About his ankles,
He brushed rocks
The waves had flung.
He ran in armour.
He led the four-yoked chariot
He had challenged to the foot-race.
Emelos steered
And touched each horse with pointed goad.

I saw the horses:
Each beautiful head was clamped with gold.

Silver streaked the centre horses.
They were fastened to the pole.
The outriders swayed to the road-stead.
Colour spread up from ankle and steel-hoof.
Bronze flashed.

And Achilles, set with brass,
Bent forward,
Level with the chariot-rail.

If a god should stand here
He could not speak
At the sight of ships
Circled with ships.

This beauty is too much
For any woman.
It is burnt across my eyes.
The line is an ivory-horn.
The Myrmidons in fifty quivering ships
Are stationed on the right.

These are Achilles' ships.
On the prow of each
A goddess sheds gold:
Sea-spirits are cut in tiers of gold.

5

Next, equal-oared ships
Were steered from the port of Argos
By one of the Mekistians.
Sthenelos was with him.

Then the son of Theseus
Led out sixty ships,
Prow to prow from Attica.
A great spirit keeps them—
Pallas, graved above each ship.

6

Wings bear her
And horses, iron of hoof:
The phantom and chariot
Appear to men slashed with waves.

Fifty Bœotian ships,
Heavy with bright arms,
Floated next:
The earth-god stood at the prow
With golden-headed serpent.

Leitos, born of earth,
Guided this group of ships.

74

Ships had gathered
From ports of Phokis:
The Lokrians sent as many.
Ajax left beautiful Thronion
To lead both fleets.

7

From Mykenae's unhewn rock,
Men, led out by Agamemnon,
Served beyond the breakwater
In one hundred ships.
His brother went with him—
Lover to lover.

Insult was thrown upon both.
Helen, possessed,
Followed a stranger
From the Greek courtyard.
They would avenge this.

Nestor brought ships from Pylos.
They are stamped
With Alpheus' bull-hoof.

8

There were twelve Ænian sails:
Gouneos led the twelve ships.
He is the tribe-king.
Near him were Elis' petty-chiefs—
The common people call Epians—
And Eurytos, their great chief.

Meges brought white-wood oars
From island Taphos.
He left Echinades—
Sailors find no entrance
Across the narrow rocks.

75

Ajax of Salamis
Finished the great arc:
He joined both branches
To the far border
With twelve ships,
Strung of flexible planks.

9

I have heard all this.
I have looked too
Upon this people of ships.
You could never count the Greek sails
Nor the flat keels of the foreign boats.

I have heard—
I myself have seen the floating ships
And nothing will ever be the same—
The shouts,
The harrowing voices within the house.
I stand apart with an army:
My mind is graven with ships.

II

Paris came to Ida.
He grew to slim height
Among the silver-hoofed beasts.
Strange notes made his flute
A Phrygian pipe.
He caught all Olympus
In his bent reeds.
While his great beasts
Cropped the grass,
The goddesses held the contest
Which sent him among the Greeks.

He came before Helen's house.
He stood on the ivory steps.
He looked upon Helen and brought
Desire to the eyes
That looked back—
The Greeks have snatched up their spears.
They have pointed the helms of their ships
Toward the bulwarks of Troy.

III

1

The crowd of the Greek force
With stacked arms and with troop-ships
Will come to Simois—
The strait, furrowed deep with silver.

They will enter Troy.
The sun-god built the porticoes.
Kassandra shakes out her hair—
Its gold clasped
With half-opened laurel-shoots—
When the god strikes her
With his breath.

They will stand on Pergamos.
They will crowd about the walls.

They will lift their shields,
Riveted with brass,
As they enter Simois
In their painted ships.

Two brothers of Helen are spirits
And dwell apart in the air,
Yet the shieldsmen will take her,
And men, alert with spear-shaft,
Will carry her to the Greek coast.

And Pergamos,
City of the Phrygians,
Ancient Troy
Will be given up to its fate.
They will mark the stone-battlements
And the circle of them
With a bright stain.
They will cast out the dead—
A sight for Priam's queen to lament
And her frightened daughters.

And Helen, child of Zeus,
Will cry aloud for the mate
She has left in that Phrygian town.

May no child of mine,
Nor any child of my child
Ever fashion such a tale
As the Phrygians shall murmur,
As they stoop at their distaffs,
Whispering with Lydians,
Splendid with weight of gold—

"Helen has brought this.
They will tarnish our bright hair.
They will take us as captives
For Helen—born of Zeus
When he sought Leda with bird-wing
And touched her with bird-throat—
If men speak truth.

"But still we lament our state,
The desert of our wide courts,
Even if there is no truth
In the legends cut on ivory
Nor in the poets
Nor the songs."

IV

1

Burnished-head
By burnished-head,
Pierides sought the bride:
They touched the flute-stops
And the lyre-strings for the dance,

They made the syrinx-notes
Shrill through the reed-stalk.
They cut gold sandal-prints
Across Pelion
Toward the gods' feast.

They called Pelios
From steep centaur-paths,
And Thetis
Among forest trees:
They chanted at the feast
Where Phrygian Ganymede,
Loved of Zeus,
Caught the measure of wine
In the circle of the golden cups.

While fifty sea-spirits
Moved and paused
To mark the beat
Of chanted words
Where light flashed
Below them on the sand.

2

A centaur-herd,
Wild-horses, crowned with grass,
Swept among the feasting gods
With fir-shoots
Toward the wine-jars.

And Chiron,
Inspired by the rites of song,
Cried with a loud voice:

"From Thessaly,
The great light
Whom Thetis will beget,"
(He spoke his name)
"Will come with the Myrmidons
Spearsmen and hosts with shields,
Golden and metal-wrought,
To scatter fire
Over Priam's beautiful land."

Therefore the spirits blessed
The fair-fathered,
The Nereid,
And chanted at Pelios' feast.

3

(*To Iphigeneia.*)
Your hair is scattered light:
The Greeks will bind it with petals.

And like a little beast,
Dappled and without horns,
That scampered on the hill-rocks,
They will leave you
With stained throat—
Though you never cropped hill-grass
To the reed-cry
And the shepherd's note.

Some Greek hero is cheated
And your mother's court
Of its bride.

And we ask this—where truth is,
Of what use is valour and is worth?

For evil has conquered the race,
There is no power but in base men,
Nor any man whom the gods do not hate.

V

IPH.   It is not for me, the day,
Nor this light of sun.
Ah, mother, mother,
The same terror is cast on us both.

Alas for that Phrygian cleft,
Beaten by snow,
The mountain-hill, Ida,
Where Priam left the young prince,
Brought far from his mother
To perish on the rocks:
Paris who is called
Idaeos, Idaeos
In the Phrygian court.

Would that he had never thrived,
Would that he had not kept the flocks
O that he had not dwelt
At that white place of the water-gods:
In meadows,
Thick with yellow flower-sprays
And flowers, tint of rose,
And the hyacinth we break for gods.

For Pallas came there,
And Kypris, crafty-heart,
And Hera and Hermes, legate of god
(Beautiful Kypris,
Pallas with spear-hilt,
Hera, queen, wed with Zeus.)
It was a hated judgment, O slender-girls.
The contest of beautiful-face by beautiful-face
Has brought this:
I am sent to death
To bring honour to the Greeks.

CH.   For Ilium, for Ilium
       Artemis exacts sacrifice.

IPH.   O wretched, wretched,—
       I know you, Helen, sharp to do hurt.
       I am slaughtered for your deceit.

       O I am miserable:
       You cherished me, my mother,
       But even you desert me.
       I am sent to an empty place.

       O that Aulis had not harboured
       These beaked ships,
       Nor sheltered their brazen prows
       As they floated toward Troy:
       O that Zeus had not turned them
       Nor wafted their splendour
       Through the straits:
       For Zeus strikes different winds
       To each ship,
       So that some men laugh
       With the light flap of the sails,
       Some bend with anger
       At their work:

       Some haul up the sheets,
       Some knot the great ropes,
       Some dash through the spray
       To quick death.

       And each man is marked for toil,
       Much labour is his fate,
       Nor is there any new hurt
       That may be added to the race.

VI

IPH.   Now sing, O slight girls,
       Without change of note,
       My death-paeon and Artemis' chant.

Stand silent, you Greeks.
The fire kindles.
They step to do sacrifice
With reed-basket of salt-cakes:
I come—I free Hellas.
My father, as priest awaits me
At the right altar-step.

Hail me now.
I destroy Phrygia and all Troy.
Clasp on the flower-circlet.
Wind it through the locks just caught with it.
Bear water in a deep bowl.
Stand around the temple-front
And the altar of heaped earth.
For I come to do sacrifice,
To break the might of the curse,
To honour the queen, if she permit,
The great one, with my death.

CH.   O, mother, high-born,
Of proud birth,
Will you not weep for us?
For we may not cry out
In the splendour of this holy place.

IPH.   Slight girls, stand forth,
Chant Artemis—Artemis:
She fronts the coast,
She stands opposite Chalkis—
For spears will clash in the contest
My fame has brought
In the shelter of these narrow straits.

Hail, land of my birth.
Hail Mykenae, where I once dwelt—

CH.   (She calls upon the city of Perseos,
Built of unchiselled rock.)

IPH. —you brought me to the Greek light
And I will not hold you guilty
For my death.

CH.   Your name will never be forgotten,
Your honour will always last.

IPH. Alas, day, you brought light,
You trailed splendour
You showed us god:
I salute you, most precious one,
But I go to a new place,
Another life.

CH.   Alas, she steps forward
To destroy Ilium and the Phrygians.
A wreath is about her head,
She takes water in a dish.

She comes to meet death,
To stain the altar of the goddess,
To hold her girl-throat
Toward the knife-thrust.

The land-springs await
And the sacred bowls,
And the Greek host, eager to depart.
But let us not forget
With our past happiness,
Artemis, daughter of god,
Queen among the great,
But cry out:
Artemis, rejoicer in blood-sacrifice,
Send the force of the Greeks
To Troy and the Phrygian court.

And grant that Agamemnon may clasp
Fame, never to be forgot
Upon his brow—encircled
By Greek spear-shafts,
May he gain honour for all the Greeks.

From the *Hippolytus* of Euripides

I

THERAPONTES.
Daemon initiate, spirit
of the god-race, Artemis,
Latona's daughter,
child of Zeus,
of all maids loveliest,
we greet you, mistress:
you dwell in your father's house,
the gold-wrought porches of Zeus,
apart in the depth of space.

HIPPOLYTUS.
Of all maids, loveliest,
I greet you, Artemis,
loveliest upon Olympus:
dearest, to you this gift,
flower set by flower and leaf,
broken by uncut grass,
where neither scythe has dipped
nor does the shepherd yet
venture to lead his sheep;
there it is white and fragrant,
the wild-bee swirls across;
as a slow rivulet,
mystic peace broods and drifts:

Ah! but my own, my dearest,
take for your gold-wrought locks
from my hands these flowers,
as from a spirit.

II

CHORUS OF TROIZENIAN WOMEN.

At high-tide,
the sea—they say—
left a deep pool
below the rock-shelf:

85

in that clear place
where the women dip
their water-jars,
my friend steeped her veils
and spread the scarlet stuff
across the hot ridge
of sun-baked rocks:
she first brought word
of my mistress:

"She lies sick,
faint on her couch
within the palace;
her thin veils
cast a shadow
across her bright locks.
I count three days
since her beautiful lips
touched the fine wheat—
her frail body
disdains nourishment:
she suffers—
some secret hurt
hastens her death."

Surely, O young queen,
you are possessed
by Pan, by Hecate,
by some spirit
of the Corybantic rites,
or by Cybele
from the hill-rocks!
or have you sinned
that you suffer thus,
against Artemis?
Have you offered
no sacrificial cakes
to the huntress?

For she walks above earth,
along the sea-coast,
and across the salt trail
of the sea-drift.

Or is it that your lord,
born of Erechtheus,
the king most noble in descent,
neglects you in the palace
and your bride-couch
for another in secret?
Or has some sea-man,
landing at our port,
friendly to ships,
brought sad news from Crete?
For some great hurt
binds you to your couch,
broken in spirit.

III

PHAEDRA.   Lift my head, help me up,
I am bruised, bone and flesh;
chafe my white hands, my servants:
this weight about my forehead?
Ah, my veil—loose it—
spread my hair across my breast.

TROPHOS.   There, do not start,
child, nor toss about;
only calm and high pride
can help your hurt:
fate tries all alike.

PHAEDRA.   Ai, ai! to drink deep
of spring water
from its white source;
ai, ai! for rest—black poplars—
thick grass—sleep.

TROPHOS.	What is this you ask, wild words, mad speech— hide your hurt, my heart, hide your hurt before these servants.
PHAEDRA.	Take me to the mountains! O for woods, pine tracts, where hounds athirst for death, leap on the bright stags! God, how I would shout to the beasts with my gold hair torn loose; I would shake the Thessalian dart, I would hurl the barbed arrow from my grasp.
TROPHOS.	Why, so distraught, child, child, why the chase and this cold water you would ask: but we may get you that from deep rills that cut the slopes before the gate.
PHAEDRA.	Artemis of the salt beach and of the sea-coast, mistress of the race-course, trodden of swift feet, O for your flat sands where I might mount with goad and whip the horses of Enetas.

IV

O Spirit,
spark by spark,
you instil fire
through the sight:
to hearts you attack
you grant rare happiness!

Do not front me with grief,
yourself discord manifest!

For neither lightning-shaft
nor yet stars shot
from a distant place
can equal the love-dart,
sped from your hands,
child of God, Eros.

In vain along Alpheos,
in vain (if we defy Eros)
are the Greek altars
bright with blood,
and the Pythian rocks
with beasts slain
for Helios:
Aphrodite's child
is man's chief absolute:
he protects love's portal
and love's rite,
or ruthlessly betrays men,
destroying them
in his flight.

So at Occhalie,
that girl, chaste—
a wild colt,
mateless, uncaught—
was betrayed by Kupris:
Heracles dragged her,
a bacchante, hell-loosed,
from her palace
to his ship:
there was flame and blood spilt
for the bride-chant,
for rapture, unhappiness.

O Thebes,
high-built and chaste,
O Dirke's river-bank,
you can tell how Kupris strikes:
for with thunder-bolt,
alight at both points,
she slew the mother of Bacchus,
child of Zeus!
Ah evil wedlock! Ah fate!
she incites all to evil,
she flutters over all things,
like a bee in flight.

V

O for wings,
swift, a bird,
set of God
among the bird-flocks!
I would dart
from some Adriatic precipice,
across its wave-shallows and crests,
to Eradanus' river-source;
to the place
where his daughters weep,
thrice-hurt for Phaeton's sake,
tears of amber and gold which dart
their fire through the purple surface.

I would seek
the song-haunted Hesperides
and the apple-trees
set above the sand drift:
there the god
of the purple marsh
lets no ships pass;
he marks the sky-space
which Atlas keeps—
that holy place
where streams,

fragrant as honey,
pass to the couches spread
in the palace of Zeus:
there the earth-spirit,
source of bliss,
grants the gods happiness.

O ship
white-sailed of Crete,
you brought my mistress
from her quiet palace
through breaker and crash of surf
to love-rite of unhappiness!
Though the boat swept
toward great Athens,
though she was made fast
with ship-cable and ship-rope
at Munychia the sea-port,
though her men stood
on the main-land,
(whether unfriended by all alike
or only by the gods of Crete)
it was evil—the auspice.

On this account
my mistress,
most sick at heart,
is stricken of Kupris
with unchaste thought:
helpless and overwrought,
she would fasten
the rope-noose about the beam
above her bride-couch
and tie it to her white throat:
she would placate the daemon's wrath,
still the love-fever in her breast,
and keep her spirit inviolate.

No more, O my spirit,
are we flawless,
we have seen evil undreamt
I myself saw it:
the Greek, the most luminous,
the Athenian, the star-like,
banished through his father's hate
to a country far distant.

O sand dunes and sand-stretches
of the Athenian coast,
O mountain-thickets
where you climbed,
following the wild beasts,
with hounds, delicate of feet,
hunting with the daemon, Artemis!

No more
will you mount your chariot,
yoked with horses of Enetas,
nor spur forward your steed
toward the stadium at Limnas,
and your chant, ever rapturous,
and the answering lyre-note,
shall cease in the king's house:
far in the forest depth
in the glades where she loves to rest,
Latona's child shall be crownless:
at your flight
the contest of the maidens will cease,
and their love-longing, comfortless.

And because of your fate,
I accept bitter hurt,
and weep:
ai, ai, poor mother,
your birth-pangs were fruitless:
I am wroth with these spirits:

alas, Karites, never-separate,
why, why have you sent him forth,
the unfortunate, blameless,
from his palace,
from his own gates?

VII

Men you strike
and the gods'
dauntless spirits alike,
and Eros helps you, O Kupris,
with wings' swift
interplay of light:
now he flies above earth,
now above sea-crash
and whirl of salt:
he enchants beasts
who dwell in the hills
and shoals in the sea-depth:
he darts gold wings
maddening their spirits:
he charms all born of earth,
(all whom Helios visits,
fiery with light)
and men's hearts:
you alone, Kupris,
creator of all life,
reign absolute.

Odyssey

Muse,
tell me of this man of wit,
who roamed long years
after he had sacked
Troy's sacred streets.

93

All the rest
who had escaped death,
returned,
fleeing battle and the sea;
only Odysseus,
captive of a goddess,
desperate and home-sick,
thought but of his wife and palace;
but Calypso,
that nymph and spirit,
yearning in the furrowed rock-shelf,
burned
and sought to be his mistress;
but years passed,
the time was ripe,
the gods decreed,
(although traitors plot
to betray him in his own court),
he was to return
to Ithaca;
and all the gods pitied him;
but Poseidon
steadfast to the last
hated
god-like Odysseus.

The sea-god visited
a distant folk,
Ethiopians,
who at the edge of earth
are divided into two parts,
(half watch the sun rise,
half, the sun set),
there the hecatomb
of slain sheep and oxen
await his revels:
and while he rejoiced,
seated at the feast,
the rest of the gods
gathered in the palace of Olympian Zeus;

94

and the father of men and of gods spoke thus:
(for he remembered bright Egisthus,
slain of Agamemnon's child,
great Orestes:)

O you spirits,
how men hate the gods,
for they say evil comes of us,
when they themselves,
by their own wickedness,
court peril
beyond their fate;
so Egisthus, defiant,
sought Agamemnon's wife
and slew Agamemnon
returning to his own palace,
though we ourselves
sent bright Hermes,
slayer of Argos,
to warn him
lest Orestes,
attaining to man's estate,
demand his inheritance
and take vengeance:
we forbade him to strike the king,
we warned him to respect his wife;
but could Hermes
of gracious aspect,
subtle with kindly speech,
thus avert the foul work?

Then the grey-eyed Athene,
the goddess, spoke:
O my father, Kronos begot,
first among the great,
his death at least was just,
so may all perish who err thus;
but my heart is rent
for the prudent Odysseus,
who, exiled from his friends,

95

is kept too long distressed
in an island, sea swept,
in the sea midst,
a forest island,
haunt of a spirit,
child of Atlas,
crafty of thought,
who knows the sea depth,
who supports the high pillars
which cut sky from earth;
it is his child
who keeps Odysseus
lamenting with broken heart,
ceaseless to tempt him
with soft and tender speech,
that he forget Ithaca;
but Odysseus,
yearning to see but the smoke
drift above his own house,
prefers death;
your heart, is it not touched,
O Olympian?
did not Odysseus please you
when he made sacrifice
before the Grecian ships
in great Troy?
why are you angry, Zeus?

Then Zeus,
keeper of the clouds,
answering her, spoke:
O my child
what quaint words
have sped your lips,
for how could I forget
the god-like Odysseus,
a spirit surpassing men,
first to make sacrifice
to the deathless
in the sky-space?

but Poseidon,
girder of earth,
though yet he spares his life,
nurtures unending hate;
he goads him from place to place
because of the Cyclops
blinded of Odysseus,
Polyphemus, half-god,
greatest of the Cyclops,
whom the nymph Thoosa,
child of Phorcys,
king of the waste sea, begot
when she lay with Poseidon
among the shallow rocks:
but come,
let us plot
to reinstate Odysseus,
and Poseidon must abandon his wrath;
for what can one god accomplish,
striving alone
to defy all the deathless?

Then the grey-eyed Athene,
the goddess, spoke:
O my father, Kronos begot,
first among the great,
if then it seems just
to the highest,
that Odysseus return
to his own house,
let us swiftly send
Hermes, slayer of Argos,
your attendant,
that he state
to the fair-haired nymph,
our irrevocable wish,
that Odysseus,
valiant of heart,
be sent back:
and I will depart to Ithaca,

97

to incite his son,
to put courage in his heart,
that he call to the market-place
the long-haired Greeks
and shut his gates
to the pretendants
who ceaselessly devour his flocks,
sheep and horned oxen
of gentle pace:
that he strive
for his father's sake
and gain favour
in men's thoughts,
I will send him to Sparta,
to Pylos' sandy waste.

*She spoke
and about her feet
clasped bright sandals,
gold-wrought, imperishable,
which lift her above sea,
across the land stretch,
wind-like,
like the wind breath.*

Hymen
1921

For Bryher and Perdita

They said:
she is high and far and blind
in her high pride,
but now that my head is bowed
in sorrow, I find
she is most kind.

We have taken life, they said,
blithely, not groped in a mist
for things that are not—
are if you will, but bloodless—
why ask happiness of the dead?
and my heart bled.

Ah, could they know
how violets throw strange fire,
red and purple and gold,
how they glow
gold and purple and red
where her feet tread.

Hymen

As from a temple service, tall and dignified, with slow
pace, each a queen, the sixteen matrons from the temple of
Hera pass before the curtain—a dark purple hung between
Ionic columns—of the porch or open hall of a palace. Their
hair is bound as the marble hair of the temple Hera. Each
wears a crown or diadem of gold.

They sing—the music is temple music, deep, simple, chanting notes:

From the closed garden
Where our feet pace
Back and forth each day,
This gladiolus white,
This red, this purple spray—
Gladiolus tall with dignity
As yours, lady—we lay
Before your feet and pray:

Of all the blessings—
Youth, joy, ecstasy—
May one gift last
(As the tall gladiolus may
Outlast the wind-flower,
Winter-rose or rose),
One gift above,
Encompassing all those;

For her, for him,
For all within these palace walls,
Beyond the feast,
Beyond the cry of Hymen and the torch,
Beyond the night and music
Echoing through the porch till day.

The music, with its deep chanting notes, dies away. The curtain hangs motionless in rich, full folds. Then from this background of darkness, dignity and solemn repose, a flute gradually detaches itself, becomes clearer and clearer, pipes alone one shrill, simple little melody.

From the distance, four children's voices blend with the flute, and four very little girls pass singly before the curtain, small maids or attendants of the sixteen matrons. Their hair is short and curls at the back of their heads like the hair of the chryselephantine Hermes. They sing:

Where the first crocus buds unfold
We found these petals near the cold
  Swift river-bed.

Beneath the rocks where ivy-frond
Puts forth new leaves to gleam beyond
  Those lately dead:

The very smallest two or three
Of gold (gold pale as ivory)
  We gathered.

When the little girls have passed before the curtain, a wood-wind weaves a richer note into the flute melody; then the two blend into one song. But as the wood-wind grows in mellowness and richness, the flute gradually dies away into a secondary theme and the wood-wind alone evolves the melody of a new song.

Two by two—like two sets of medallions with twin profiles distinct, one head slightly higher, bent forward a little—the four figures of four slight, rather fragile taller children, are outlined with sharp white contour against the curtain.

The hair is smooth against the heads, falling to the shoulders, but slightly waved against the nape of the neck. They are looking down, each at a spray of winter-rose. The tunics fall to the knees in sharp marble folds. They sing:

Never more will the wind
Cherish you again,
Never more will the rain.

Never more
Shall we find you bright
In the snow and wind.

The snow is melted,
The snow is gone,
And you are flown:

Like a bird out of our hand,
Like a light out of our heart,
You are gone.

*As the wistful notes of the wood-wind gradually die
away, there comes a sudden, shrill, swift piping.*

*Free and wild, like the wood-maidens of Artemis, is this
last group of four—very straight with heads tossed back.
They sing in rich, free, swift notes. They move swiftly before
the curtain in contrast to the slow, important pace of the
first two groups. Their hair is loose and rayed out like that
of the sun-god. They are boyish in shape and gesture. They
carry hyacinths in baskets, strapped like quivers to their
backs. They reach to draw the flower sprays from the baskets,
as the Huntress her arrows.*

*As they dart swiftly to and fro before the curtain, they
are youth, they are spring—they are the Chelidonia, their
song is the swallow-song of joy:*

Between the hollows
Of the little hills
The spring spills blue—
Turquoise, sapphire, lapis-lazuli—
On a brown cloth outspread.

Ah see,
How carefully we lay them now,
Each hyacinth spray,
Across the marble floor—
A pattern your bent eyes
May trace and follow
To the shut bridal door.

Lady, our love, our dear,
Our bride most fair,
They grew among the hollows
Of the hills;
As if the sea had spilled its blue,

As if the sea had risen
From its bed,
And sinking to the level of the shore,
Left hyacinths on the floor.

There is a pause. Flute, pipe and wood-wind blend in a full, rich movement. There is no definite melody but full, powerful rhythm like soft but steady wind above forest trees. Into this, like rain, gradually creeps the note of strings.

As the strings grow stronger and finally dominate the whole, the bride-chorus passes before the curtain. There may be any number in this chorus. The figures—tall young women, clothed in long white tunics—follow one another closely, yet are all distinct like a procession of a temple frieze.

The bride in the center is not at first distinguishable from her maidens; but as they begin their song, the maidens draw apart into two groups, leaving the veiled symbolic figure standing alone in the center.

The two groups range themselves to right and left like officiating priestesses. The veiled figure stands with her back against the curtain, the others being in profile. Her head is swathed in folds of diaphanous white, through which the features are visible, like the veiled Tanagra.

When the song is finished, the group to the bride's left turns about; also the bride, so that all face in one direction. In processional form they pass out, the figure of the bride again merging, not distinguishable from the maidens.

STROPHE   But of her
Who can say if she is fair?
Bound with fillet,
Bound with myrtle
Underneath her flowing veil,
Only the soft length
(Beneath her dress)
Of saffron shoe is bright
As a great lily-heart
In its white loveliness.

ANTISTROPHE   But of her
We can say that she is fair.
We bleached the fillet,
Brought the myrtle;
To us the task was set
Of knotting the fine threads of silk:
We fastened the veil,
And over the white foot
Drew on the painted shoe
Steeped in Illyrian crocus.

STROPHE   But of her,
Who can say if she is fair?
For her head is covered over
With her mantle
White on white,
Snow on whiter amaranth,
Snow on hoar-frost,
Snow on snow,
Snow on whitest buds of myrrh.

ANTISTROPHE   But of her,
We can say that she is fair;
For we know underneath
All the wanness,
All the heat
(In her blanched face)
Of desire
Is caught in her eyes as fire
In the dark center leaf
Of the white Syrian iris.

The rather hard, hieratic precision of the music—its stately pause and beat—is broken now into irregular lilt and rhythm of strings.

Four tall young women, very young matrons, enter in a group. They stand clear and fair, but this little group entirely lacks the austere precision of the procession of maidens just preceding them. They pause in the center of the stage; turn, one three-quarter, two in profile and the fourth full face;

106

they stand, turned as if confiding in each other like a Tanagra group.

They sing lightly, their flower trays under their arms.

Along the yellow sand
Above the rocks
The laurel-bushes stand.
Against the shimmering heat
Each separate leaf
Is bright and cold,
And through the bronze
Of shining bark and wood
Run the fine threads of gold.

Here in our wicker-trays,
We bring the first faint blossoming
Of fragrant bays:

Lady, their blushes shine
As faint in hue
As when through petals
Of a laurel-rose
The sun shines through,
And throws a purple shadow
On a marble vase.

(Ah, love,
So her fair breasts will shine
With the faint shadow above.)

The harp chords become again more regular in simple definite rhythm. The music is not so intense as the bride-chorus; and quieter, more sedate, than the notes preceding the entrance of the last group.

Five or six slightly older serene young women enter in processional form; each holding before her, with precise bending of arms, coverlets and linen, carefully folded, as if for the bride couch. The garments are purple, scarlet and deep blue, with edge of gold.

They sing to blending of wood-wind and harp.

107

From citron-bower be her bed,
Cut from branch of tree a-flower,
Fashioned for her maidenhead.

From Lydian apples, sweet of hue,
Cut the width of board and lathe.
Carve the feet from myrtle-wood.

Let the palings of her bed
Be quince and box-wood overlaid
With the scented bark of yew.

That all the wood in blossoming,
May calm her heart and cool her blood
For losing of her maidenhood.

*The wood-winds become more rich and resonant. A tall
youth crosses the stage as if seeking the bride door. The
music becomes very rich, full of color.*

*The figure itself is a flame, an exaggerated symbol; the
hair a flame; the wings, deep red or purple, stand out
against the curtains in a contrasting or almost clashing
shade of purple. The tunic, again a rich purple or crimson,
falls almost to the knees. The knees are bare; the sandals
elaborately strapped over and over. The curtain seems a rich
purple cloud, the figure, still brighter, like a flamboyant
bird, half emerged in the sunset.*

*Love pauses just outside the bride's door with his gift, a
tuft of black-purple cyclamen. He sings to the accompani-
ment of wood-winds, in a rich, resonant voice:*

The crimson cover of her bed
Is not so rich, nor so deeply bled
The purple-fish that dyed it red,
As when in a hot sheltered glen
There flowered these stalks of cyclamen:

(Purple with honey-points
Of horns for petals;
Sweet and dark and crisp,
As fragrant as her maiden kiss.)

108

There with his honey-seeking lips
The bee clings close and warmly sips,
And seeks with honey-thighs to sway
And drink the very flower away.

(Ah, stern the petals drawing back;
Ah rare, ah virginal her breath!)

Crimson, with honey-seeking lips,
The sun lies hot across his back,
The gold is flecked across his wings.
Quivering he sways and quivering clings
(Ah, rare her shoulders drawing back!)
One moment, then the plunderer slips
Between the purple flower-lips.

Love passes out with a crash of cymbals. There is a momentary pause and the music falls into its calm, wave-like rhythm.

A band of boys passes before the curtain. They pass from side to side, crossing and recrossing; but their figures never confuse one another, the outlines are never blurred. They stand out against the curtain with symbolic gesture, stooping as if to gather up the wreaths, or swaying with long stiff branch as if to sweep the fallen petals from the floor.

There is no marked melody from the instruments, but the boys' voices, humming lightly as they enter, gradually evolve a little dance song. There are no words but the lilt up and down of the boys' tenor voices.

Then, as if they had finished the task of gathering up the wreaths and sweeping the petals, they stand in groups of two before the pillars where the torches have been placed. They lift the torches from the brackets. They hold them aloft between them, one torch to each two boys. Their figures are cut against the curtain like the simple, triangular design on the base of a vase or frieze—the boys' heads on a level, the torches above them.

They sing in clear, half-subdued voices:

Where love is king,
Ah, there is little need
To dance and sing,
With bridal-torch to flare
Amber and scatter light
Across the purple air,
To sing and dance
To flute-note and to reed.

Where love is come
(Ah, love is come indeed!)
Our limbs are numb
Before his fiery need;
With all their glad
Rapture of speech unsaid,
Before his fiery lips
Our lips are mute and dumb.

Ah, sound of reed,
Ah, flute and trumpet wail,
Ah, joy decreed—
The fringes of her veil
Are seared and white;
Across the flare of light,
Blinded the torches fail.
(Ah, love is come indeed!)

At the end of the song, the torches flicker out and the figures are no longer distinguishable in the darkness. They pass out like shadows. The purple curtain hangs black and heavy.

The music dies away and is finally cut short with a few deep, muted chords.

Demeter

I

Men, fires, feasts,
steps of temple, fore-stone, lintel,
step of white altar, fire and after-fire,
slaughter before,
fragment of burnt meat,
deep mystery, grapple of mind to reach
the tense thought,
power and wealth, purpose and prayer alike,
(men, fires, feasts, temple steps)—useless.

Useless to me who plant
wide feet on a mighty plinth,
useless to me who sit,
wide of shoulder, great of thigh,
heavy in gold, to press
gold back against solid back
of the marble seat:
useless the dragons wrought on the arms,
useless the poppy-buds and the gold inset
of the spray of wheat.

Ah they have wrought me heavy
and great of limb—
she is slender of waist,
slight of breast, made of many fashions;
they have set *her* small feet
on many a plinth;
she they have known,
she they have spoken with,
she they have smiled upon,
she they have caught
and flattered with praise and gifts.

But useless the flattery
of the mighty power
they have granted me:

for I will not stay in her breast,
the great of limb,
though perfect the shell they have
fashioned me, these men!

Do I sit in the market-place—
do I smile, does a noble brow
bend like the brow of Zeus—
am I a spouse, his or any,
am I a woman, or goddess or queen,
to be met by a god with a smile—and left?

II

Do you ask for a scroll,
parchment, oracle, prophecy, precedent;
do you ask for tablets marked with thought
or words cut deep on the marble surface,
do you seek measured utterance or the mystic trance?

Sleep on the stones of Delphi—
dare the ledges of Pallas
but keep me foremost,
keep me before you, after you, with you,
never forget when you start
for the Delphic precipice,
never forget when you seek Pallas
and meet in thought
yourself drawn out from yourself
like the holy serpent,
never forget
in thought or mysterious trance—
I am greatest and least.

Soft are the hands of Love,
soft, soft are his feet;
you who have twined myrtle,
have you brought crocuses,
white as the inner
stript bark of the osier,

have you set
black crocus against the black
locks of another?

III

Of whom do I speak?
Many the children of gods
but first I take
Bromios, fostering prince,
lift from the ivy brake, a king.

Enough of the lightning,
enough of the tales that speak
of the death of the mother:
strange tales of a shelter
brought to the unborn,
enough of talc, myth, mystery, precedent—
a child lay on the earth asleep.

Soft are the hands of Love,
but what soft hands
clutched at the thorny ground,
scratched like a small white ferret
or foraging whippet or hound,
sought nourishment and found
only the crackling of ivy,
dead ivy leaf and the white
berry, food for a bird,
no food for this who sought,
bending small head in a fever,
whining with little breath.

Ah, small black head,
ah, the purple ivy bush,
ah, berries that shook and spilt
on the form beneath,
who begot you and left?

Though I begot no man child
all my days,
the child of my heart and spirit,
is the child the gods desert
alike and the mother in death—
the unclaimed Dionysos.

IV

What of her—
mistress of Death?

Form of a golden wreath
were my hands that girt her head,
fingers that strove to meet,
and met where the whisps escaped
from the fillet, of tenderest gold,
small circlet and slim
were my fingers then.

Now they are wrought of iron
to wrest from earth
secrets; strong to protect,
strong to keep back the winter
when winter tracks too soon
blanch the forest:
strong to break dead things,
the young tree, drained of sap,
the old tree, ready to drop,
to lift from the rotting bed
of leaves, the old
crumbling pine tree stock,
to heap bole and knot of fir
and pine and resinous oak,
till fire shatter the dark
and hope of spring
rise in the hearts of men.

What of her—
mistress of Death—
what of his kiss?

114

Ah, strong were his arms to wrest
slight limbs from the beautiful earth,
young hands that plucked the first
buds of the chill narcissus,
soft fingers that broke
and fastened the thorny stalk
with the flower of wild acanthus.

Ah, strong were the arms that took
(ah, evil the heart and graceless),
but the kiss was less passionate!

Simaetha

Drenched with purple,
drenched with dye, my wool,
bind you the wheel-spokes—
turn, turn, turn my wheel!

Drenched with purple,
steeped in the red pulp
of bursting sea sloes—
turn, turn, turn my wheel!

(Ah did he think
I did not know,
I did not feel—
what wrack, what weal for him:
golden one, golden one,
turn again Aphrodite with the yellow zone,
I am cursed, cursed, undone!
Ah and my face, Aphrodite,
beside your gold,
is cut out of white stone!)

Laurel blossom and the red seed
of the red vervain weed,
burn, crackle in the fire,
burn, crackle for my need!
Laurel leaf, O fruited
branch of bay,
burn, burn away
thought, memory and hurt!

(Ah when he comes,
stumbling across my sill,
will he find me still,
fragrant as the white privet,
or as a bone,
polished in wet and sun,
worried of wild beaks,
and of the whelps' teeth—
worried of flesh,
left to bleach under the sun,
white as ash bled of heat,
white as hail blazing in sheet-lightning,
white as forked lightning
rending the sleet?)

Thetis

I

On the paved parapet
you will step carefully
from amber stones to onyx
flecked with violet,
mingled with light,
half showing the sea-grass
and sea-sand underneath,

116

reflecting your white feet
and the gay strap crimson
as lily-buds of Arion,
and the gold that binds your feet.

II

You will pass
beneath the island disk
(and myrtle-wood,
the carved support of it)
and the white stretch
of its white beach,
curved as the moon crescent
or ivory when some fine hand
chisels it:
when the sun slips
through the far edge,
there is rare amber
through the sea,
and flecks of it
glitter on the dolphin's back
and jewelled halter
and harness and bit
as he sways under it.

III

You will pause
where the coral-lily roots
thread amber about
gold grain and pebble of wrought
crystal or purple rock;
green water dark
with the blue from the pools beneath;
and between the bands of water,
each day your feet will tread,
climbing from purple to blue,
from blue to sea-red,
step upon step,

laid crosswise,
uneven, sloping gradually,
then steep and high
to the sun-light overhead.

IV

Should the sun press
too heavy a crown,
should dawn cast
over-much loveliness,
should you tire as you laugh,
running from wave to wave-crest,
gathering the sea-flower to your breast,
you may dive down
to the uttermost sea depth,
where no great fish venture
nor small fish glitter and dart,
only the anemones and flower
of the wild sea-thyme
cover the silent walls
of an old sea-city at rest.

Circe

It was easy enough
to bend them to my wish,
it was easy enough
to alter them with a touch,
but you
adrift on the great sea,
how shall I call you back?

Cedar and white ash,
rock-cedar and sand plants
and tamarisk
red cedar and white cedar
and black cedar from the inmost forest,
fragrance upon fragrance
and all of my sea-magic is for nought.

It was easy enough—
a thought called them
from the sharp edges of the earth;
they prayed for a touch,
they cried for the sight of my face,
they entreated me
till in pity
I turned each to his own self.

Panther and panther,
then a black leopard
follows close—
black panther and red
and a great hound,
a god-like beast,
cut the sand in a clear ring
and shut me from the earth,
and cover the sea-sound
with their throats,
and the sea-roar with their own barks
and bellowing and snarls,
and the sea-stars
and the swirl of the sand,
and the rock-tamarisk
and the wind resonance—
but not your voice.

It is easy enough to call men
from the edges of the earth.
It is easy enough to summon them to my feet
with a thought—

it is beautiful to see the tall panther
and the sleek deer-hounds
circle in the dark.
It is easy enough
to make cedar and white ash fumes
into palaces
and to cover the sea-caves
with ivory and onyx.

But I would give up
rock-fringes of coral
and the inmost chamber
of my island palace
and my own gifts
and the whole region
of my power and magic
for your glance.

Leda

Where the slow river
meets the tide,
a red swan lifts red wings
and darker beak,
and underneath the purple down
of his soft breast
uncurls his coral feet.

Through the deep purple
of the dying heat
of sun and mist,
the level ray of sun-beam
has caressed
the lily with dark breast,
and flecked with richer gold
its golden crest.

120

Where the slow lifting
of the tide,
floats into the river
and slowly drifts
among the reeds,
and lifts the yellow flags,
he floats
where tide and river meet.

Ah kingly kiss—
no more regret
nor old deep memories
to mar the bliss;
where the low sedge is thick,
the gold day-lily
outspreads and rests
beneath soft fluttering
of red swan wings
and the warm quivering
of the red swan's breast.

Hippolytus Temporizes

I worship the greatest first—
(it were sweet, the couch,
the brighter ripple of cloth
over the dipped fleece;
the thought: her bones
under the flesh are white
as sand which along a beach
covers but keeps the print
of the crescent shapes beneath:
I thought:
between cloth and fleece,
so her body lies.)

I worship first, the great—
(ah, sweet, your eyes—
what God, invoked in Crete,
gave them the gift to part
as the Sidonian myrtle-flower
suddenly, wide and swart,
then swiftly,
the eye-lids having provoked our hearts—
as suddenly beat and close.)

I worship the feet, flawless,
that haunt the hills—
(ah, sweet, dare I think,
beneath fetter of golden clasp,
of the rhythm, the fall and rise
of yours, carven, slight
beneath straps of gold that keep
their slender beauty caught,
like wings and bodies
of trapped birds.)

I worship the greatest first—
(suddenly into my brain—
the flash of sun on the snow,
the fringe of light and the drift,
the crest and the hill-shadow—
ah, surely now I forget,
ah splendour, my goddess turns:
or was it the sudden heat,
beneath quivering of molten flesh,
of veins, purple as violets?)

Cuckoo Song

Ah, bird,
our love is never spent
with your clear note,

nor satiate our soul;
not song, not wail, not hurt,
but just a call summons us
with its simple top-note
and soft fall;

not to some rarer heaven
of lilies over-tall,
nor tuberose set against
some sun-lit wall,
but to a gracious
cedar-palace hall;

not marble set with purple
hung with roses and tall
sweet lilies—such
as the nightingale
would summon for us
with her wail—

(surely only unhappiness
could thrill
such a rich madrigal!)
not she, the nightingale
can fill our souls
with such a wistful joy as this:

nor, bird, so sweet
was ever a swallow note—
not hers, so perfect
with the wing of lazuli
and bright breast—
nor yet the oriole
filling with melody
from her fiery throat
some island-orchard
in a purple sea.

Ah dear, ah gentle bird,
you spread warm length
of crimson wool
and tinted woven stuff
for us to rest upon,
nor numb with ecstasy
nor drown with death:

only you soothe, make still
the throbbing of our brain:
so through her forest trees,
when all her hope was gone
and all her pain,
Calypso heard your call—
across the gathering drift
of burning cedar-wood,
across the low-set bed
of wandering parsley and violet,
when all her hope was dead.

The Islands

I

What are the islands to me,
what is Greece,
what is Rhodes, Samos, Chios,
what is Paros facing west,
what is Crete?

What is Samothrace,
rising like a ship,
what is Imbros rending the storm-waves
with its breast?

What is Naxos, Paros, Milos,
what the circle about Lycia,
what, the Cyclades'
white necklace?

What is Greece—
Sparta, rising like a rock,
Thebes, Athens,
what is Corinth?

What is Euboia
with its island violets,
what is Euboia, spread with grass,
set with swift shoals,
what is Crete?

What are the islands to me,
what is Greece?

II

What can love of land give to me
that you have not—
what do the tall Spartans know,
and gentler Attic folk?

What has Sparta and her women
more than this?

What are the islands to me
if you are lost—
what is Naxos, Tinos, Andros,
and Delos, the clasp
of the white necklace?

III

What can love of land give to me
that you have not,
what can love of strife break in me
that you have not?

Though Sparta enter Athens,
Thebes wrack Sparta,
each changes as water,
salt, rising to wreak terror
and fall back.

IV

"What has love of land given to you
that I have not?"

I have questioned Tyrians
where they sat
on the black ships,
weighted with rich stuffs,
I have asked the Greeks
from the white ships,
and Greeks from ships whose hulks
lay on the wet sand, scarlet
with great beaks.
I have asked bright Tyrians
and tall Greeks—
"what has love of land given you?"
And they answered—"peace."

V

But beauty is set apart,
beauty is cast by the sea,
a barren rock,
beauty is set about
with wrecks of ships,
upon our coast, death keeps
the shallows—death waits
clutching toward us
from the deeps.

Beauty is set apart;
the winds that slash its beach,
swirl the coarse sand
upward toward the rocks.

Beauty is set apart
from the islands
and from Greece.

VI

In my garden
the winds have beaten
the ripe lilies;
in my garden, the salt
has wilted the first flakes
of young narcissus,
and the lesser hyacinth,
and the salt has crept
under the leaves of the white hyacinth.

In my garden
even the wind-flowers lie flat,
broken by the wind at last.

VII

What are the islands to me
if you are lost,
what is Paros to me
if your eyes draw back,
what is Milos
if you take fright of beauty,
terrible, torturous, isolated,
a barren rock?

What is Rhodes, Crete,
what is Paros facing west,
what, white Imbros?

What are the islands to me
if you hesitate,
what is Greece if you draw back
from the terror
and cold splendour of song
and its bleak sacrifice?

At Baia

I should have thought
in a dream you would have brought
some lovely, perilous thing,
orchids piled in a great sheath,
as who would say (in a dream)
I send you this,
who left the blue veins
of your throat unkissed.

Why was it that your hands
(that never took mine)
your hands that I could see
drift over the orchid heads
so carefully,
your hands, so fragile, sure to lift
so gently, the fragile flower stuff—
ah, ah, how was it

You never sent (in a dream)
the very form, the very scent,
not heavy, not sensuous,
but perilous—perilous—
of orchids, piled in a great sheath,
and folded underneath on a bright scroll
some word:

Flower sent to flower;
for white hands, the lesser white,
less lovely of flower leaf,

or

Lover to lover, no kiss,
no touch, but forever and ever this.

Sea Heroes

Crash on crash of the sea,
straining to wreck men, sea-boards, continents,
raging against the world, furious,
stay at last, for against your fury
and your mad fight,
the line of heroes stands, god-like:

Akroneos, Oknolos, Elatreus,
helm-of-boat, loosener-of-helm, dweller-by-sea,
Nauteus, sea-man,
Prumneos, stern-of-ship,
Agchialos, sea-girt,
Elatreus, oar-shaft:
lover-of-the-sea, lover-of-the-sea-ebb,
lover-of-the-swift-sea,
Ponteus, Proreus, Ooos:
Anabesncos, one caught between
wave-shock and wave-shock:
Eurualos, broad sea-wrack,
like Ares, man's death,
and Naubolides, best in shape,
of all first in size:
Phaekous, seas' thunderbolt—
ah, crash on crash of great names—
man-tamer, man's-help, perfect Laodamos:
and last the sons of great Alkinoos,
Laodamos, Halios and god-like Clytomeos.

Of all nations, of all cities,
of all continents,
she is favoured among the rest,
for she gives men as great as the sea,
valorous to the fight,
to battle against the elements and evil:
greater even than the sea,
they live beyond wrack and death of cities,
and each god-like name spoken
is as a shrine in a godless place.

129

But to name you,
we reverent are breathless,
weak with pain and old loss,
and exile and despair—
our hearts break but to speak
your name, Oknaleos—
and may we but call you in the feverish wrack
of our storm-strewn beach, Eretmeos,
and our hurt is quiet and our hearts tamed,
as the sea may yet be tamed,
and we vow to float great ships,
named for each hero,
and oar-blades, cut out of mountain-trees
as such men might have shaped:
Eretmeos and the sea is swept,
baffled by the lordly shape,
Akroneos has pines for his ship's keel;
to love, to mate the sea?
Ah there is Ponteos,
the very deeps roar,
hailing you dear—
they clamour to Ponteos,
and to Proeos
leap, swift to kiss, to curl, to creep,
lover to mistress.

What wave, what love, what foam,
for Ooos who moves swift as the sea?
Ah stay, my heart, the weight
of lovers, of loneliness
drowns me,
alas that their very names
so press to break my heart
with heart-sick weariness,
what would they be,
the very gods,
rearing their mighty length
beside the unharvested sea?

Fragment 113

"Neither honey nor bee for me."—Sappho.

Not honey,
not the plunder of the bee
from meadow or sand-flower
or mountain bush;
from winter-flower or shoot
born of the later heat:
not honey, not the sweet
stain on the lips and teeth:
not honey, not the deep
plunge of soft belly
and the clinging of the gold-edged
pollen-dusted feet;

not so—
though rapture blind my eyes,
and hunger crisp
dark and inert my mouth,
not honey, not the south,
not the tall stalk
of red twin-lilies,
nor light branch of fruit tree
caught in flexible light branch;

not honey, not the south;
ah flower of purple iris,
flower of white,
or of the iris, withering the grass—
for fleck of the sun's fire,
gathers such heat and power,
that shadow-print is light,
cast through the petals
of the yellow iris flower;

not iris—old desire—old passion—
old forgetfulness—old pain—
not this, nor any flower,
but if you turn again,

seek strength of arm and throat,
touch as the god;
neglect the lyre-note;
knowing that you shall feel,
about the frame,
no trembling of the string
but heat, more passionate
of bone and the white shell
and fiery tempered steel.

Evadne

I first tasted under Apollo's lips
love and love sweetness,
I Evadne;
my hair is made of crisp violets
or hyacinth which the wind combs back
across some rock shelf;
I Evadne
was mate of the god of light.

His hair was crisp to my mouth
as the flower of the crocus,
across my cheek,
cool as the silver cress
on Erotos bank;
between my chin and throat
his mouth slipped over and over.

Still between my arm and shoulder,
I feel the brush of his hair,
and my hands keep the gold they took
as they wandered over and over
that great arm-full of yellow flowers.

Song

You are as gold
as the half-ripe grain
that merges to gold again,
as white as the white rain
that beats through
the half-opened flowers
of the great flower tufts
thick on the black limbs
of an Illyrian apple bough.

Can honey distill such fragrance
as your bright hair—
for your face is as fair as rain,
yet as rain that lies clear
on white honey-comb,
lends radiance to the white wax,
so your hair on your brow
casts light for a shadow.

Why Have You Sought?

Why have you sought the Greeks, Eros,
when such delight was yours
in the far depth of sky:
there you could note bright ivory
take colour where she bent her face,
and watch fair gold shed gold
on radiant surface of porch and pillar:
and ivory and bright gold,
polished and lustrous grow faint
beside that wondrous flesh
and print of her foot-hold:
Love, why do you tempt the Grecian porticoes?

Here men are bent with thought
and women waste fair moments
gathering lint and pricking coloured stuffs
to mar their breasts,
while she, adored,
wastes not her fingers,
worn of fire and sword,
wastes not her touch
on linen and fine thread,
wastes not her head
in thought and pondering;
Love, why have you sought the horde
of spearsmen, why the tent
Achilles pitched beside the river-ford?

White World

The whole white world is ours,
and the world, purple with rose-bays,
bays, bush on bush,
group, thicket, hedge and tree,
dark islands in a sea
of grey-green olive or wild white-olive,
cut with the sudden cypress shafts,
in clusters, two or three,
or with one slender, single cypress-tree.

Slid from the hill,
as crumbling snow-peaks slide,
citron on citron fill
the valley, and delight
waits till our spirits tire
of forest, grove and bush
and purple flower of the laurel-tree.

Yet not one wearies,
joined is each to each
in happiness complete
with bush and flower:
ours is the wind-breath
at the hot noon-hour,
ours is the bee's soft belly
and the blush of the rose-petal,
lifted, of the flower.

Phaedra

Think, O my soul,
of the red sand of Crete;
think of the earth; the heat
burnt fissures like the great
backs of the temple serpents;
think of the world you knew;
as the tide crept, the land
burned with a lizard-blue
where the dark sea met the sand.

Think, O my soul—
what power has struck you blind—
is there no desert-root, no forest-berry
pine-pitch or knot of fir
known that can help the soul
caught in a force, a power,
passionless, not its own?

So I scatter, so implore
Gods of Crete, summoned before
with slighter craft;
ah, hear my prayer:
Grant to my soul
the body that it wore,

135

trained to your thought,
that kept and held your power,
as the petal of black poppy,
the opiate of the flower.

For art undreamt in Crete,
strange art and dire,
in counter-charm prevents my charm
limits my power:
pine-cone I heap,
grant answer to my prayer.

No more, my soul—
as the black cup, sullen and dark with fire,
burns till beside it, noon's bright heat
is withered, filled with dust—
and into that noon-heat
grown drab and stale,
suddenly wind and thunder and swift rain,
till the scarlet flower is wrecked
in the slash of the white hail.

The poppy that my heart was,
formed to bind all mortals,
made to strike and gather hearts
like flame upon an altar,
fades and shrinks, a red leaf
drenched and torn in the cold rain.

She Contrasts with Herself Hippolyta

Can flame beget white steel—
ah no, it could not take
within my reins its shelter;
steel must seek steel,
or hate make out of joy
a whet-stone for a sword;

136

sword against flint,
Theseus sought Hippolyta;
she yielded not nor broke,
sword upon stone,
from the clash leapt a spark,
Hippolytus, born of hate.

What did she think
when all her strength
was twisted for his bearing;
did it break,
even within her sheltered heart, a song,
some whispered note,
distant and faint as this:

Love that I bear
within my breast
how is my armour melted
how my heart:
as an oak-tree
that keeps beneath the snow,
the young bark fresh
till the spring cast
from off its shoulders
the white snow
so does my armour melt.

Love that I bear
within my heart, O speak;
tell how beneath the serpent-spotted shell,
the cygnets wait,
how the soft owl
opens and flicks with pride,
eye-lids of great bird-eyes,
when underneath its breast
the owlets shrink and turn.

You have the power,
(then did she say) Artemis,
benignity to grant
forgiveness that I gave
no quarter to an enemy who cast
his armour on the forest-moss,
and took, unmatched in an uneven contest,
Hippolyta who relented not,
returned and sought no kiss.

Then did she pray: Artemis,
grant that no flower
be grafted alien on a broken stalk,
no dark flame-laurel on the stricken crest
of a wild mountain-poplar;
grant in my thought,
I never yield but wait,
entreating cold white river,
mountain-pool and salt:
let all my veins be ice,
until they break
(strength of white beach,
rock of mountain land,
forever to you, Artemis, dedicate)
from out my reins,
those small, cold hands.

She Rebukes Hippolyta

Was she so chaste?

Swift and a broken rock
clatters across the steep shelf
of the mountain slope,
sudden and swift
and breaks as it clatters down
into the hollow breach
of the dried water-course:

far and away
(through fire I see it,
and smoke of the dead, withered stalks
of the wild cistus-brush)
Hippolyta, frail and wild,
galloping up the slope
between great boulder and rock
and group and cluster of rock.

Was she so chaste,
(I see it, sharp, this vision,
and each fleck on the horse's flanks
of foam, and bridle and bit,
silver, and the straps,
wrought with their perfect art,
and the sun,
striking athwart the silver-work,
and the neck, strained forward, ears alert,
and the head of a girl
flung back and her throat.)

Was she so chaste—
(Ah, burn my fire, I ask
out of the smoke-ringed darkness
enclosing the flaming disk
of my vision)
I ask for a voice to answer:
was she chaste?

Who can say—
the broken ridge of the hills
was the line of a lover's shoulder,
his arm-turn, the path to the hills,
the sudden leap and swift thunder
of mountain boulders, his laugh.

She was mad—
as no priest, no lover's cult
could grant madness;
the wine that entered her throat
with the touch of the mountain rocks
was white, intoxicant:
she, the chaste,
was betrayed by the glint
of light on the hills,
the granite splinter of rocks,
the touch of the stone
where heat melts
toward the shadow-side of the rocks.

Egypt

(To E. A. Poe)

Egypt had cheated us,
for Egypt took
through guile and craft
our treasure and our hope,
Egypt had maimed us,
offered dream for life,
an opiate for a kiss,
and death for both.

White poison flower we loved
and the black spike
of an ungarnered bush—
(a spice—or without taste—
we wondered—then we asked
others to take and sip
and watched their death)
Egypt we loved, though hate
should have withheld our touch.

Egypt had given us knowledge,
and we took, blindly,
through want of heart,
what Egypt brought;
knowing all poison,
what was that or this,
more or less perilous,
than this or that.

We pray you, Egypt,
by what perverse fate,
has poison brought with knowledge,
given us this—
not days of trance,
shadow, fore-doom of death,
but passionate grave thought,
belief enhanced,
ritual returned and magic;

Even in the uttermost black pit
of the forbidden knowledge,
wisdom's glance,
the grey eyes following
in the mid-most desert—
great shaft of rose,
fire shed across our path,
upon the face grown grey, a light,
Hellas re-born from death.

Prayer

White, O white face—
from disenchanted days
wither alike dark rose
and fiery bays:
no gift within our hands,

141

nor strength to praise,
only defeat and silence;
though we lift hands, disenchanted,
of small strength, nor raise
branch of the laurel
or the light of torch,
but fold the garment
on the riven locks,
yet hear, all-merciful, and touch
the fore-head, dim, unlit of pride and thought,
Mistress—be near!

Give back the glamour to our will,
the thought; give back the tool,
the chisel; once we wrought
things not unworthy,
sandal and steel-clasp;
silver and steel, the coat
with white leaf-pattern
at the arm and throat:
silver and metal, hammered for the ridge
of shield and helmet-rim;
white silver with the darker hammered in,
belt, staff and magic spear-shaft
with the gilt spark at the point and hilt.

Helios

Helios makes all things right:—
night brands and chokes
as if destruction broke
over furze and stone and crop
of myrtle-shoot and field-wort,
destroyed with flakes of iron,

the bracken-stems,
where tender roots were sown,
blight, chaff and waste
of darkness to choke and drown.

A curious god to find,
yet in the end faithful;
bitter, the Kyprian's feet—
ah flecks of whited clay,
great hero, vaunted lord—
ah petal, dust and wind-fall
on the ground—queen awaiting queen.

Better the weight, they tell,
the helmet's beaten shell,
Athene's riven steel,
caught over the white skull,
Athene sets to heal
the few who merit it.

Yet even then, what help,
should he not turn and note
the height of forehead and the mark of conquest,
draw near and try the helmet;
to left—reset the crown
Athene weighted down,
or break with a light touch
mayhap the steel set to protect;
to slay or heal.

A treacherous god, they say,
yet who would wait to test
justice or worth or right,
when through a fetid night
is wafted faint and nearer—
then straight as point of steel
to one who courts swift death,
scent of Hesperidean orange-spray.

Heliodora
1924

[Author's] Note

The poem Lais has in italics a translation of the Plato epigram in the Greek Anthology. Heliodora has in italics the two Meleager epigrams from the Anthology. In Nossis is the translation of the opening lines of the Garland of Meleager and the poem of Nossis herself in the Greek Anthology. The four Sappho fragments are re-worked freely. The Ion is a translation of the latter part of the first long choros of the Ion of Euripides.

Wash of cold river
in a glacial land,
Ionian water,
chill, snow-ribbed sand,
drift of rare flowers,
clear, with delicate shell-
like leaf enclosing
frozen lily-leaf,
camellia texture,
colder than a rose;

wind-flower
that keeps the breath
of the north-wind—
these and none other;

intimate thoughts and kind
reach out to share
the treasure of my mind,

147

intimate hands and dear
drawn garden-ward and sea-ward
all the sheer rapture
that I would take
to mould a clear
and frigid statue;

rare, of pure texture,
beautiful space and line,
marble to grace
your inaccessible shrine.

Holy Satyr

Most holy Satyr,
like a goat,
with horns and hooves
to match thy coat
of russet brown,
I make leaf-circlets
and a crown of honey-flowers
for thy throat;
where the amber petals
drip to ivory,
I cut and slip
each stiffened petal
in the rift
of carven petal;
honey horn
has wed the bright
virgin petal of the white
flower cluster: lip to lip
let them whisper,
let them lilt, quivering.

Most holy Satyr,
like a goat,
hear this our song,
accept our leaves,
love-offering,
return our hymn,
like echo fling
a sweet song,
answering note for note.

Lais

Let her who walks in Paphos
take the glass,
let Paphos take the mirror
and the work of frosted fruit,
gold apples set
with silver apple-leaf,
white leaf of silver
wrought with vein of gilt.

Let Paphos lift the mirror,
let her look
into the polished centre of the disk.

Let Paphos take the mirror;
did she press
flowerlet of flame-flower
to the lustrous white
of the white forehead?
did the dark veins beat
a deeper purple
than the wine-deep tint
of the dark flower?

149

Did she deck black hair
one evening, with the winter-white
flower of the winter-berry,
did she look (reft of her lover)
at a face gone white
under the chaplet
of white virgin-breath?

Lais, exultant, tyrannizing Greece,
Lais who kept her lovers in the porch,
lover on lover waiting,
(but to creep
where the robe brushed the threshold
where still sleeps Lais)
so she creeps, Lais,
to lay her mirror at the feet
of her who reigns in Paphos.

Lais has left her mirror
for she sees no longer in its depth
the Lais' self
that laughed exultant
tyrannizing Greece.

Lais has left her mirror,
for she weeps no longer,
finding in its depth,
a face, but other
than dark flame and white
feature of perfect marble.

Lais has left her mirror,
(so one wrote)
to her who reigns in Paphos;
Lais who laughed a tyrant over Greece,
Lais who turned the lovers from the porch,
that swarm for whom now
Lais has no use;
Lais is now no lover of the glass,
seeing no more the face as once it was,
wishing to see that face and finding this.

Heliodora

He and I sought together,
over the spattered table,
rhymes and flowers,
gifts for a name.

He said, among others,
I will bring
(and the phrase was just and good,
but not as good as mine,)
"the narcissus that loves the rain."

We strove for a name,
while the light of the lamps burnt thin
and the outer dawn came in,
a ghost, the last at the feast
or the first,
to sit within
with the two that remained
to quibble in flowers and verse
over a girl's name.

He said, "the rain, loving,"
I said, "the narcissus, drunk,
drunk with the rain."

Yet I had lost
for he said,
"the rose, the lover's gift,
is loved of love,"
he said it,
"loved of love;"
I waited, even as he spoke,
to see the room filled with a light,
as when in winter
the embers catch in a wind
when a room is dank;

so it would be filled, I thought,
our room with a light
when he said
(and he said it first,)
"the rose, the lover's delight,
is loved of love,"
but the light was the same.

Then he caught,
seeing the fire in my eyes,
my fire, my fever, perhaps,
for he leaned
with the purple wine
stained on his sleeve,
and said this:
"did you ever think
a girl's mouth
caught in a kiss,
is a lily that laughs?"

I had not.
I saw it now
as men must see it forever afterwards;
no poet could write again,
"the red-lily,
a girl's laugh caught in a kiss;"
it was his to pour in the vat
from which all poets dip and quaff,
for poets are brothers in this.

So I saw the fire in his eyes,
it was almost my fire,
(he was younger,)
I saw the face so white,
my heart beat,
it was almost my phrase;
I said, "surprise the muses,
take them by surprise;

it is late,
rather it is dawn-rise,
those ladies sleep, the nine,
our own king's mistresses."

A name to rhyme,
flowers to bring to a name,
what was one girl faint and shy,
with eyes like the myrtle,
(I said: "her underlids
are rather like myrtle,")
to vie with the nine?

Let him take the name,
he had the rhymes,
"the rose, loved of love,
the lily, a mouth that laughs,"
he had the gift,
"the scented crocus,
the purple hyacinth,"
what was one girl to the nine?

He said:
"I will make her a wreath;"
he said:
"I will write it thus:

I will bring you the lily that laughs,
I will twine
with soft narcissus, the myrtle,
sweet crocus, white violet,
the purple hyacinth, and last,
the rose, loved-of-love,
that these may drip on your hair
the less soft flowers,
may mingle sweet with the sweet
of Heliodora's locks,
myrrh-curled."

(He wrote myrrh-curled,
I think, the first.)

I said:
"they sleep, the nine,"
when he shouted swift and passionate:
"that for the nine!
above the hills
the sun is about to wake,
and to-day white violets
shine beside white lilies
adrift on the mountain side;
to-day the narcissus opens
that loves the rain."

I watched him to the door,
catching his robe
as the wine-bowl crashed to the floor,
spilling a few wet lees,
(ah, his purple hyacinth!)
I saw him out of the door,
I thought:
there will never be a poet
in all the centuries after this,
who will dare write,
after my friend's verse,
"a girl's mouth
is a lily kissed."

Helen

All Greece hates
the still eyes in the white face,
the lustre as of olives
where she stands,
and the white hands.

All Greece reviles
the wan face when she smiles,
hating it deeper still
when it grows wan and white,
remembering past enchantments
and past ills.

Greece sees unmoved,
God's daughter, born of love,
the beauty of cool feet
and slenderest knees,
could love indeed the maid,
only if she were laid,
white ash amid funereal cypresses.

Nossis

I thought to hear him speak
the girl might rise
and make the garden silver,
as the white moon breaks,
"Nossis," he cried, "a flame."

I said:
"a girl that's dead
some hundred years;
a poet—what of that?
for in the islands,
in the haunts of Greek Ionia,
Rhodes and Cyprus,
girls are cheap."

I said, to test his mood,
to make him rage or laugh or sing or weep,
"in Greek Ionia and in Cyprus,
many girls are found
with wreaths and apple-branches."

"Only a hundred years or two or three,
has she lain dead
yet men forget;"
he said,
"I want a garden,"
and I thought
he wished to make a terrace on the hill,
bend the stream to it,
set out daffodils,
plant Phrygian violets,
such was his will and whim,
I thought,
to name and watch each flower.

His was no garden
bright with Tyrian violets,
his was a shelter
wrought of flame and spirit,
and as he flung her name
against the dark,
I thought the iris-flowers
that lined that path
must be the ghost of Nossis.

"Who made the wreath,
for what man was it wrought?
speak, fashioned all of fruit-buds,
song, my loveliest,
say Meleager brought to Diocles,
(a gift for that enchanting friend)
memories with names of poets.
He sought for Moero, lilies,
and those many,
red-lilies for Anyte,
for Sappho, roses,

with those few, he caught
that breath of the sweet-scented
leaf of iris,
the myrrh-iris,
to set beside the tablet
and the wax
which Love had burnt,
when scarred across by Nossis:"

when she wrote:

"I Nossis stand by this:
I state that love is sweet:
if you think otherwise
assert what beauty
or what charm
after the charm of love,
retains its grace?

"Honey," you say:
honey? I say "I spit
honey out of my mouth:
nothing is second-best
after the sweet of Eros."

I Nossis stand and state
that he whom Love neglects
has naught, no flower, no grace,
who lacks that rose, her kiss."

I thought to hear him speak
the girl might rise
and make the garden silver
as the white moon breaks,
"Nossis," he cried, "a flame."

Centaur Song

Now that the day is done,
now that the night creeps soft
and dims the chestnut clusters'
radiant spike of flower,
O sweet, till dawn
break through the branches
of our orchard-garden,
rest in this shelter
of the osier-wood and thorn.

They fall,
the apple-flowers;
nor softer grace has Aphrodite
in the heaven afar,
nor at so fair a pace
open the flower-petals
as your face bends down,
while, breath on breath,
your mouth wanders
from my mouth o'er my face.

What have I left
to bring you in this place,
already sweet with violets?
(those you brought
with swathes of earliest grass,
forest and meadow balm,
flung from your giant arms
for us to rest upon.)

Fair are these petals
broken by your feet;
your horse's hooves
tread softer than a deer's;
your eyes, startled,
are like the deer eyes
while your heart
trembles more than the deer.

O earth, O god,
O forest, stream or river,
what shall I bring
that all the day hold back,
that Dawn remember Love
and rest upon her bed,
and Zeus, forgetful not of Danae or Maia,
bid the stars shine forever.

Thetis

He had asked for immortal life
in the old days and had grown old,
now he had aged apace,
he asked for his youth,
and I, Thetis, granted him

freedom under the sea
drip and welter of weeds,
the drift of the fringing grass,
the gift of the never-withering moss,
and the flowering reed,

and most,
beauty of fifty nereids,
sisters of nine,
I one of their least,
yet great and a goddess,
granted Pelius,

love under the sea,
beauty, grace infinite:

so I crept, at last,
a crescent, a curve of a wave,
(a man would have thought,
had he watched for his nets
on the beach)
a dolphin, a glistening fish,
that burnt and caught for its light,
the light of the undercrest
of the lifting tide,
a fish with silver for breast,
with no light but the light
of the sea it reflects.

Little he would have guessed,
(had such a one
watched by his nets,)
that a goddess flung from the crest
of the wave the blue of its own
bright tress of hair,
the blue of the painted stuff
it wore for dress.

No man would have known save he,
whose coming I sensed as I strung
my pearl and agate and pearl,
to mark the beat and the stress
of the lilt of my song.

Who dreams of a son,
save one,
childless, having no bright
face to flatter its own,
who dreams of a son?

Nereids under the sea,
my sisters, fifty and one,
(counting myself)
they dream of a child
of water and sea,
with hair of the softest,

to lie along the curve
of fragile, tiny bones,
yet more beautiful each than each,
hair more bright and long,
to rival its own.

Nereids under the wave,
who dreams of a son
save I, Thetis, alone?

Each would have for a child,
a stray self, furtive and wild,
to dive and leap to the wind,
to wheedle and coax
the stray birds bright and bland
of foreign strands,
to crawl and stretch on the sands,
each would have for its own,
a daughter for child.

Who dreams, who sings of a son?
I, Thetis, alone.

When I had finished my song,
and dropped the last seed-pearl,
and flung the necklet
about my throat
and found it none too bright,
not bright enough nor pale
enough, not like the moon that creeps
beneath the sea,
between the lift of crest and crest,
had tried it on
and found it not
quite fair enough
to fill the night
of my blue folds of bluest dress
with moon for light,
I cast the beads aside and leapt,

161

myself all blue
with no bright gloss
of pearls for crescent light;

but one alert, all blue and wet,
I flung myself, an arrow's flight,
straight upward
through the blue of night
that was my palace wall,
and crept to where I saw the mark
of feet, a rare foot-fall:

Achilles' sandal on the beach,
could one mistake?
perhaps a lover or a nymph,
lost from the tangled fern and brake,
that lines the upper shelf of land,
perhaps a goddess or a nymph
might so mistake
Achilles' footprint for the trace
of a bright god alert to track
the panther where he slinks for thirst
across the sand;

perhaps a goddess or a nymph,
might think a god had crossed the track
of weed and drift,
had broken here this stem of reed,
had turned this sea-shell to the light:

so she must stoop, this goddess girl,
or nymph, with crest of blossoming wood
about her hair for cap or crown,
must stoop and kneel and bending down,
must kiss the print of such a one.

Not I, the mother, Thetis self,
I stretched and lay, a river's slim
dark length,
a rivulet where it leaves the wood,
and meets the sea,
I lay along the burning sand,
a river's blue.

At Ithaca

Over and back,
the long waves crawl
and track the sand with foam;
night darkens and the sea
takes on that desperate tone
of dark that wives put on
when all their love is done.

Over and back,
the tangled thread falls slack,
over and up and on;
over and all is sewn;
now while I bind the end,
I wish some fiery friend
would sweep impetuously
these fingers from the loom.

My weary thoughts
play traitor to my soul
just as the toil is over;
swift while the woof is whole,
turn now my spirit, swift,
and tear the pattern there,
the flowers so deftly wrought,
the border of sea-blue,
the sea-blue coast of home.

The web was over-fair,
that web of pictures there,
enchantments that I thought
he had, that I had lost;
weaving his happiness
within the stitching frame,
weaving his fire and fame,
I thought my work was done,
I prayed that only one
of those that I had spurned,
might stoop and conquer this
long waiting with a kiss.

But each time that I see
my work so beautifully
inwoven and would keep
the picture and the whole,
Athene steels my soul,
slanting across my brain,
I see as shafts of rain
his chariot and his shafts,
I see the arrows fall,
I see my lord who moves
like Hector, lord of love,
I see him matched with fair
bright rivals and I see
those lesser rivals flee.

We Two

We two are left:
I with small grace reveal
distaste and bitterness;
you with small patience
take my hands;
though effortless,

you scald their weight
as a bowl, lined with embers,
wherein droop
great petals of white rose,
forced by the heat
too soon to break.

We two are left:
as a blank wall, the world,
earth and the men who talk,
saying their space of life
is good and gracious,
with eyes blank
as that blank surface
their ignorance mistakes
for final shelter
and a resting-place.

We two remain:
yet by what miracle,
searching within the tangles of my brain,
I ask again,
have we two met within
this maze of daedal paths
in-wound mid grievous stone,
where once I stood alone?

Fragment Thirty-six

I know not what to do:
  my mind is divided.—Sappho.

I know not what to do,
my mind is reft:
is song's gift best?
is love's gift loveliest?

I know not what to do,
now sleep has pressed
weight on your eyelids.

Shall I break your rest,
devouring, eager?
is love's gift best?
nay, song's the loveliest:
yet were you lost,
what rapture
could I take from song?
what song were left?

I know not what to do:
to turn and slake
the rage that burns,
with my breath burn
and trouble your cool breath?
so shall I turn and take
snow in my arms?
(is love's gift best?)
yet flake on flake
of snow were comfortless,
did you lie wondering,
wakened yet unawake.

Shall I turn and take
comfortless snow within my arms?
press lips to lips
that answer not,
press lips to flesh
that shudders not nor breaks?

Is love's gift best?
shall I turn and slake
all the wild longing?
O I am eager for you!
as the Pleiads shake
white light in whiter water
so shall I take you?

166

My mind is quite divided,
my minds hesitate,
so perfect matched,
I know not what to do:
each strives with each
as two white wrestlers
standing for a match,
ready to turn and clutch
yet never shake muscle nor nerve nor tendon;
so my mind waits
to grapple with my mind,
yet I lie quiet,
I would seem at rest.

I know not what to do:
strain upon strain,
sound surging upon sound
makes my brain blind;
as a wave-line may wait to fall
yet (waiting for its falling)
still the wind may take
from off its crest,
white flake on flake of foam,
that rises,
seeming to dart and pulse
and rend the light,
so my mind hesitates
above the passion
quivering yet to break,
so my mind hesitates
above my mind,
listening to song's delight.

I know not what to do:
will the sound break,
rending the night
with rift on rift of rose
and scattered light?

will the sound break at last
as the wave hesitant,
or will the whole night pass
and I lie listening awake?

Flute Song

Little scavenger away,
touch not the door,
beat not the portal down,
cross not the sill,
silent until
my song, bright and shrill,
breathes out its lay.

Little scavenger avaunt,
tempt me with jeer and taunt,
yet you will wait to-day;
for it were surely ill
to mock and shout and revel;
it were more fit to tell
with flutes and calathes,
your mother's praise.

After Troy

We flung against their gods,
invincible, clear hate;
we fought;
frantic, we flung the last
imperious, desperate shaft

and lost:
we knew the loss
before they ever guessed
fortune had tossed to them
her favour and her whim;
but how were we depressed?
we lost yet as we pressed
our spearsmen on their best,
we knew their line invincible
because there fell
on them no shiverings
of the white enchantress,
radiant Aphrodite's spell:

we hurled our shafts of passion,
noblest hate,‾
and knew their cause was blest,
and knew their gods were nobler,
better taught in skill,
subtler with wit of thought,
yet had it been God's will
that *they* not we should fall,
we know those fields had bled
with roses lesser red.

Cassandra

O Hymen king.

Hymen, O Hymen king,
what bitter thing is this?
what shaft, tearing my heart?
what scar, what light, what fire
searing my eye-balls and my eyes with flame?
nameless, O spoken name,
king, lord, speak blameless Hymen.

Why do you blind my eyes?
why do you dart and pulse
till all the dark is home,
then find my soul
and ruthless draw it back?
scaling the scaleless,
opening the dark?
speak, nameless, power and might;
when will you leave me quite?
when will you break my wings
or leave them utterly free
to scale heaven endlessly?

A bitter, broken thing,
my heart, O Hymen lord,
yet neither drought nor sword
baffles men quite,
why must they feign to fear
my virgin glance?
feigned utterly or real
why do they shrink?
my trance frightens them,
breaks the dance,
empties the market-place;
if I but pass they fall
back, frantically;
must always people mock?
unless they shrink and reel
as in the temple
at your uttered will.

O Hymen king,
lord, greatest, power, might,
look for my face is dark,
burnt with your light,
your fire, O Hymen lord;
is there none left
can equal me
in ecstasy, desire?

is there none left
can bear with me
the kiss of your white fire?
is there not one,
Phrygian or frenzied Greek,
poet, song-swept, or bard,
one meet to take from me
this bitter power of song,
one fit to speak, Hymen,
your praises, lord?

May I not wed
as you have wed?
may it not break, beauty,
from out my hands, my head, my feet?
may Love not lie beside me
till his heat
burn me to ash?
may he not comfort me, then,
spent of all that fire and heat,
still, ashen-white and cool
as the wet laurels,
white, before your feet
step on the mountain-slope,
before your fiery hand
lift up the mantle
covering flower and land,
as a man lifts,
O Hymen, from his bride,
(cowering with woman eyes,) the veil?
O Hymen lord, be kind.

Epigrams

1

O ruthless, perilous, imperious hate,
you can not thwart
the promptings of my soul,
you can not weaken nay nor dominate
Love that is mateless,
Love the rite,
the whole measure of being:
would you crush with bondage?
nay, you would love me not
were I your slave.

2

Torture me not with this or that or this,
Love is my master,
you his lesser self;
while you are Love,
I love you generously,
be Eros,
not a tyrannous, bitter mate:
Love has no charm
when Love is swept to earth:
you'd make a lop-winged god,
frozen and contrite,
of god up-darting,
winged for passionate flight.

Fragment Forty

Love . . . bitter-sweet.—Sappho.

1

Keep love and he wings,
with his bow,
up, mocking us,
keep love and he taunts us
and escapes.

Keep love and he sways apart
in another world,
outdistancing us.

Keep love and he mocks,
ah, bitter and sweet,
your sweetness is more cruel
than your hurt.

Honey and salt,
fire burst from the rocks
to meet fire
spilt from Hesperus.

Fire darted aloft and met fire:
in that moment
love entered us.

2

Could Eros be kept?
he were prisoned long since
and sick with imprisonment;
could Eros be kept?
others would have broken
and crushed out his life.

173

Could Eros be kept?
we too sinning, by Kypris,
might have prisoned him outright.

Could Eros be kept?
nay, thank him and the bright goddess
that he left us.

3

Ah, love is bitter and sweet,
but which is more sweet,
the sweetness
or the bitterness?
none has spoken it.

Love is bitter,
but can salt taint sea-flowers,
grief, happiness?

Is it bitter to give back
love to your lover
if he crave it?

Is it bitter to give back
love to your lover
if he wish it
for a new favourite?
who can say,
or is it sweet?

Is it sweet
to possess utterly?
or is it bitter,
bitter as ash?

4

I had thought myself frail;
a petal,
with light equal
on leaf and under-leaf.

I had thought myself frail;
a lamp,
shell, ivory or crust of pearl,
about to fall shattered,
with flame spent.

I cried:
"I must perish,
I am deserted,
an outcast, desperate
in this darkness,"
(such fire rent me with Hesperus,)
then the day broke.

5

What need of a lamp
when day lightens us,
what need to bind love
when love stands
with such radiant wings
over us?

What need—
yet to sing love,
love must first shatter us.

Toward the Piraeus

Slay with your eyes, Greek,
men over the face of the earth,
slay with your eyes, the host,
puny, passionless, weak.

Break as the ranks of steel
broke when the Persian lost:
craven, we hated them then:
now we would count them Gods
beside these, spawn of the earth.

Grant us your mantle, Greek!
grant us but one
to fright (as your eyes) with a sword,
men, craven and weak,
grant us but one to strike
one blow for you, passionate Greek.

1

You would have broken my wings,
but the very fact that you knew
I had wings, set some seal
on my bitter heart, my heart
broke and fluttered and sang.

You would have snared me,
and scattered the strands of my nest;
but the very fact that you saw,
sheltered me, claimed me,
set me apart from the rest

Of men—of *men*, made you a god,
and me, claimed me, set me apart
and the song in my breast,
yours, yours forever—
if I escape your evil heart.

2

I loved you:
men have writ and women have said
they loved,
but as the Pythoness stands by the altar,
intense and may not move,

176

till the fumes pass over;
and may not falter or break,
till the priest has caught the words
that mar or make
a deme or a ravaged town;

so I, though my knees tremble,
my heart break,
must note the rumbling,
heed only the shuddering
down in the fissure beneath the rock
of the temple floor;

must wait and watch
and may not turn nor move,
nor break from my trance to speak
so slight, so sweet,
so simple a word as love.

3

What had you done
had you been true,
I can not think,
I may not know.

What could we do
were I not wise,
what play invent,
what joy devise?

What could we do
if you were great?

(Yet were you lost,
who were there then,
to circumvent
the tricks of men?)

177

What can we do,
for curious lies
have filled your heart,
and in my eyes
sorrow has writ
that I am wise.

4

If I had been a boy,
I would have worshipped your grace,
I would have flung my worship
before your feet,
I would have followed apart,
glad, rent with an ecstasy
to watch you turn
your great head, set on the throat,
thick, dark with its sinews,
burned and wrought
like the olive stalk,
and the noble chin
and the throat.

I would have stood,
and watched and watched
and burned,
and when in the night,
from the many hosts, your slaves,
and warriors and serving men
you had turned
to the purple couch and the flame
of the woman, tall like the cypress tree
that flames sudden and swift and free
as with crackle of golden resin
and cones and the locks flung free
like the cypress limbs,
bound, caught and shaken and loosed,
bound, caught and riven and bound
and loosened again,
as in rain of a kingly storm
or wind full from a desert plain.

So, when you had risen
from all the lethargy of love and its heat,
you would have summoned me,
me alone,
and found my hands,
beyond all the hands in the world,
cold, cold, cold,
intolerably cold and sweet.

5

It was not chastity that made me cold nor fear,
only I knew that you, like myself, were sick
of the puny race that crawls and quibbles and lisps
of love and love and lovers and love's deceit.

It was not chastity that made me wild, but fear
that my weapon, tempered in different heat,
was over-matched by yours, and your hand
skilled to yield death-blows, might break

With the slightest turn—no ill will meant—
my own lesser, yet still somewhat fine-wrought,
fiery-tempered, delicate, over-passionate steel.

At Eleusis

*What they did,
they did for Dionysos,
for ecstasy's sake:*

now take the basket,
think;
think of the moment you count
most foul in your life;

179

conjure it,
supplicate,
pray to it;
your face is bleak, you retract,
you dare not remember it:

stop;
it is too late.
The next stands by the altar step,
a child's face yet not innocent,
it will prove adequate, but you,
I could have spelt your peril at the gate,
yet for your mind's sake,
though you could not enter,
wait.

What they did,
they did for Dionysos,
for ecstasy's sake:

Now take the basket—
(ah face in a dream,
did I not know your heart,
I would falter,
for each that fares onward
is my child;
ah can you wonder
that my hands shake,
that my knees tremble,
I a mortal, set in the goddess' place?)

Fragment Forty-one

. . . thou flittest to Andromeda.—Sappho.

1

Am I blind alas,
am I blind?
I too have followed
her path.
I too have bent at her feet.
I too have wakened to pluck
amaranth in the straight shaft,
amaranth purple in the cup,
scorched at the edge to white.

Am I blind?
am I the less ready for her sacrifice?
am I the less eager to give
what she asks,
she the shameless and radiant?

Am I quite lost,
I towering above you and her glance,
walking with swifter pace,
with clearer sight,
with intensity
beside which you two
are as spent ash?

Nay, I give back to the goddess the gift
she tendered me in a moment
of great bounty.
I return it. I lay it again
on the white slab of her house,
the beauty she cast out
one moment, careless.

Nor do I cry out:
"why did I stoop?
why did I turn aside
one moment from the rocks
marking the sea-path?
Aphrodite, shameless and radiant,
have pity, turn, answer us."

Ah no—though I stumble toward
her altar-step,
though my flesh is scorched and rent,
shattered, cut apart,
slashed open;
though my heels press my own wet life
black, dark to purple,
on the smooth, rose-streaked
threshold of her pavement.

2

Am I blind alas, deaf too
that my ears lost all this?
nay, O my lover,
shameless and still radiant,
I tell you this:

I was not asleep,
I did not lie asleep on those hot rocks
while you waited.
I was not unaware when I glanced
out toward the sea
watching the purple ships.

I was not blind when I turned.
I was not indifferent when I strayed aside
or loitered as we three went
or seemed to turn a moment from the path
for that same amaranth.

I was not dull and dead when I fell
back on our couch at night.
I was not indifferent when I turned
and lay quiet.
I was not dead in my sleep.

3

Lady of all beauty,
I give you this:
say I have offered small sacrifice,
say I am unworthy your touch,
but say not:
"she turned to some cold, calm god,
silent, pitiful, in preference."

Lady of all beauty,
I give you this:
say not:
"she deserted my altar-step,
the fire on my white hearth
was too great,
she fell back at my first glance."

Lady, radiant and shameless,
I have brought small wreaths,
(they were a child's gift,)
I have offered myrrh-leaf,
crisp lentisk,
I have laid rose-petal
and white rock-rose from the beach.

But I give now a greater,
I give life and spirit with this.
I render a grace
no one has dared to speak,
lest men at your altar greet him
as slave, callous to your art;

I dare more than the singer
offering her lute,
the girl her stained veils,
the woman her swathes of birth,
or pencil and chalk,
mirror and unguent box.

I offer more than the lad
singing at your steps,
praise of himself,
his mirror his friend's face,
more than any girl,
I offer you this:
(grant only strength
that I withdraw not my gift,)
I give you my praise and this:
the love of my lover
for his mistress.

Telesila

In Argos—that statue of her;
at her feet the scroll of her
love-poetry, in her hand a helmet.

War is a fevered god
who takes alike
maiden and king and clod,
and yet another one,
(ah withering peril!)
deprives alike,
with equal skill,
alike indifferently,
hoar spearsman of his shaft,

wan maiden of her zone,
even he,
Love who is great War's
very over-lord.

War bent
and kissed the forehead,
yet Love swift,
planted on chin
and tenderest cyclamen lift
of fragrant mouth,
fevered and honeyed breath,
breathing o'er and o'er
those tendrils of her hair,
soft kisses
like bright flowers.

Love took
and laid the sweet,
(being extravagant,)
on lip and chin and cheek,
but, ah, he failed
even he,
before the luminous eyes
that dart
no suave appeal,
alas, impelling me
to brave incontinent,
grave Pallas' high command.

And yet the mouth!
ah Love ingratiate,
how was it you,
so poignant, swift and sure,
could not have taken all
and left me free,
free to desert the Argives,
let them burn,

free yet to turn
and let the city fall:
yea, let high War
take all his vengeful way,
for what am I?
I cannot save nor stay
the city's fall.

War is a fevered god,
(yet who has writ as she
the power of Love?)
War bent and kissed the forehead,
that bright brow,
ignored the chin
and the sweet mouth,
for that and the low laugh were his,
Eros ingratiate,
who sadly missed
in all the kisses count,
those eyebrows
and swart eyes,
O valiant one
who bowed
falsely and vilely trapped us
traitorous lord.

And yet,
(remembrance mocks,)
should I have bent the maiden
to a kiss?
Ares the lover
or enchanting Love?
but had I moved
I feared
for that astute regard;
for that bright vision,
how might I have erred?
I might have marred and swept
another not so sweet
into my exile;

186

I might have kept a look
recalling many and many a woman's look,
not this alone,
astute, imperious, proud.

And yet
I turn and ask
again, again, again,
who march to death,
what was it worth,
reserve and pride and hurt?
what is it worth
to such as I
who turn to meet
the invincible Spartans'
massed and serried host?
what had it cost, a kiss?

Fragment Sixty-eight

. . . even in the house of Hades.—Sappho.

1

I envy you your chance of death,
how I envy you this.
I am more covetous of him
even than of your glance,
I wish more from his presence
though he torture me in a grasp,
terrible, intense.

Though he clasp me in an embrace
that is set against my will
and rack me with his measure,
effortless yet full of strength,

and slay me
in that most horrible contest,
still, how I envy you your chance.

Though he pierce me—imperious—
iron—fever—dust—
though beauty is slain
when I perish,
I envy you death.

What is beauty to me?
has she not slain me enough,
have I not cried in agony of love,
birth, hate,
in pride crushed?

What is left after this?
what can death loose in me
after your embrace?
your touch,
your limbs are more terrible
to do me hurt.

What can death mar in me
that you have not?

2

What can death send me
that you have not?
you gathered violets,
you spoke:
"your hair is not less black,
nor less fragrant,
nor in your eyes is less light,
your hair is not less sweet
with purple in the lift of lock;"
why were those slight words
and the violets you gathered
of such worth?

How I envy you death;
what could death bring,
more black, more set with sparks
to slay, to affright,
than the memory of those first violets,
the chance lift of your voice,
the chance blinding frenzy
as you bent?

3

So the goddess has slain me
for your chance smile
and my scarf unfolding
as you stooped to it;
so she trapped me
with the upward sweep of your arm
as you lifted the veil,
and the swift smile and selfless.

Could I have known?
nay, spare pity,
though I break,
crushed under the goddess' hate,
though I fall beaten at last,
so high have I thrust my glance
up into her presence.

Do not pity me, spare that,
but how I envy you
your chance of death.

Lethe

Nor skin nor hide nor fleece
    Shall cover you,
Nor curtain of crimson nor fine
Shelter of cedar-wood be over you,
    Nor the fir-tree
    Nor the pine.

Nor sight of whin nor gorse
    Nor river-yew,
Nor fragrance of flowering bush,
Nor wailing of reed-bird to waken you,
    Nor of linnet,
    Nor of thrush.

Nor word nor touch nor sight
    Of lover, you
Shall long through the night but for this:
The roll of the full tide to cover you
    Without question,
    Without kiss.

Charioteer

In that manner (archaic) he finished the statue of his brother. It stands mid-way in the hall of laurels . . . between the Siphnians' offering and the famous tripod of Naxos.

Only the priest
of the inmost house
has such height,
only the faun
in the glade
such light, strong ankles,

only the shade of the bay-tree
such rare dark
as the darkness
caught under the fillet
that covers your brow,
only the blade
of the ash-tree
such length, such beauty
as thou,
O my brother;
and only the gods
have such love
as I bring you;
but now,
taut with love,
more than any bright lover,
I vowed
to the innermost
god of the temple,
this vow.

God of beauty, I cried,
as the four stood alert,
awaiting the shout
at the goal
to be off;
god of beauty,
I cried to that god,
if he merit the laurel,
I dedicate all of my soul
to you; to you
all my strength and my power;
if he merit the bay,
I will fashion a statue
of him, of my brother,
out of thought,
and the strength of my wrist
and the fire of my brain;
I will strive night and day
till I mould from the clay,

till I strike from the bronze,
till I conjure the rock,
the chisel, the tool,
to embody this image;
an image to startle,
to capture men's hearts,
to make all other bronze,
all art to come after,
a mock,
all beauty to follow,
a shell that is empty;
I'll stake all my soul
on that beauty,
till God shall awake
again in men's hearts,
who have said he is dead,
our King and our Lover.

Then the start,
ah the sight,
ah but dim, veiled with tears,
(so Achilles must weep
who finds his friend dead,)
will he win?
then the ring of the steel
as two met at the goal,
entangled and foul,
misplaced at the start,
who, who blunders? not you?
what omens are set?
alas, gods of the track,
what ill wreaks its hate,
speak it clear,
let me know
what evil, what fate?
for the ring of sharp steel
told two were in peril,
two, two, one is you,
already involved

with the fears of defeat;
two grazed;
which must go?

As the wind,
Althaia's beauty came;
as one after a cruel march,
catches sight,
toward the cold dusk,
of the flower
that's her name-sake,
strayed apart
toward the road-dust,
from the stream
in the wood-depth,
so I in that darkness,
my mouth bitter
with sheer loss,
took courage,
my heart spoke,
remembering how she spoke:
"I will seek hour by hour
fresh cones, resin
and pine-flowers,
flower of pine,
laurel flower;
I will pray:
'let him come
back to us,
to our home,
with the trophy of zeal,
with the love and the proof
of the favour of god;
let him merit the bay.'
(I expect it,)

I myself on earth pray
that our father may pray;
his voice nearer the gods
must carry beyond
my mere mortal prayer:
'O my father beyond,
look down, and be proud,
ask this thing
that we win,
ask it straight of the gods.'"

Was he glad,
did he know?
for the strength
of his prayer and her prayer
met me now
in one flame,
all my head, all my brow
was one flame,
taut and beaten
and faintly aglow,
as the wine-cup
encrusted and beaten and fine
with the pattern of leaves,
(so my brow,)
yet metallic and cool,
as the gold of the frigid metal
that circles the heat
of the wine.

Then the axle-tree cleft,
not ours, gods be blest;
now but three of you left,
three alert and abreast,
three—one streak of what fire?
three straight for the goal:
ah defeat,
ah despair,
still fate tricked our mares,

194

for they swerved,
flanks quivering and wet,
as the wind
at the mid-stretch
caught and fluttered a white scarf;
a veil shivering,
only the fluttering
of a white band,
yet unnerved and champing,
they turned,
(only knowing the swards of Achaea)
and he, O my love,
that stranger,
his stallions
stark frenzied and black,
had taken the inmost course,
overtook,
overcame,
overleapt,
and crowded you back.

O those horses
we loved and we prized;
I had gathered Alea mint
and soft branch
of the vine-stock in flower,
I had stroked Elaphia;
as one prays to a woman
"be kind,"
I had prayed Daphnaia;
I had threatened Orea
for her trick
of out-pacing the three,
even these,
I had almost despaired
at her fleet, proud pace,
O the four,
O swift mares of Achaea.

Should I pray them again?
or the gods of the track?
or Althaia at home?
or our father who died for Achaea?
or our fathers beyond
who had vanquished the east?
should I threaten or pray?

The sun struck the ridge of white marble
before me:
white sun on white marble
was black:
the day was of ash,
blind, unrepentant, despoiled,
my soul cursed the race and the track,
you had lost.

You, lost at the last?

Ah fools,
so you threatened to win?
ah fools,
so you knew my brother?
Greeks all,
all crafty and feckless,
even so, had you guessed
what ran in his veins and mine,
what blood of Achaea,
had you dared,
dared enter the contest,
dared aspire with the rest?

You had gained,
you outleapt them;
a sudden, swift lift of the reins,
a sudden, swift, taut grip of the reins,
as suddenly loosed,
you had gained.

196

When death comes
I will see
no vision of after,
(as some count
there may be an hereafter,)
no thought of old lover,
no girl, no woman,
neither mother,
nor yet my father
who died for Achaea,
neither God with the harp
and the sun on His brow,
but thou,
O my brother.

When death comes,
instead of a vision,
(I will catch it in bronze)
you will stand
as you stood at the end,
(as the herald announced it,
proclaiming aloud,
"Achaea has won,")
in-reining them now,
so quiet,
not turning to answer
the shout of the crowd.

The Look-out

Better the wind, the sea, the salt
in your eyes,
than this, this, this.

You grumble and sweat;
my ears are acute
to catch your complaint,
almost the sea's roar is less
than your constant threat
of "back and back to the shore,
and let us rest."

You grumble and curse your luck
and I hear:
"O Lynceus,
aloft by the prow,
his head on his arms,
his eyes half closed,
almost asleep,
to watch for a rock,
(and hardly ever we need
his 'to left' or 'to right')
let Lynceus have my part,
let me rest like Lynceus."

"Rest like Lynceus!"
I'd change my fate for yours,
the very least,
I'd take an oar with the rest.

"Like Lynceus,"
as if my lot were the best.

O God, if I could speak,
if I could taunt the lot
of the wretched crew,
with my fate, my work.

But I may not,
I may not tell
of the forms that pass and pass,
of that constant old, old face
that leaps from each wave
to wait underneath the boat
in the hope that at last she's lost.

Could I speak,
I would tell of great mountains
that flow, great weeds
that float and float
to tangle our oars
if I fail "to left, to right;"
where the dolphin leaps
you saw a sign from the god,
I saw why he leapt from the deep.

"To right, to left;"
it is easy enough
to lean on the prow, half asleep,
and you think,
"no work for Lynceus."
No work?

If only you'd let me take an oar,
if only my back could break with the hurt,
if the sun could blister my feet,
pain, pain that I might forget
the face that just this moment
passed through the prow
when you said, "asleep."

Many and many a sight
if I could speak,
many and many tales I'd tell,
many and many a struggle,
many a death,
many and many my hurts
and my pain so great,
I'd gladly die
if I did not love the quest.

Grumble and swear and curse,
brother, god and the boat,
and the great waves,

but could you guess
what strange terror lurks in the sea-depth,
you'd thank the gods for the ship,
the timber and giant oars, god-like,
and the god-like quest.

If you could see as I,
what lurks in the sea-depth,
you'd pray to the ropes
and the solid timbers
like god, like god;

you'd pray to the oars and your work,
you'd pray and thank
the boat for her very self;
timber and oar and plank
and sail and the sail-ropes,
these are beautiful things and great.

But Lynceus at the prow
has nothing to do but wait
till we reach a shoal or some rocks
and then he has only to lift his arms,
right, left;
O brother,
I'd change my place
for the worst seat
in the cramped bench,
for an oar, for an hour's toil,
for sweat and the solid floor.

I'd change my place
as I sit with eyes half closed,
if only I could see just the ring
cut by the boat,
if only I could see just the water,
the crest and the broken crest,
the bit of weed that rises on the crest,
the dolphin only when he leaps.

But Lynceus,
though they cannot guess
the hurt, though they do not thank
the oars for the dead peace
of heart and brain worn out,
you must wait,
alert, alert, alert.

From the Masque

Hyacinth

1

Your anger charms me,
and yet all the time
I think of chaste, slight hands,
veined snow;
snow craters filled
with first wild-flowerlets;
glow of ice-gentian,
whitest violet;
snow craters
and the ice ridge
spilling light;
dawn and the lover
chaste dawn leaves bereft—
I think of these
and snow-cooled Phrygian wine.

Your anger charms me subtly
and I know
that you would take
the still hands
where I'd rest;

you would despoil
for very joy of theft;
list, lady,
I would give you one last hint:
quench your red mouth
in some cold forest lake,
cover your russet locks
with arum leaf,
quench out the colour,
still the fevered glance,
cover your want,
your fire insatiate,
I can not match your fervour,
nay, nor still my ache
with any
but white hands inviolate.

2

Take the red spoil
of grape and pomegranate,
the red camellia,
the most, most red rose;
take all the garden spills,
inveterate,
prodigal spender
just as summer goes,
the red scales of the deep in-folded spice,
the Indian, Persian and the Syrian pink,
their scent undaunted
even in that faint,
unmistakable fragrance
of the late tuberose,
(heavy its petals,
eye-lids of dark eyes
that open languorous
and more languorous close—the east,
further than scent
of our wind-smitten isle,)
take these:

O lady, take them,
prodigal
I cull and offer this and this and these
last definite whorls
of clustered peonies,
the last, the first
that stained our stainless ledge
of blue and white
and the white foam of sea,
rocks,
and that strait ledge
whiter than the rock
the Parians break
from their enchanted hill;
take, lady,
but leave me with my weed and shell
and those slight, hovering gull-wings that recall
silver of far Hymettus' asphodel.

3

Take all
for you have taken everything,
but do not let me see you taking this;
Adonis lying spent with Venus' care,
Adonis dying were a lesser ache
than this,
to have even your slightest breath
breathe in the crystal air
where he takes breath.

Take all
for you have taken everything,
save the broad ledge of sea
which no man takes,
take all
for you have taken mirth and ease
and all the small delights
of simple poets,
the lilt of rhyme,

the sway and lift and fall,
the first spring gold
your fire has scorched to ash,
the fresh winds
that go halt
where you have passed,
the Tyrian iris
I so greatly loved,
its dark head speared
through its wet spray of leaves.

Take all,
but ah, lady, a fool, a poet
may even know when you have taken all:
up on the mountain slope
one last flower cleaves
to the wet marge of ice,
the blue of snow,
keep all your riot
in the swales below,
of grape and autumn,
take all, taking these,
for you and autumn yet
can not prevail
against that flame, that flower,
(ice, spark or jewel,)
the cyclamen,
parting its white cyclamen leaves.

4

O, I am ill with dust
as you with stain,
O, I am worthless,
weary, world-bedraggled,
nevertheless to mountains
still the rain
falls on the tangle
of dead under-brush,
freshens the loam,

the earth and broken leaves
for that hoar-frost
of later star or flower,
the fragile host
of Greek anemones.

Say I am little meet
to call the youth,
say I have little magic
to enchant,
but is that reason
why your flaring will
should sweep and scorch,
should lap and seethe and fill
with last red flame
the tender ditch and runnel
which the spring freshet
soon must fill again?

White violets
have no place
on your hot brow;
how can I bring you
what the spring must bring?
what can I offer?
lush and heady mallow?
the fire-grass
or the serpent-spotted
fire-flower?
O take them,
for I stand a ruinous cloud
between you
and the chaste uplifted hill.

O take them swiftly
and more swiftly go,
for spring is distant yet,
for spring is far;
you have your tense, short space
of blazing sun,

your melons, vines,
your terraces of fruit;
now all you have,
all, all I gladly give
who long but for the ridge,
the crest and hollow,
the lift and fall,
the reach and distant ledge
of the sun-smitten,
wind-indented snow.

The bird-choros of

Ion

Birds from Parnassus,
swift
you dart
from the loftiest peaks;
you hover, dip,
you sway and perch
undaunted on the gold-set cornice;
you eagle,
god's majestic legate,
who tear, who strike
song-birds in mid-flight,
my arrow whistles toward you,
swift
be off;

ah drift,
ah drift
so soft, so light,
your scarlet foot so deftly placed
to waft you neatly
to the pavement,

swan, swan
and do you really think
your song
that tunes the harp of Helios,
will save you
from the arrow-flight?
turn back,
back
to the lake of Delos;

lest all the song notes
pause and break
across a blood-stained throat
gone songless,
turn back,
back
ere it be too late,
to wave-swept Delos.

Alas, and still another,
what?
you'd place your mean nest
in the cornice?
sing, sing
my arrow-string,
tell to the thief
that plaits its house
for fledglings
in the god's own house,
that still the Alpheus
whispers sweet
to lure
the birdlets to the place,
that still the Isthmus
shines with forests;
on the white statues
must be found
no straw nor litter
of bird-down,
Phœbus must have his portal fair;

and yet, O birds,
though this my labour
is set,
though this my task is clear,
though I must slay you,
I, god's servant,
I who take here
my bread and life
and sweep the temple,
still I swear
that I would save you,
birds or spirits,
winged songs
that tell to men god's will;

still, still
the Alpheus whispers clear
to lure the bird-folk
to its waters,
ah still
the Isthmus
blossoms fair;
lest all the song notes
pause and break
across a blood-stained throat
gone songless,
turn back,
back
ere it be too late,
to wave-swept Delos.

RED ROSES FOR BRONZE
1931

Red Roses for Bronze

I

If I might take a weight of bronze
and sate
my wretched fingers
in ecstatic work,
if I might fashion
eyes and mouth and chin,
if I might take dark bronze
and hammer in
the line beneath your underlip
(the slightly mocking,
slightly cynical smile
you choose to wear)
if I might ease my fingers and my brain
with stroke,
stroke,
stroke,
stroke,
stroke at—something (stone, marble, intent,
    stable, materialized)
peace,
even magic sleep
might come again.

II

All very well
while all the others smirked,
to turn and smile:
you thought that I might see your joke,
would do
(fault of a better)
for the moment anyhow;
you knew
that I would prove too strange, too proud,
for just the ordinary sort of come and go,
the little half-said thing,

the half-caught smile,
the subtle little sort of differentiating
between the thing that's said
and that's said not;
the "have I seen you somewhere else?
forgot? impossible,"
the half-caught back half-smile,
the interrupted nod,
"a clod
may hold the rarest flower,
so I?"
the question that's an answer
and the thing
that means that what's said
isn't answering;
this,
this,
or this,
or this thing
or this other;
the casual sort of homage that you care
to flick toward this
or this odd passing whim;
the one above the second on the marble stair,
the smaller (or the taller) of those two,
chattering,
chattering
by the fountain-rim.

III

I count most men ignoble by your height,
neither too tall,
for some taste
none too slight,
but sensing underneath the garment seam
ripple and flash and gleam
of indrawn muscle
and of those more taut,

212

I feel that I must turn and tear and rip
the fine cloth
from the moulded thigh and hip,
force you to grasp my soul's sincerity,
and single out
me,
me,
something to challenge,
handle differently.

IV

I'd say,
come let me start the thing at once,
to-day—
to-morrow will not do at all;
I've got a studio
near the Olympieum,
it's cold in winter,
in summer—well
the heat
forbids an adequate comparison;
they say discomfort
prods the ardent soul on;
why must they vent on artists
all their venom?
though that, of course, is all
beside the question—
I mean
come now,
to-day;
forgive me; your dark hair
catches the light
in serpent curves,
here,
there;
that shimmer on the bay-leaf
where the sun
catches the bronze-green glint,

213

bay-leaf
or palm,
the sort of thing that spreads its ripple on
over across the helmets
to the stars;

you might be Mars
or maybe Actaeon
the Huntress
bids her hounds
to leap upon.

V

I'd hide my fervour in
"that sort of thing,
you know how tiresome it is,"
begin my mastery
in ironic wise,
making of mouth and eyes
a thing of mystery
and invidious lure,
so that all, seeing it, would stare,
so that all men (seeing it)
would forsake all women
(chattering)
I'd make a thing at last,
downright,
not in the least
subtle
or insinuating;

such is my jealousy and such my hate
though I would state it otherwise,
say;
"as a favour,
just that turn of chin,
something I've waited for,
you know the judges at the Pythian games,
the classic note,

the touch the world proclaims
perfection;
tiresome?
but I must finish what I have begun,
the tall god standing
where the race is run";

such is my jealousy
(that I discreetly veil
with just my smile)
that I would clear so fiery a space
that no mere woman's love could long endure;
and I would set your bronze head in its place,
about the base,
my roses would endure,
while others,
those, for instance,
she might proffer,
standing by the stair,
or any tentative offers of white flowers
or others lesser purple at the leaf,
must fall and sift and pale
in (O so short a space)
to ashes and a little heap of dust.

In the Rain

I

I said,
"the town bird
lifts a lordlier head,"
you said,
"the wild-swan only is kingly";

had I run less swiftly
across the square
(in the rain)
I had had breath to explain;
I did not deign to stammer,
"but this,
but this—"
O kiss
that you did not give,
O name of tenderness
that you did not name.

II

I am glad;
the cold is a cloak,
the gold on the wet stones
is a carpet laid;
my hands clutch at the rain,
no pain in my heart
but gold,
gold,
gold
on my head,
a crown;
while the rain pours down
and the gutters run,
(the lake is over-flowing
and sodden)
I say to myself,
"I am glad he never said good-bye
nor questioned me why
I was late."

III

I'm late to-day,
you were late yesterday,
but he didn't say,
"I'm sorry,

216

I kept you waiting,"
(the rain beats in my eyes again)
I lifted my face,
surprised
to see no answer in his,
no kiss,
(love is a trap,
a snare)
a bird
lifted a passionless wing;
nothing,
nothing was ever so fair
as the wonder that clutched at me there,
unaware,
under the rain;
my brain sang
a rhythm I never dreamt to sing,
"I will be gay and laugh and sing,
he is going away,"
I sang and sang under my breath,
"can death offer a sweeter thing?
I am free;
O pavements spread me your gold,
I am young,
I am young,
I am young
whom Love
had made old."

IV

I will be free,
no lover's kiss
to bind me to earth,
no bliss of love
to counteract
actual bliss,

(the wind,
the rain)
no pain of love
to cut the fibre of joy
that the wind is cold,
that the old, old streets
are beautiful
and the way to the temple,
that the court will yet be bountiful
with box-tree
and myrtle,
that the grove has recompense
of dedmet
and mehet-tree incense,
that some day
I will care:

then,
the air
will be full of multiple wings;
the fountain-basin, bare
of ripple and circlet, will spring
into life,
will duplicate ring
on translucent ring
of amethyst water,
purple
and rare
crimson;
the naked pillar will show
vermilion;
in the empty square;
the God will stand
with his bow
and intimate arrows;
my heart will quiver and bow,
I will start,
remember
the touch of your hand on my brow,

(it was burning,
you healed it,
it was parched
and you cooled it)
but now,
I can walk by the shrine
and the sacred rows
of transplanted apples,
(Cydonian?)
a barbarian,
an ignorant stranger
who knows
nothing of love.

V

Doves
circle and glitter and flare
wing and feather,
very-stars
of the upper air
(where Love is)
do I care?
I seek sustenance
otherwhere;
elsewhere
I find
shelter;
I bind
the dark, dark fibre
of laurel;
spite of you,
spite of all,
to spite
and in respite,
I will bow
to one God;

(O intimate song,
my Lord,
O fire
and the Word);
I will leave
your personified things,
find strength
by an empty altar.

VI

Don't come there,
don't come,
you have all the world,
go anywhere,
everywhere,
you have cloak and wings and a rod,
all the paths are yours,
all, all the altars
save one,
this one
of my intimate God;
don't come near,
go here,
there,
where you will,
you are Hermes,
Lord-of-the-dead,
you are a man,
feigning the godhead,
or a god pretending a man's weakness,
a man's wiles;
frowning
or swift to smile,
you are a god above
and a god below,
Hermes,
treading the track of the dead;
you said,
"you were late yesterday";

had a staunch heart bled
at a casual word
from a casual man?
a god said,
"you were late";

you go to the under-world
or the gate of heaven,
while I tread
an earth,
devoid of your touch,
(unutterable bliss)
thank God,
devoid of your kiss.

VII

Your head
is bound with the myrtle,
is bound with the bay,
is bound with the red
rose;
God knows
(being God)
why you stay with us,
why you trifle and traffic
and play
with us;
if you lose,
if you gain,
do you care?

a snare is Love,
a shame,
who are maimed with Love,
totter and falter and stare,
lost in a world
defamed,

bound round the ankles with violets,
with myrrh
and with half-opened myrrh,
trailing unutterable sweet
and lost,
lost,
lost;
a wreck,
a circumscribed thing
is a man's heart,
touched by the wing
of immortal ecstasy,
we are maimed and weak,
and yet—

I was dead
and you woke me,
now you are gone,
I am dead.

If You Will Let Me Sing

If you will let me sing,
That God will be
gracious to each of us,
who found his own wild Daphne
in a tree,
who set
on desolate plinth,
image
of Hyacinth.

Choros Translations

from *The Bacchae*

I

Who is there,
who is there in the road?
who is there,
who is there in the street?
back,
back, each to his house,
let no one,
no one speak;
chasten your tongues;
O cease
from murmuring,
for swift,
I cry with every note
of concentrated speech
my song to Dionysos.

O happy, happy each
man whom predestined fate
leads to the holy rite
of hill and mountain worship;
O blessed, blessed spirit
who seeks the mountain goddess,
Cybele mother-spirit,
who carrying aloft
the thyrsus, ivy-wrapt,
waits upon
Dionysos.

Bacchantes,
swift,
be swift,
invoke and draw him back
from Phrygian mountain-peaks,

(God's son whom God begot)
back to the broad-paved
sacred towns
of Greece.

II

O Thebes,
Semele's nurse,
crown,
crown yourself
with pine branch,
with ivy
and the bright
fruit
of the flowering smilax;
Thebes,
crown yourself with oak leaf
and dance,
dance,
dance
ecstatic;
bind white wool
to the deer pelt,
lift high
the sacred narthex,
and dance until the earth dance;
the earth must dance
when Bromios
conducts
his sacred high priests
from hill
to distant hill peak,
(those women whom the distaff
no longer claims
nor spun cloth)
driven mad,
mad,
mad
by Bacchus.

III

Ah, it is sweet on the hills,
to dance in sacred faun-pelt,
to dance until one falls faint,
to beat the sacred dance-beat
until one drops down
worn out;
ah, it is sweet to rush
on, then,
to Phrygian hill-peaks,
to taste the sacred raw flesh
of mystic sacred goat-meat;
ah, it is sweet,
ah, sweet
the Lydian hills with Bromios;
Evoe,
Bromios leads us,
bearing aloft the narthex,
himself
even as the pine-torch,
himself the flame and torch-light,
cries,
on,
on,
on;
the fields drip
honey
and wine
and white milk;
the torches smell of incense;
on,
on,
cries Bacchus, Bromios,
rousing the wandering wild pack,
enchanting them with glad shouts,
tossing his glorious hair loose;
he chants,
he cries,

O, O forth
golden
as gold-decked Tmolos;
Bacchantes,
beat deep drum-note,
with Phrygian chant,
sing Evius,
with sacred flute
and sweet note,
incite,
incite our wild dance
from hill
to distant hill-peak;

so hearing him,
Bacchantes,
leap out
and as the wild-colt
at meadow,
round its mare's feet,
they beat
ecstatic dance-beat.

IV

STROPHE. Again,
again in the night,
shall I beat white feet in delight
of the dance
of Dionysos?
shall I bear my throat to the night
air
and the dew in the night?
again shall my pulses beat
like the deer
escaped from the net,
from the knots
and the huntsman's shouts,
from the hounds
and the hunting riot?

shall I lie in the meadows sweet,
escaped,
escaped from the lot
of men,
like a faun in the desert,
like a wind
by the river bank?
again,
again
shall I rest
ecstatic in loneliness,
apart in the haunted forest,
hidden by leaf
and leaf-branch?
O which of the gifts of the gods
is the best gift?
this,
this,
this,
this;
escape
from the power of the hunting pack,
and to know that wisdom is best
and beauty
sheer holiness.

ANTISTROPHE.   Hard,
hard it is to wake the gods,
but once awake,
hard,
hard,
hard is the lot
of the ignorant man,
fanatic,
saying the gods are not;
cunning,
cunning their nets,
hiding time's long, long tracks,
snaring the wretch;

think not
by thought, to escape
predestined fate;
it is so easy to know
wisdom is right,
easy,
easy to bow
to God in His might;
doubt not,
rather accept;
daemons have strength,
ritual is rooted in earth,
ancient and blest.

O which of the gifts of the gods
is the best gift?
this,
this,
this,
this;
escape
from the power of the hunting pack
and to know that wisdom is best
and beauty
sheer holiness.

EPODE.   Hope
has manifold power,
hope,
hope
has manifold face
to manifest men,
each different;
some win,
some fail;
happy, happy he
who, safe from the sea,
finds his sea-port
and home;

happy, happy he
who rests,
when his work is done;
happy the man of wealth,
happy of power,
but happier, happier far
I count
mysterious,
mystical happiness,
this one
who finds
day by day,
hour by hour,
mysterious,
mystical,
not to be spoken
bliss.

V

STROPHE.   Stalk,
stalk the prey,
away,
away to the hills,
hell-hounds of madness,
swift;
leap toward the hideous freak,
this monster of wickedness,
track Pentheus down,
the clown,
mimic in woman's dress;
on to the hills,
the rest
leave to his mother first,
leave to the dancing host,
let the wild Maenads press
toward him who would betray;
hear,
hear his mother cry:

229

arise,
arise and slay
incarnate wickedness,
a godless man
and unjust;
who, who has borne this beast,
no woman,
rather see
whelp of a desert lion
or Lybian Gorgoness;
who,
who has dared appear?
(hear,
hear his mother first,
spying him from the covert,
from the steep ledge of hillock)
hear,
hear,
O Bacchus,
see
who desecrates the hills;
the hills belong to us,
invoke,
invoke
armed Justice;
let Diké stand forth manifest,
let her step forth and slay,
slash him across the throat,
this monster,
Gorgon born,
Echion born
and born of earth.

VI

AGAVE.　Take me,
my guardians,
where I shall look upon
no,
no,
no Cithaeron;

my sisters and me,
one in our misery
shall re-invoke no old
passions and mysteries;
the thyrsus shall pass on
to other Dionysians;
O let me never see
haunted, mad Cithaeron
nor Cithaeron
see me.

Chance Meeting

I

Take from me something,
be it all too fine
and untranslatable and worthless
for your purpose,
take it,
it's mine;
no one can give as I give,
none can say,
"take bountifully and smile
and go away,
then, hate for ever;
do not stoop to send
the little missive
that might slay or end
this pain for ever."

Your one word might stay
the pain;
but do not send it;
keep yourself out of it,
intransient;

finish what you have begun,
write swiftly
with a stylus
dipped in sun
and tears
and blood,
rain,
hail
and snow;
dip stylus in the beauty of the translatable
    things you know;
the things I have
are nameless,
old and true;
they may not be named;
few may live and know.

II

Our hands that did not touch,
might have met once,
might just have gathered
this one in this one;
impersonal fire, beyond us,
might have rushed
into our fingers;
we'd have known then
(being true)
one of the other;
our hands might have crushed
red petal
of an island rose,
have done
with vanity of written word
and rhyme,
might have known once
(just in those fingers)
other leaves and stones,
touched Miletus,
known Samos,

lifted stones
from a small shelf
at Delos,
let grass slip
and seaweed,
(dead ten thousand years ago
that withers never)
in between our hands,
laughed
even;
heaven is a near
translatable thing;
it's here,
it's there . . .

III

I thought my thought
might spoil your thought,
being fierce and rare,
holding bright points
as stars in the mid-air,
slaying and hating
that which it loves most,
even as the sun
the host of stars of night;
even as the sun
must slay the stars
by day,
I thought my thought
would slay;

I thought your thought
was rare,
made maps for men,
the words you write
are chart and rudder in a storm
or bright
as light-house,
set above the shoals;

I thought your stars
must shine for men,
while mine,
must shine alone,
invisible,
to dominate me at noon
while others say,
"the stars are gone,
how odd to see
even a whisp of moon,
by day";
I say,
I thought that you might share my thought,
might cry,
"the stars are shining,
ringed about with the intolerable light
of the sun."

IV

Why did I think of others,
(being untrue)
say to myself,
"this one
and this,
and this
were wrecked by you,"
say,
"you have taken
ruthless and with power,
a burning glass
that concentrates;
the fire,
once stolen,
you reject the ash,
you take the spirit,
let the body go,
to wander like the ghosts
Achilles knew":

why did I hesitate?
I heard a voice,
reiterate an oracle that gravely spoke:
"you took and did not give,
you praised and knew
the song they made was worthless
and the note,
they sung
was dross,
heavy and leaden by your silver-note,
the throat they lifted to bared winds
was slain
by voices in the wind;
you heard,
they did not hear;
you used them as the oracle, the seer
that speaks numb and unheeding what he says,
you bled them of their genius,
being dear
to oracle and altar of the Sun;
we say,
you took whatever fire there was
and left them without love
and without power;

desire crept to your knees,
you took it not to warm yourself
but to tempt near
the things that otherwise must perish
in the wind
and fire."

V

You didn't know
those Gods that pass,
those feet that come and go,
the parting of the curtain
where waves swell,

the holy sands,
the sunken holy well,
the wave that burns
and breaks a sharper blue
because for just one moment
some deft thought
severed the curtain
of that "then" and "now."

You thought as poets think,
suavely it's true,
and you could turn
intricate river-runnels into words,
tell
wave-lengths in brave metres;
all the same,
the spell
had passed you,
left you comfortless;
you did not sense the wings beyond the gate;
you could not see,
you could not touch and feel,
actually the sea-sand
and the sea-shell.
If you had caught my hand,
we would have dipped
our fingers
in any icy river,
sipped
a nectar
that had spoiled your life,
slain sister,
daughter,
mother,
friend and wife,
demanded headier loves
than your heart knew.

Sea-Choros

from *Hecuba*

Wind of the sea,
O where,
where,
where,
through the salt and spray,
do you bear me,
in misery?
where,
where,
shall I be brought,
bought as a slave
for what house,
shall it be Thessaly?
shall I wander along the creeks
where Apidanus breaks
myriad water-ways,
or sold
to some Doric sea-mart?
O wind,
wind,
turn to me,
you who are swift to pace
beside the deep-sea ships,
who are swift to race
from crest to thundering sea-crest,
speak to me,
sea-wind,
hear;
where,
where in the land of the Greek,
do you take me,
to what seaport,
exiled,
unfortunate?

Wind of the sea,
O where,
where,
where,
through the salt and spray,
do you bear me
in misery?
wind,
sea-wind,
shall it be
where first the bay and palm-tree
blossomed in mystic leaf,
sacrosanct to protect
fair Leto for the birth,
twin-born,
begot of High Zeus?
wind,
wind,
shall I grow old
where the palm-trees still unfold
myrrh of leaf
and the laurel-tree;
shall I sing,
chant in ecstasy,
with maidens, in the set dance,
gold arrows of the goddess,
her gold bow
and her head-dress?
wind,
wind,
wind,
shall it be
that the sea-oars,
sweeping the sea,
take the roadway
to Delos?

Wind of the sea,
O where,
where,
where,
through the salt and spray,
do you bear me
in misery?
or nearer,
or further,
shall I
be claimed by another
and find
the shuttle,
the needle,
the loom
my fate?
am I doomed
to the court
of far Pallas?
what thread,
glowing crocus and red,
shall I thread
upon multiple thread,
till the pattern unfold
to depict
great Zeus,
son of ever-great Cronos?
shall I prick
out
the flight of the giants,
the fire-bolt,
Athena's yoked chariot?

Wind,
wind,
here I stand,
wind,
wind,
at an end;

Hymen has left me for Death;
love passes,
light passes
my hearth;
I face Europe
from Asia,
this lost land;
wind,
wind,
wind,
were it best
to die
in great Asia's death?
wind,
wind,
wind,
were it wise
to leave my children, my home,
my people (death's people)
to roam
afar
on the gathering wave-crests?

Wind of the sea,
O where,
where,
where,
through the salt and spray,
do you bear me
in misery?
or further,
or nearer,
I cry;
I am lost,
I am dead
whether I
thread the shuttle for Pallas
or praise
the huntress,

the flower of my days
is stricken,
is broken,
is gone
with my fathers,
my child
and my home;
wind,
wind,
we have found an end
in the sword of the Greek
and his fire-brand.

Wine Bowl

I will rise
from my troth
with the dead,
I will sweeten my cup
and my bread
with a gift;
I will chisel a bowl for the wine,
for the white wine
and red;
I will summon a Satyr to dance,
a Centaur,
a Nymph
and a Faun;
I will picture
a warrior King,
a Giant,
a Naiad,
a Monster;
I will cut round the rim of the crater,
some simple
familiar thing,

vine leaves
or the sea-swallow's wing;
I will work at each separate part
till my mind is worn out
and my heart:
in my skull,
where the vision had birth,
will come wine,
would pour song
of the hot earth,
of the flower and the sweet
of the hill,
thyme,
meadow-plant,
grass-blade and sorrel;
in my skull,
from which vision took flight,
will come wine
will pour song
of the cool night,
of the silver and blade of the moon,
of the star,
of the sun's kiss at mid-noon;
I will challenge the reed-pipe
and stringed lyre,
to sing sweeter,
pipe wilder,
praise louder
the fragrance and sweet
of the wine-jar,
till each lover
must summon another,
to proffer a rose
where all flowers are,
in the depths of the exquisite crater;
flower will fall upon flower
till the red shower
inflame all
with intimate fervour;
till:

men who travel afar
will look up,
sensing grape
and hill-slope
in the cup;
men who sleep by the wood
will arise,
hearing ripple and fall
of the tide,
being drawn by the spell of the sea;
the bowl will ensnare and enchant
men who crouch by the hearth
till they want
but the riot of stars in the night;
those who dwell far inland
will seek ships;
the deep-sea fisher,
plying his nets,
will forsake them
for wheat-sheaves and loam;
men who wander
will yearn for their home,
men at home
will depart.

I will rise
from my troth with the dead,
I will sweeten my cup
and my bread
with a gift;
I will chisel a bowl for the wine,
for the white wine
and red.

Trance

The floor
of the temple
is bright
with the rain,
the porch and lintel,
each pillar,
plain
in its sheet of metal;
silver,
silver flows
from the laughing Griffins;
the snows of Pentelicus
show dross beside
the King of Enydicus
and his bride,
Lycidoë,
outlined in the torch's flare;
beware, I say,
the loverless,
the sad,
the lost,
the comfortless;
I care
only for happier things,
the bare, bare open court,
(geometric,
with circumspect wing)
the naked plinth,
the statue's rare,
intolerant grace;
I am each of these,
I stare
till my eyes are a statue's eyes,
set in,
my eye-balls are glass,
my limbs marble,
my face fixed
in its marble mask;

only the wind
now fresh from the sea,
flutters a fold,
then lets fall a fold
on my knee.

Myrtle Bough

"I'll wreathe my sword in a myrtle-bough."—Harmodius
and Aristogiton

I

Your hands
make Pallas wonder,
yet your face
is dawn-spilled,
dew over
wild myrtle-flowers;
strange dissonance—
intolerant eyes flare out,
steel glistens
on the field of desperate Mars;
white myrtle and blue myrtle
and the sword,
wreathed with their tender stems,
Harmodius.

Then let me be a brother
to your need,
shoulder to steel-clad shoulder;
let me take
the helmet
and the buckler
and the greaves, Aristogiton,
to your slender grace;

let women fall beside us,
and men frown,
let us be soul and brother,
having won
the bitter wisdom
of Love's bitterest greed.

Love, beyond men and women;
having won
love beyond joy and sighing;
now be done,
O Perseus,
drop the Gorgon head, delay
your task
of making stones of men;
having proved all your immaculate strength,
Harmodius,
be gone,
and hurl your armour and your greaves away,
tall,
feverish,
alert
Aristogiton.

II

And turn,
turn,
turn,
Narcissus,
from your reeds,
having stripped off
your weight of chastened, burnished armour,
see
your greaves
covered an ankle
wrought of goodlier stuff,
ivory;

your chrysalis
of steel and silver
withers at the breath
of that wild thing it covers,
flower
whose scent
copies Assyrian odours,
while most sweet,
imperilled with the touch of Zephyrus,
in turns and shivers,
knowing its one bliss
to see itself,
itself,
itself
is this:

myself
who cast my silver-self afar,
armour and greaves and helmet,
for one star
rises above the sand-dunes,
one star lights
the pool above the marshes,
the fresh weeds;
arise;
delight
yourself in your own image,
Hesperus.

III

Yourself in myself,
mirror for a star,
star for a mirror,
water and wild, wild fervour,
some night-bird
crying to the impervious moon,

Cynthia
come soon,
Cynthia
come soon,
come soon:

see Love with Love is wedded for a day,
man with a maid?
maid with a man?
come, say—
are these two maids
or pages with bright shoon?
O traitorous moon,
who hide your visage
in a starry veil,
woven of fire and blossom,
pause and tell
your secret to us
by this citron tree
that reaches skyward
to enchant your car,
tangling your axle
with its bloom;
O star,
grant us the secret of your wanderings,
hold converse with us,
bid us to be wise;
advise
Love whether Love is only man or maid,
or child or prince or god
or merely staid
warrior
with silver
bright
cuirass
for light.

IV

For you are armed
although you cast aside
your mounted gear,
helmet
and princely wear,
stamped with your rare
insignia of pride;
nor can my manifold power
of song
and verse
and prayer
quell your stark will;
you remain silver still;
your flowers are not endangered
by my fever,
tall,
slender
and perverse young god,
Hermes
or Diomed,
or that one panting by the lapis water,
seeing alone the beauty
that must break
even his adamant heart
and make him kneel,
sensing at last the stark and perilous ache
that gods and mortals feel:

arise, O sleeping ivory,
and awake,
O open eyes
bluer than that blue lake
wherein you trace
each feature,
written clear;
O fair and dear,
your stricken body
must die fretfully,

unless you rouse your marble self
and greet
your live self,
filled with fervour
in my face.

V

For you are graved indelibly
in each trait;
your mouth
is my mouth
and your throat,
my throat;
O dare the mouth,
sip nectar,
let the note
that brands and burns my utterance
be your song;
O feel as I feel,
brush your lips along
my eyelids,
open wide
beneath your frigid kisses;
let my pride sustain me,
passionless, rigid steel;
then having proved my inviolate strength,
support me,
let me reel,
nerveless and fragile,
fainting on slight stem,
toward you another wind-flower,
swept of rain;
two wind-flowers, loved of Cyprus,
two bright heads,
inscribed with the same script
that says
Adon
is dead;

or Hyacinth
has fled the earthly vale,
wan Hyacinth;
let your bright splendour pale
as that one's did
before the fiery pain
and holy rapture
of his lord and king;
so pitiful,
so beautifully adored
by him who left him on the wind-swept grass
crying alas,
again,
alas,
alas,
must all I touch
wither to nothingness?

VI

For I must find
your vulnerable heel,
must burn and mark you
with a like rare steel
that burns and marks
each contour of my pride;
how can you turn,
how can you think to hide
from Him
who struck great Helios,
who brought low
God?
the eagle could not seek an eerier crag
but he must mock him
with a warier wing;
God loosing Love
saw foot-holds unto hell
scarring remote Olympus,

and hell mocked
even high Zeus' most radiant palaces
when he delayed
bidding wan Orpheus sing;

sing
and your hell is heaven,
your heaven less hell,
sing;
let my own retarded rapture tell
you of the pulse,
the throb,
the quivering
that bade great Helios
drop the golden string
and spurn the lyre for ever;
let song break
your icy cover,
O wild myrtle-frond,
wild myrtle grafted
with a Syrian bud,
bud of dark purple
in an ivory cup
of fragrant petal;
O Tyrian shoot,
I would impregnate you
with sacredness
so that you never, never could be free
but loom
and waver
and waft terribly
white wings and wings of gold
across bright skies
be Eros to all eyes.

Choros Sequence

from *Morpheus*

"Dream—dark-winged."

I

Give me your poppies,
poppies, one by one,
red poppies,
white ones,
red ones set by white;
I'm through with protestation;
my delight
knows nothing of the mind
or argument;
let me be done
with brain's intricacies;
your insight
has driven deeper
than the lordliest tome
of Attic thought
or Cyrenian logic;
O strange, dark Morpheus,
covering me with wings,
you give the subtle fruit
Odysseus scorned
that left his townsmen fainting on the sands,
you bring the siren note,
the lotus-land;
O let me rest
at last,
at last,
at last;
your touch is sweeter
than the touch of Death;
O I am tired of measures
like deft oars;
the beat and ringing
of majestic song;

give me your poppies;
I would lie along
hot rocks, listening;
still my ambition
that would rear and chafe
like chariot horses
waiting for the race;
let me forget
the spears of Marathon.

II

Give me your poppies,
red with rarer white,
give me your just-unfolded
poppy-flowers;
how strange—much longer
than a decade lost
is this one moment
when your breath is close;
sustained,
held tense,
munificent strength delays
the ultimate profusion;
long hours
trail in their purple
and long years are lost
in just this moment
while our souls are near,
our mouths separate;
never another like this one
that holds our mouths asunder;
hail and rain
and visible storm
and thunder
fled through the rocks
that our two beings made,
strong I
and you stronger;
two crashing rocks;

Charybdis
and that other,
ever twain,
apart,
ever sundered,
Scylla;

give me your poppies
(new flowers spring from this)
fire breaks from Ætna
and a sheath of iris,
wild small dart-iris
and the headier sweet
(to heal us,
chill narcissus)
curl and drop
another offering
for your impetuous feet,
bull-throated god
or Pluto leaving Hell
for a white goddess.

III

I would forego
my snowfields for your sun,
I would surrender
crocus
and ice-gentian
and all the lilies
rising one by one,
one after one,
and then another one
like star that flames white fire
to star
as beacon;

I would forget
the holy marjoram
and all the little speedwells
and low thrift
for just one grain
of your enchantment; lift
the veil,
dividing me from me,
and heal the scar
my searing helmet made,
and lure me forth
radiant,
unafraid
as the immortals;

we near heaven's hills with this,
God's asphodels;
O stay,
stay close,
bend down;
bend down my dream, my Morpheus,
breathe my soul
straight into you;
I would revive the whole
of Ilium
and in sacred trance,
show Helen
who made Troy
a barren town.

IV

Again,
again,
again,
I would be done
with state and grandeur,
trailing through long rooms
in Tyrian colour
toward the Spartan throne;

again,
again,
again,
I would strip off
the girdle
and the rare embroidery
of gold and silver;
see, again I tear
the jewelled circlet
from my myrrh-bound hair;
again,
again,
again,
I hear
the sea-wind raging
and again I seek
the sea-road leading
to the mightier sea;
again
we round the sea-coast perilously;
wind-beaten spume
and all the headier froth
conceal us
as we front the perilous north,
while Aphrodite's veil,
our talisman,
is lifted,
wafting us from dangerous shoal;
again,
again,
again,
the blunt prow slips
over the sea-road
to your native land;
warm sand
under my naked feet,
forgetfulness;

257

then, sweet,
nothing but kisses
while the warriors shout
and Troy burns
and tall Greeks rush in and out
under charred gateways
back to weightier ships.

V

Phrygian and oriental,
now be gone,
Paris;
and you,
you,
you,
give me your poppies,
O return to me
as if the very-god had come
straight from Euboea,
in his hand
a cone
of pine;
I, mistress of the oft-imperilled zone,
translucent,
wrought of many colours,
step
ardent yet temperate
from my luminous throne;
he smiles
and all the effrontery of all my race
rises to meet his smiling, cynical face,
and all my effrontery and all my wiles
blanch and wither
beside his enchanting smiles;
and all the gold woven about my veil
and all the pearls, entwined
for their sorcery,
fail
beside the devouring embers
of his touch;

258

I pale
beside him
who has vine and plant for dower,
I but a white rose,
one white rose
in flower;

and Cyprus will not help me if I call,
for I am she
and she has chosen inimitably
(her way)
subtly,
subtle in mystery,
me for a while,
me for a vase, an urn, a thing for her only,
for her to prove
that men still live
and gods still deign
to love.

VI

Give me your poppies,
mightier, priestly state
must live with them;
Demeter at the gate
of hell,
awaiting springtime
and the host
of maidens chanting;
the Eleusinian coast
must flower again
with torch
and mystery;
the lost and lovely Daughter
must arise
and God must quicken hell
and Paradise
must be revealed to all;

give me your poppies,
let their radiance spill
rapture
for ever;
love me,
O love me,
never let me go;
beauty must spring
like violets out of snow
and children smile before us
as we pass
and faded loves
recall old happiness;

O give some poppies
to these lonelier ones,
let us not darken
all this luminous sun
with any thought
of jealousy or hate;
O love, befriend this one
and this lost one;
I shall not rate you for inconstancy;
this flower is waiting for a little touch,
this one will wither in the casual blight
of sudden winter;
give to the dead-alive,
the living dead;
let them not mope in anger any more;
O let them laugh and live
and praise God's ways
at once the hopeless ghosts
in ecstasy
murmured and gathered
(covering dazzled eyes)
to see the spread of wings
before hell's door,
the quivering
of Psyche's butterflies.

VII

So give me poppies,
nectar is less sweet;
this is no venomous fruit
nor poisonous leaf
but bread and wine
and lilies in broad cups;
O praise me dying,
lift me,
raise me up;
say I have loved you
in some holy wise;
say I have given more than woman could
and say you love me
as, in holy wood,
Orion bent
to shelter Artemis;
say I am wild and passionate
yet chaste;
kiss me
and say
you never kissed and never could again
a face so stricken in its rapturous pain;
now give me poppies,
drive the hurt away;
there is no unguent
of the Thracian vine
can give me half
you give,
no anodyne
from any Syrian orchard
can give more;
my love,
the shore
even of sainted
distant holy Crete
lies spread like parchment
unrolled
at your feet;

you waken all the sealed past
with your touch,
the hills of Ida
are the yellow sands;
so shrive me,
grant the magic of your hands
as Paeon once, benignant, might have done
to one who died
of loving over-much.

VIII

So having died,
raise me again,
again;
give me more poppies,
out of sleep, new flowers
rise fresh,
as rimming
river-wild Eurotas;
give me more poppies;
out of sleep and sleep,
the fringe of consciousness is lined with bright
wild,
wild,
wild,
wild,
white arums
and the night-lily,
feigning with narcotic breath,
the sacred peace
and holiness of death;
give me more poppies'
scarlet, delicate bloom;
kiss me;
my room
merges with precinct
and the palace hall
seems to lend lustre
and ennoble
all,

all my trivial, simple little things;
kiss me;
the gloom
is edged with palpitant fire
where Love amazed
pauses in flight
to witness our desire,
for this, this, this
he sees
is something other,
mayhap (he thinks)
some potent visiting star,
flaming from aether,
from the middle-space
where Phoebus' horses
blaze their track
towards Dawn;

how far,
how far,
a kiss may bear us
like a travelling ship;
I slip
out of the borderland of consciousness,
kiss me again,
again.

IX

I live,
I live,
I live,
you give me that;
this gift of ecstasy
is rarer,
dearer
than any monstrous pearl
from tropic water;
I live,
I live,
I live,

I quaff a cup
that Lenaeus' happy troop
might stoop to offer,
skimming the surface of the purple vat
with wine-wreathed crater;
I live,
I live,
I live,
O hear
and champion him
you dear
and sainted Dryades,
grant him your dream,
ecstatic revelry;
reveal him to himself
as he himself to me,
who broke the clasp
to set the parchment free;
unroll before him too his hierarchy,
show him his gods from Asia,
his Assyrian
goddesses;
define on parchment the bright sorcery,
outlined, with katha-flower
and martagon;

hear,
hear,
you good and potent deities,
let him go free
of ancient superstition,
let him lift straight to sunlight
and bright skies,
as from the river-bed of Meroë,
the lotus lifts
its fiery passionate head.

X

I live,
I live,
I live,
you give me that;
one grain of your beguilement
has more might
than all the contents
of Assyrian phials,
laid, by an Eastern magnate,
at the feet
of an enchanter
of the Median rites;
I live,
I live,
I live,
O paragon,
who make the dead smile,
let me laugh again;
give me a robe
such as I might have worn
below the sea,
cherishing the just-born
Achilles
with bright tales
and phantasies,
told in the same
monotonous little song,
like water going over and over and on,
on, on to mightier lakes
and stranger seas;
let me forget the words that women say,
let me forget the very voice,
employ
water and wind
to tell the mystery
of love that comes to lovers being dead;

O let me say the things
that Thetis said
to him when he had grown to lustihood
of warrior grandeur:
let me be the lover-mother,
lay again
your head here, here;
there is no pain,
no disenchantment, no, nor evil spell
can ever touch you;
see I tell
and tell and tell the same thing over again,
over and over
in monotonous tone,
I love you,
love you,
love you,
dear-my-own.

XI

Achilles stayed a moment and is gone,
man,
man,
and child,
the warrior,
all are one;
I charmed the three
to unity in my arms,
I would re-make,
re-break them
and re-charm;
go,
this perfection leads to ultimate death:
hemlock
(they say)
refines the deepest bliss;

the night of ultimate darkness
waits us
who can fail
the quest,
the golden morrow
for a dream—slight
interim of madness;
love,
this love I feel
craves anodine of hatred,
loneliness—fir and pine,
the crest of hill-tops,
scent of the wild cedar;

I would be free,
be free;
go
for I fear
lest I strike swift
as she, the lynx and bear;
the Huntress claims me even amid the dream,
the breath of Artemis
stays this latter kiss.

XII

Medes,
Greeks
and Phrygians
suddenly are gone,
there is no lover,
no child
but a song;
song wrought enchantment,
said "you are a god,"
song made its sequence,
man
and man
and child;

267

now you have been a father to yourself,
let poppies wither
for this lovelier crown;
see,
I would pluck the olive
from my own
chaplet
to name you,
poet with the rest;
lover and lover,
man-child and a god,
all that is over;
see the kingly rod
is twined with laurel,
sacrosanct
and blest:

let us be gone,
remember what is best:
remembering this god last;
though I was tired of measures like deft oars,
now I return,
a beggar,
crave far shores,
would take my place upon the rower's seat;
avail myself of crumbs from hero's fare,
take lees of wine;
steal, cringe,
slave with the rest,
only to beat time with them,
but to feel
intimately
of them, Argonites,
who scale
the Delphic head-land
on the Delphic quest.

XIII

Which
nevertheless,
through toil
and dreariness,
brings only bliss;
which
nevertheless,
through pain
and definite loss,
brings only happiness,
alone
sanctity;
His fiery kiss
must burn away this kiss
(this
and the one next after
and the next);
His fiery touch
must burn away the dross
of dreams of Medes and Grecians,
and the host,
flying with Helen,
and the frenzied troop
even of mad Iacchus;
His ultimate kiss
alone must comfort us
who place love foremost,
then find song is best;

love
is a garment
riven in the light
that rises from Parnassus,
showing
the night is over;

see
He strikes,
as sunlight through a purple cloud,
and takes Love to him,
lover
and the shroud
of past endeavour.

Halcyon

"Bird—loved of sea-men."

I

I'm not here,
everything's vague, blurred everywhere,
then you are blown
into a room;

the sea comes where a carpet
laid red and purple,
and where the edge showed marble,
there is seaweed;

sedge breaks the wall
where the couch stands,
the hands of strange people,
twisting tassel and fringe

of rich cloth, become clear;
I understand the people,
they aren't hateful but dear;
over all

a shrill wind, clear sky;
O why, why, why
am I fretful, insecure;
why am I vague, unsure

until you are blown,
unexpected, small, quaint, unnoticeable,
a grey gull,
into a room.

II

You're very dear,
but it isn't that,
there's no rose and myrtle,
nothing, nothing at all,

only those small, small hands,
funny little gestures,
ways no one understands,
a figure under-small,

eyes that terrify people,
unfair estimates, prejudice,
hardly any charm,
yet that isn't everything,

that isn't by any means all;
a wind has started a little whirlpool
of sand where the carpet ought to be,
and shells lie

by the preposterous feet
of that woman who frets me, annihilates me,
O she will kill me yet,
my late cousin, the wool merchant's wife.

III

That's life,
but I had grown accustomed
to disappointment,
insecurity, gloom;

271

I begged for a place in their room,
I, a shadow, sought a place
where disgrace attended
the shape of a head-band wrong,

of a misplaced comb,
where reflected light
was caught in bowl and wall,
and silver all shimmering;

"tinsel" they said the other lives were,
all those I loved,
I was forgot;
O what, what, what

sent you, all grey, unnoticeable
and small
to shatter my peace,
unconscionable little gull?

IV

Now the house shakes
(it's in the very best suburb),
the town, the town-hall,
the agora, the market-stalls;

the whole place is besieged
with a host of flying wings,
already they lie ruined—
all the consequent things,

and the rich, all those
whose place is with the best,
even the general's wife
and the pro-consul's widow

are reft of dignity;
how can sand fly in hair
so carefully dyed
so rare a red?

272

how can shells lie by sandals
so beautifully sewn
with cornelian
and Tryphlia-stone?

V

Perhaps they said
when they sent you here,
"no one will see,
certainly no one will care,

an elf, no Grace,
an odd little castaway,
not fit for the gods yet";
we'll let her drift

in and about the hulk
of the old world,
a dead place
and dull, beached, stranded

and thick with barnacle;
O well, perhaps not;
perhaps we were not
after all the terror and pain,

the curious betrayal,
the thousand and one things that people don't notice
(how could they?)
forgot.

VI

You're impatient, unkind,
lovers aren't that,
so it can't be love;
you're invariably blind,

273

bitter and crude to me,
cruel, whimsical;
since you don't find
this colour agrees with you

(you say my dress
makes you sick)
go find some one else
there are plenty about;

yes, I will shout,
don't say my voice displeases you,
nor my ways;
O the days, the days

without these quarrels,
what were they?
something like a desert apart
without hope of oasis

or a grot lacking water
or a bird with a broken wing
or some sort of withered Adon-garden,
O, one of all or any of all those things.

VII

Well, then, never come again
since you found me out
the last time;
I can't stay in hour after hour

and wait;
you were late;
don't tell me over and over
about that dress,

purple, wine-colour,
with belt and shoulder straps
of grape and the over-
skirt with a long fringe

of silver; it's too late.
I have no lover nor want to be
taunted with age,
I'm too staid

for grape-colour,
for fringe and belt and straps
and ear-rings perhaps
and head-band of hammered silver;

I'm ill; I want to go away
where no one can come;
O little elf, leave me alone,
don't make me suffer again,

don't ask me to be slim and tall,
radiant and lovely
(that's over)
and beautiful.

VIII

O for you,
because you're a child—
now life will begin
all over again;

and I thought
I was through;
now I must be gay
where I was prim;

now I must smile,
now I must laugh;
(O, the grim, grim years)
O little, little gull,

let me put my head there
where the feathers turn from grey to white,
from white to grey,
and cry.

IX

You say, "lie still";
your hand is chill,
cold, unimpassioned,
inviolable;

you say, "lie back,
you won't faint";
what makes you think that?
what makes you think

I won't drift out,
get quite away?
O, you know—you say,
"you can't now,

you must wait
to keep me alive,
for if you go,
I won't stay;

I never had an illusion,
they hate me,
every one, every one,
but it's worse for you,

you're a baby, a lost star,
you never knew, nor saw,
you don't yet,
how horrible they all are."

X

No, it isn't true,
they're not all horrible,
you're always unfair;
well there you see

we quarrel again—
don't talk—dismiss happiness,
unhappiness, pain, bliss,
even thought—

what's left?
incomparable beyond belief,
white stones,
immaculate sand,

the slow move-forward of the tide
on a shallow reef,
salt and dried weed,
the wind's low hiss;

it's here in my skull
(leave your hand there)
for you—for ever—
mysterious little gull.

Songs from Cyprus

I

Gather for festival,
bright weed and purple shell;
make, on the holy sand,
pattern as one might make
who tread, with rose-red heel,
a measure
pleasureful;

such as those songs we made
in rose and myrtle shade,
where rose and myrtle fell
(shell-petal or rose-shell),
on just such holy sand;
ah, the song
musical;

give me white rose and red;
find me, in citron glade,
citron of precious weight;
spread gold before her feet;
ah, weave the citron flower;
hail goddess,
beautiful.

II

White rose, O white,
white rose and honey-coloured,
tell me again,
tell me the thing she whispered;

red rose, O wine,
fragrant, O subtly flavoured,
cyclamen stain,
how, how has your fire differed

from rose so white?
swift, swift, O Eros-favoured,
part, meet, part—then
rose, be rose-white, unsevered.

III

Bring fluted asphodel,
take strip and bar of silver,
fling them before Love's shrine;

see the white flowers turn red,
fragrance whereof the dead
breathe faintly by their river,

by Lethe's bank are rose,
and all the silver bars
shape to taut bows and arrows,

wherewith Love fronts his foes,
(ah, friend, beware his quiver)
wherewith Love fronts his foes.

IV

Where is the nightingale,
in what myrrh-wood and dim?
ah, let the night come back,
for we would conjure back
all that enchanted him,
all that enchanted him.

Where is the bird of fire?
in what packed hedge or rose?
in what roofed ledge of flower?
no other creature knows
what magic lurks within,
what magic lurks within.

Bird, bird, bird, bird, we cry,
hear, pity us in pain:
hearts break in the sunlight,
hearts break in daylight rain,
only night heals again,
only night heals again.

V

Bring myrrh and myrtle bud,
bell of the snowy head
of the first asphodel;

frost of the citron flower,
petal on petal, white
wax of faint love-delight;

flower, flower and little head
of tiny meadow-floret,
white, where no bee has fed;

full of its honey yet
spilling its scented sweet;
spread them before her feet;

white citron, whitest rose,
(myrrh leaves, myrrh leaves enclose),
and the white violet.

VI

In Cyprus,
we sought lilies for her shrine,
(white and dark-petalled where Adonis bled)
but, here in Greece,
for one white lilies,
for another red,
nor any peace.

In Cyprus,
we nursed love within our hearts,
and sang and with the song we wove the dance,
but here in Greece,
love is a torment
and they drive him out, far out,
and sue for peace.

In Cyprus,
peace is not where love has left;
I do not understand
the ways that seek white lilies for one love,
(casting aside the darker
scarred with fire)
and for another, red.

All flowers are hers
who rules the immeasurate seas,
in Cyprus, purple and white lilies tall;
how were it other?
there is no escape
from her who nurtures,
who imperils all.

Let Zeus Record

I

I say, I am quite done,
quite done with this;
you smile your calm
inveterate chill smile

and light steps back;
intolerate loveliness
smiles at the ranks
of obdurate bitterness;

you smile with keen
chiselled and frigid lips;
it seems no evil
ever could have been;

so, on the Parthenon,
like splendour keeps
peril at bay,
facing inviolate dawn.

II

Men cannot mar you,
women cannot break
your innate strength,
your stark autocracy;

still I will make no plea
for this slight verse;
it outlines simply
Love's authority:

but pardon this,
that in these luminous days,
I re-invoke the dark
to frame your praise;

as one to make a bright room
seem more bright,
stares out deliberate
into Cerberus-night.

III

Sometimes I chide the manner of your dress;
I want all men to see the grace of you;
I mock your pace, your body's insolence,
thinking that all should praise, while obstinate
you still insist your beauty's gold is clay:

I chide you that you stand not forth entire,
set on bright plinth, intolerably desired;
yet I in turn will cheat, will thwart your whim,
I'll break my thought, weld it to fit your measure
as one who sets a statue on a height
to show where Hyacinth or Pan have been.

IV

When blight lay and the Persian like a scar,
and death was heavy on Athens, plague and war,
you gave me this bright garment and this ring;

I who still kept of wisdom's meagre store
a few rare songs and some philosophising,
offered you these for I had nothing more;

that which both Athens and the Persian mocked
you took, as a cold famished bird takes grain,
blown inland through darkness and withering rain.

V

Would you prefer myrrh-flower or cyclamen?
I have them, I could spread them out again;
but now for this stark moment while Love breathes
his tentative breath, as dying, yet still lives,
wait as that time you waited tense with me:

others shall love when Athens lives again,
you waited in the agonies of war;
others will praise when all the host proclaims
Athens the perfect; you, when Athens lost,
stood by her; when the dark perfidious host
turned, it was you who pled for her with death.

VI

Stars wheel in purple, yours is not so rare
as Hesperus, nor yet so great a star
as bright Aldebaran or Sirius,
nor yet the stained and brilliant one of War;

stars turn in purple, glorious to the sight;
yours is not gracious as the Pleiads' are
nor as Orion's sapphires, luminous;

yet disenchanted, cold, imperious face,
when all the others, blighted, reel and fall,
your star, steel-set, keeps lone and frigid tryst
to freighted ships, baffled in wind and blast.

VII

None watched with me
who watched his fluttering breath,
none brought white roses,
none the roses red;

many had loved,
had sought him luminous,
when he was blithe
and purple draped his bed;

yet when Love fell
struck down with plague and war,
you lay white myrrh-buds
on the darkened lintel;

you fastened blossom
to the smitten sill;
let Zeus record this,
daring Death to mar.

White Rose

White rose,
white rose,
white rose
that mocked the fire
of jasemine
and of lily
and of faint
pulse of the violet,

drained of purple fire,
(white violet,
you are no flower at all)
white rose
you are a stricken weary thing,
shaming the spring . . .

> (*ah hear him,*
> *hear him,*
> *hear him,*
> *let him sing!*)

. . . white rose
your wisdom is a simple thing,
and must we grieve who found you very fair?
white rose,
white rose,
beware,
beauty is beauty
but not, not so rare
and not so bountiful
that it may spare
a moment
to revile
Love;
a moment to repent
once Love is fled . . .

> (*see spring is gone,*
> *ah wail, ah wail in vain,*
> *for spring is dead,*
> *Love having kissed the mouth,*
> *the mouth*
> *of youth*
> *again!*)

Calliope

"And thou thyself, Calliope."—Sappho.

To climb the intricate heights
of unimpeded rapture,
is no slight
task, O my love;
yet rapture, the very loveliest,
changes,
inbreeds
blackest despair,
succeeds pure fire,
if you neglect
(as you neglect)
others;
come back;
spirit must not tempt flesh—

    Nor dark flesh spirit,
    nay, I am gone,
    gone out, out, out from this;
    what holds me?
    fervid, torturing, your kiss?
    is love enough?
    the intolerable host
    and throng of mortals spoil
    at last,
    even the most abiding, intimate
    bliss;
    intolerable stain;
    hate of the listless
    unadoring host;
    nay, I am out and lost.

O spirit, white,
and versed in mystic lore,
beware,
too soon, too soon
you think yourself exempt
from all our lower thought,

our lesser magic,
Love's exquisite revel;
grow not too soon, too bold,
return,
O sweet, bright Lydian,
loveliest,
O lily-cold.

    Nay,
    cheat me not with time,
    with the dull ache of flesh,
    for all flesh turns,
    even the loveliest
    ankle and frail thigh,
    to bitterest dust,
    I would be off;
    I long for the white throng,
    the host of the immortals;
    nay,
    fondle me not,
    I must
    break from your trammels—

Your wings,
O sweet, O sweet,
are not yet grown,
what were you
mid the great, eternal host?
a beggar lost;
what were you
without shield of valorous flesh?
mine, mine;
my song it is that aches
to set you free;
my verse would break
the fleshly portal down;
I, I it is
that tends and spares your light,
lamp sheltering—

Nay, I am gone,
what is your flesh to me?
what is your chant, your song?
mid the immortals
all, as stars, swing free
and need no lamp of silver work or bronze;
I would escape;
in the high portals
of imperial Zeus,
no veils of baser flesh
chafe at us grievously,
see—
I am gone.

All Mountains

"Give me all mountains."—Hymn to Artemis.

Give me all mountains:
city,
town,
the precinct
of temple,
the crowded town-gate,
I have no love for:
walls must crush or hide
whether of market,
palace court
or precinct:
give me the stream's cold path,
the grove of pine,
for garden terrace
the unclaimed,
bleak
wild stretches
of the mountain side.

Give me no earth,
crushed flat
with crude layer
of fitted square
or meted length,
but boulders
unhewn
and set apart
as secret altars,
high in the loveliest
alder grove
or poplar;
give me for altar fire
the wild azalia;
let Phoebus keep
the fervid market place.

Give him white marble,
him the luminous white
of sheltering porch,
carved pillar,
portico;
give him the wharf,
the quay,
the street,
the market,
street corner
and the corner of the street;
nor do I envy him
my fiery brother,
who count as fair
only the reach of snow,
set stark
in mid air.

Marble of islands,
snow of distant points,
threatened with wave of pine,
with wash of alder;

my islands
shift and change,
now here, now there,
dazzling,
white,
granite,
silver
in blue aether;
I swim
who tread the mountain path as air.

Let Phoebus keep the market,
let white Love
claim all the islands
of seaport or river
would I contend with these?
nay,
I would rather pity him, my brother,
pity white passionate Love
who only knows
the promptings
of the restless, thwarted seas,
(shivering in porches
from the bitter air);
ah Zeus,
ennoble,
shelter these
thy children,
but give me the islands of the upper air,
all mountains
and the towering mountain trees.

Triplex

A Prayer

Let them not war in me,
these three;
Saviour-of-cities,
Flower-of-destiny
and she,
Twinborn-with-Phoebus,
fending gallantly.

Let them not hate in me,
these three;
Maid
of the luminous grey-eyes,
Mistress
of honey and marble implacable white thighs
and Goddess,
chaste daughter of Zeus,
most beautiful in the skies.

Let them grow side by side in me,
these three;
violets,
dipped purple in stark Attic light,
rose,
scorched (on Cyprus coast)
ambrosial white
and wild
exquisite hill-crocus
from Arcadian snows.

Birds in Snow

See,
how they trace
across the very-marble
of this place,
bright sevens and printed fours,
elevens and careful eights,
abracadabra
of a mystic's lore
or symbol
outlined
on a wizard's gate;

like plaques of ancient writ
our garden flags now name
the great and very-great;
our garden flags acclaim
in carven hieroglyph,
here king and kinglet lie,
here prince and lady rest,
mystical queens sleep here
and heroes that are slain

in holy righteous war;
hieratic, slim and fair,
the tracery written here,
proclaims what's left unsaid
in Egypt of her dead.

Chance

Chance says,
come here,
chance says,
can you bear

to part?
chance says,
sweetheart,
we haven't loved

for almost a year,
can you bear
this loneliness?
I can't;

apart from you,
I fear
wind,
bird,

sea,
wave,
low places
and the high air;

I hear
dire threat
everywhere;
I start

at wind
in sycamores,
I can't bear
anything

further;
chance says,
dear,
I'm here,

don't you want me
any more?

When I Am a Cup

When I am a cup
lifted up,
can you hear
echo in a seashell?

*When you are a cup
there is no sigh nor song,
only the weed, the weed,
trailing along.*

When I am a cup
made of shell,
O, can you hear
distant, ringing sea-bells?

*When you are a cup
there is no sound,
but of seaweed trailing
across sandy ground.*

Sigil

I

Ground
under a maple-tree
breeds parasite,

so I
bear tentacles, as it were,
from you, tree-loam;

ground
under a beech
breeds faun-lily, each

tree
spreads separate leaf-mould,
whether maple or beech,

whether paper-birch;
I come
as those parasites

out of frost almost,
Indian-pipe, hypatica
or the spotted snake-cup,

adder-root, blood-root,
or the white, white plaque
of the wild dog-wood tree;

each alone,
each separately, I come
separate parasite,

white spear-head
with implacable fragile shoot
from black loam.

II

This is my own world,
these can't see;
I hear, "this is my dower,"

I fear no man, no woman;
flower does not fear
bird, insect nor adder;

I fear neither the wind
nor viper,
familiar sound

bids me raise
frost-nipped, furred head
from winter-ground;

familiar scent
makes me say,
"I am awake";

familiar touch
makes me say, "all this was over-done,
much

was wasted, blood and bone spent
toward this last
secret

wild,
wild,
wild fulfilment."

III

For:
I am not man,
I am not woman;
I crave

you
as the sea-fish
the wave.

IV

When you turn to sleep
and love is over,
I am your own;

when you want to weep
for some never-found lover,
I come;

when you would think,
"what was the use of it,"
you'll remember

something you can't grasp
and you'll wonder
what it was

altered your mood;
suddenly, summer grass
and clover

will be spread,
and you'll whisper,
"I've forgotten something,

what was it,
what was it,
I wanted to remember?"

V

That will be me,
silver
and wild and free;

that will be me
to send a shudder through you,
cold wind

through an aspen tree;
that will be me
to bid you recover

every voice,
every sound,
every syllable

from grass-blade,
tree-toad,
from every wisp and feather

of fern
and moss
and grass,

from every wind-flower,
tethered
by a thread,

from every thread-stem
and every thread-root
and acorns half-broken

above ground
and under the ground.

VI

Confine
your measure to the boundary of the sky,
take all that, I

am quite content
with fire-fly,
with butter-fly;

take everything,
I compensate my soul
with a new rôle;

you're free
but you're only a song,
I'm free but I've gone;

298

I'm not here,
being everywhere
you are.

VII

Whether this happened before,
whether this happen again,
it's the same;

there is no magic nor lure,
there is no spell and no power
to equalise love's fire;

whether he fasten his car
with the bright doves and afar
threaten great Zeus and the stars;

or whether he cringe at my feet,
whether he beat on your eyes,
white wings, white butterflies.

Epitaph

So I may say,
"I died of living,
having lived one hour";

so they may say,
"she died soliciting
illicit fervour";

so you may say,
"Greek flower; Greek ecstasy
reclaims for ever

299

one who died
following
intricate songs' lost measure."

The Mysteries

Renaissance Choros

Dark
days are past
and darker days draw near;
darkness on this side,
darkness over there
threatens the spirit
like massed hosts
a sheer
handful
of thrice-doomed spearsmen;
enemy this side,
enemy a part
of hill
and mountain-crest
and under-hill;
nothing before of mystery,
nothing past,
only the emptiness,
pitfall of death,
terror,
the flood,
the earthquake,
stormy ill;
then voice within the turmoil,
that slight breath
that tells as one flower may
of winter past
(that kills
with Pythian bow,
the Delphic pest;)

one flower,
slight voice,
reveals
all holiness
with
"peace
be still."

II

A sceptre
and a flower-shaft
and a spear,
one flower may kill the winter,
so this rare
enchanter
and magician
and arch-mage;
one flower may slay the winter
and meet death,
so this
goes and returns
and dies
and comes to bless
again,
again;
a sceptre and a flower
and a near
protector
to the lost and impotent;
yea,
I am lost,
behold what star is near;
yea,
I am weak,
see
what enchanted armour
clothes the intrepid mind
that sheds the gear
of blighting thought;

behold what wit is here
what subtlety,
what humour
and what light;
see,
I am done,
no lover and none dear,
a voice within the fever,
that slight breath
belies our terror
and our hopelessness,
"lo,
I am here."

III

"Not to destroy,
nay, but to sanctify
the flower
that springs
Adonis
from the dead;
behold,
behold
the lilies
how they grow,
behold how fair,
behold how pure a red,
(so love has died)
behold the lilies
bled
for love;
not emperor nor ruler,
none may claim
such splendour;
king may never boast
so beautiful a garment
as the host
of field
and mountain lilies."

IV

"Not to destroy,
nay, but to sanctify
each flame
that springs
upon the brow of Love;
not to destroy
but to re-invoke
and name
afresh each flower,
serpent
and bee
and bird;
behold,
behold
the spotted snake
how wise;
behold the dove,
the sparrow,
not one dies
without your father;
man sets the trap
and bids the arrow fly,
man snares the mother-bird
while passing by
the shivering fledglings,
leaving them to lie
starving;
no man,
no man,
no man
may ever fear
that this one,
winnowing the lovely air,
is overtaken by a bird of prey,
that this is stricken
in its wild-wood plight,
that this dies broken
in the wild-wood snare,

I
and my father
care."

V

"Not to destroy,
nay, but to sanctify
the fervour
of all ancient mysteries;
behold the dead are lost,
the grass has lain
trampled
and stained
and sodden;
behold,
behold,
behold
the grass disdains
the rivulet
of snow and mud and rain;
the grass,
the grass
rises
with flower-bud;
the grain
lifts its bright spear-head
to the sun again;
behold,
behold
the dead
are no more dead,
the grain is gold,
blade,
stalk
and seed within;
the mysteries
are in the grass
and rain."

VI

"The mysteries remain,
I keep the same
cycle of seed-time
and of sun and rain;
Demeter in the grass
I multiply,
renew and bless
Iacchus in the vine;
I hold the law,
I keep the mysteries true,
the first of these
to name the living, dead;
I am red wine and bread.

> *I keep the law,*
> *I hold the mysteries true,*
> *I am the vine,*
> *the branches, you*
> *and you."*

UNCOLLECTED AND
UNPUBLISHED POEMS
1912–1944

Epigram

(*After the Greek*)

The golden one is gone from the banquets;
She, beloved of Atimetus,
The swallow, the bright Homonoea:
Gone the dear chatterer;
Death succeeds Atimetus.

Late Spring

We can not weather all this gold
Nor stand under the gold from elm-trees
And the re-coated sallows.
We can not hold our heads erect
Under this golden dust.

We can not stand
Where enclosures for the fruit
Drop hot—radiant—slight petals
From each branch.

We can not see:
The dog-wood breaks—white—
The pear-tree has caught—
The apple is a red blaze –
The peach has already withered its own leaves—
The wild plum-tree is alight.

309

Amaranth

I

Am I blind alas,
am I blind,
I too have followed
her path.
I too have bent at her feet.
I too have wakened to pluck
amaranth in the straight shaft,
amaranth purple in the cup,
scorched at the edge to white.

Am I blind?
am I the less ready for her sacrifice?
am I less eager to give
what she asks,
she the shameless and radiant?

Am I quite lost,
I towering above you and her glance,
walking with swifter pace,
with clearer sight,
with intensity
beside which you two
are as spent ash?

Nay I give back to my goddess the gift
she tendered me in a moment
of great bounty.
I return it. I lay it again
on the white slab of her house,
the beauty she cast out
one moment, careless.

Nor do I cry out:
"why did I stoop?
why did I turn aside
one moment from the rocks
marking the sea-path?
Andromeda, shameless and radiant,
have pity, turn, answer us."

Ah no—though I stumble toward
her altar-step,
though my flesh is scorched and rent,
shattered, cut apart,
and slashed open;
though my heels press my own wet life
black, dark to purple,
on the smooth rose-streaked
threshold of her pavement.

II

Am I blind, alas, deaf too,
that my ears lost all this?
Nay, O my lover, Atthis:
shameless and still radiant
I tell you this:

I was not asleep.
I did not lie asleep on those hot rocks
while you waited.
I was not unaware when I glanced
out toward sea,
watching the purple ships.

I was not blind when I turned.
I was not indifferent when I strayed aside
or loitered as we three went,
or seemed to turn a moment from the path
for that same amaranth.

I was not dull and dead when I fell
back on our couch at night.
I was not indifferent though I turned
and lay quiet.
I was not dead in my sleep.

III

Lady of all beauty,
I give you this:
say I have offered but small sacrifice,
say I am unworthy your touch,
but say not, I turned to some cold, calm god,
silent, pitiful, in preference.

Lady of all beauty,
I give you this:
say not, I have deserted your altar-steps,
that the fire on your white hearth
was too great,
that I fell back at your first glance.

Lady, radiant and shameless,
I have brought small wreaths,
they were a child's gift.
I have offered you white myrrh-leaf
and sweet lentisk.
I have laid rose-petals
and white rock-rose from the beach.

But I give now
a greater,
I give life and spirit with this,
I render a grace
no one has dared to speak
at your carved altar-step,
lest men point him out,
slave, callous to your art,

312

I dare more than the singer
offering her lute,
the girl her stained veils,
the woman her swathes of birth,
the older woman her pencils of chalk
and mirror and unguent box.

I offer more than the lad,
singing at your steps,
praising himself mirrored in his friend's face,
more than any girl,
I offer you this,
(grant only strength
that I withdraw not my gift)
I give you my praise for this:
the love of my lover for his mistress.

IV

Let him go forth radiant,
let life rise in his young breast,
life is radiant,
life is made for beautiful love
and strange ecstasy,
strait, searing body and limbs,
tearing limbs and body from life;
life is his if he ask,
life is his if he take it,
then let him take beauty
as his right.

Take beauty, wander apart
in the tree-shadows,
wander under wind-bowed sheaths
of golden fir-boughs,
go far, far from here
in your happiness,
take beauty for that is her wish:

313

Her wish,
the radiant and shameless.

V

But I,
how I hate you for this,
how I despise and hate,
was my beauty so slight a gift,
so soon, so soon forgot?

I hate you for this,
and now that your fault be less,
I would cry, turn back,
lest she the shameless and radiant
slay you for neglect.

Neglect of the finest beauty upon earth
my limbs, my body and feet,
beauty that men gasp
wondering that life
could rest in so burnt a face,
so scarred with her touch,
so fire-eaten, so intense.

Turn, for I love you yet,
though you are not worthy my love,
though you are not equal to it.

Turn back;
true I have glanced out
toward the purple ships
with seeming indifference.
I have fallen from the high grace
of the goddess,
for long days
I have been dulled with this grief,
but turn
before death strike,
for the goddess speaks:

314

She too is of the deathless,
she too will wander in my palaces
where all beauty is peace.

She too is of my host
that gather in groups or singly wait
by some altar apart;
she too is my poet.

Turn if you will
from her path,
turn if you must from her feet,
turn away, silent,
find rest if you wish:

find quiet
where the fir-trees
press, as you
swaying lightly above earth.

Turn if you will from her path
for one moment seek
a lesser beauty
and a lesser grace,
but you will find
no peace in the end
save in her presence.

Eros

I

Where is he taking us
now that he has turned back?

315

Where will this take us,
this fever,
spreading into light?

Nothing we have ever felt,
nothing we have dreamt,
or conjured in the night
or fashioned in loneliness,
can equal this.

Where is he taking us,
Eros,
now that he has turned back?

II

My mouth is wet with your life,
my eyes blinded with your face,
a heart itself which feels
the intimate music.

My mind is caught,
dimmed with it,
(where is love taking us?)
my lips are wet with your life.

In my body were pearls cast,
shot with Ionian tints, purple,
vivid through the white.

III

Keep love and he wings
with his bow,
up, mocking us,
keep love and he taunts us
and escapes.

Keep love and he sways apart
in another world,
outdistancing us.

Keep love and he mocks,
ah, bitter and sweet,
your sweetness is more cruel
than your hurt.

Honey and salt,
fire burst from the rocks
to meet fire
spilt from Hesperus.

Fire darted aloft and met fire,
and in that moment
love entered us.

IV

Could Eros be kept,
he was prisoned long since
and sick with imprisonment,
could Eros be kept,
others would have taken him
and crushed out his life.

Could Eros be kept,
we had sinned against the great god,
we too might have prisoned him outright.

Could Eros be kept,
nay, thank him and the bright goddess
that he left us.

V

Ah love is bitter and sweet,
but which is more sweet
the bitterness or the sweetness,
none has spoken it.

317

Love is bitter,
but can salt taint sea-flowers,
grief, happiness?

Is it bitter to give back
love to your lover if he crave it?

Is it bitter to give back
love to your lover if he wish it
for a new favourite,
who can say,
or is it sweet?

Is it sweet to possess utterly,
or is it bitter,
bitter as ash?

VI

I had thought myself frail,
a petal
with light equal
on leaf and under-leaf.

I had thought myself frail;
a lamp,
shell, ivory or crust of pearl,
about to fall shattered,
with flame spent.

I cried:

"I must perish,
I am deserted in this darkness,
an outcast, desperate,"
such fire rent me with Hesperus,

Then the day broke.

318

VII

What need of a lamp
when day lightens us,
what need to bind love
when love stands
with such radiant wings over us?

What need—
yet to sing love,
love must first shatter us.

Envy

I

I envy you your chance of death,
how I envy you this.
I am more covetous of him
even than of your glance,
I wish more from his presence
though he torture me in a grasp
terrible, intense.

Though he clasp me in an embrace
that is set against my will,
and rack me with his measure,
effortless yet full of strength,
and slay me
in that most horrible contest,
still, how I envy you your chance.

Though he pierce me with his lust,
iron, fever and dust,
though beauty is slain
when I perish,
I envy you death.

319

What is beauty to me?
has she not slain me enough,
have I not cried in agony of love,
birth, hate,
in pride crushed?

What is left after this?
what can death loose in me
after your embrace?
your touch,
your limbs are more terrible
to do me hurt.

What can death mar in me
that you have not?

II

What can death send me
that you have not?
You gathered violets,
you spoke:
"your hair is not less black
nor less fragrant,
nor in your eyes is less light,
your hair is not less sweet
with purple in the lift of locks;"
why were those slight words
and the violets you gathered
of such worth?

How I envy you death;
what could death bring,
more black, more set with sparks
to slay, to affright,
than the memory of those first violets,
the chance lift of your voice,
the chance blinding frenzy
as you bent?

III

Could I have known
you were more male than the sun-god,
more hot, more intense,
could I have known?
for your glance all-enfolding,
sympathetic, was selfless
as a girl's glance.

Could I have known?
I whose heart,
being rent, cared nothing,
was unspeakably indifferent.

IV

So the goddess has slain me
for your chance smile
and my scarf unfolding
as you stooped to it,
so she trapped me,
for the upward sweep of your arm,
as you lifted the veil,
was the gesture of a tall girl
and your smile was as selfless.

Could I have known?
nay, spare pity,
though I break,
crushed under the goddess' hate,
though I fall beaten at last,
so high have I thrust my glance
up into her presence.

Do not pity me, spare that,
but how I envy you
your chance of death.

I Said

(1919)

I

I said:
"think how Hymettus pours divine honey,
think how dawn vies
in the shelter of Hymettus,
with the clusters of field-violet,
(rill on rill of violets!
parted and crested fire!)
think of Hymettus
and the tufted spire of thyme,
hyacinth, wild wind-flower,
think of Hymettus
beyond mist," I said, "and rain,"
and you,
"'twere better, better being dead."

"But what grave heart," I said,
"of beauty dies if you die:
at Marathon there bled
souls such as yours,
such souls as yours
stained those pale violets red,
her violets beyond Athens,
and they fled,
spearsmen of lesser force than ours,
being but a thousand, thousand,
that vast horde,
without *her* spearhead
glittering at their head,
being a million, million and they fled
at Marathon"—
"I am no Greek," you said.

Whether you are a Greek or a Syrian or Mede,
to-day we are one in our need for beauty.

But it seems to me Greek rather
to live as you lived,
outwardly telling lies,
inwardly without swerving or doubt—
"if I can not have beauty about me
and people of my own sort,
I will not live,
I will not compromise"—
and though I have heard many people
talk about life
and the indubitable comfort of being dead,
your words alone of them all
rang unutterably true,
you meant what you said.

The race may or may not be to the swift,
but tell me, is it likely
that the fight will be entrusted to the dead?
you may not seem a Greek to yourself,
you may not seem a Greek to another,
but anyone who stands alone,
so tenaciously determined
if fate over-rule a desire to live,
at least to die for beauty,
anyone to-day who can contemplate
the idea of death, abstract death,
(romantic though he be,
young without doubt, mad perhaps)
anyone to-day who can die for beauty,
(even though it be mere romance
or a youthful geste)
is and must be my brother.

III

Ah, the long path down from that hill,
the very rocks broken,
scattered, rain of sand,
rocks clutched—sliding down—
shield, helmet, light as fire—
ah yes, he had made them, Hephaestos,
he had wrought and hammered for us
the lance and the shield,
the helmet that rested as light
as the silver under-side of the grape-leaf
that Bacchos strips
from the tough, warped wood-stem,
where the leaf shows its fine, tender, white fibre
where it joins the rough threads
of the brown wood-fibre of the vine.

Ah the gold in our hearts,
and the shrill pain in our hearts
that was not pain;
yet who could say it was joy?
it was beyond any words;
there were no words
even in our glorious speech
that could hint the joy we had then;
how can we to-day in a crude tongue,
in a strange land hope to say
one word that can hint at the joy we had
when the rocks broke like sand under our heels
and they fled?

Don't you understand,
as far as anything purposeful goes,
if you tear the fruit from the vine,
gloriously with violence and madness and joy,
the rough wood fibre
most likely will slash into your fingers
and leave blood on your hand?

324

Don't you understand
if you to-day in a crude speech
in a dark land hope to say,
to speak one word of the joy we had
(to people who anyway don't want to understand)
when the rocks broke like fire under our feet
and they fled,

O don't you, don't you understand,
you must count yourself now, *now* among the dead?

IV

Don't crouch at my feet in the dark,
don't crouch and tremble with the rain beating outside
and the thousand ghosts and the dead
and the people about,
don't crouch any more and cling to my knees,
don't tempt me and try me,
don't beg like a child and cry,
"you have taken my hope away."
I am not a god.
I cannot make you happy.
I might say there is some happiness
for you if you live,
there is always hope of some happiness,
but to you I won't lie.

Don't crouch on the floor
in the dark,
don't say the fear
is gnawing you and gnawing you away,
perhaps I have the same fear.

Don't tempt me any more.

Helios and Athene

The serpent does not crouch at Athene's feet. The serpent lifts a proud head under the shelter of her shield.

The serpent is marked with pattern as exquisite as the grain of the field-lily petal. He is hatched from an egg like the swan.

The baby Ion, son of Helios, was deserted by his mother. She laid him among violets. Athene, the goddess, sent serpents to protect him. These serpents fed the child with honey.

When Helios the god slays the serpent, he slays in reality not so much the serpent, as fear of the serpent. The god learns from the serpent. Be ye wise as serpents.

The serpent lifts a proud head beneath the massive shield-rim of Athene, guardian of children, patron of the city.

On one of the remote altars of Demeter at Eleusis, is a serpent carved beautifully in high bas-relief.

The Eleusinian candidate, it is thought, at one stage of initiation, walked through a black cave, the retreat of snakes.

The mind may learn, though the body cringes back.

Consider the birds. Be wise as serpents.

In Athene's hands is a winged creature, a Nike, her own soul.

Consider the birds. Consider your own soul.

II

The naked Greek, the youth in athletic contest, has set, accurately prescribed movement and posture. This convention made of him a medium or link between men in ordinary life and images of Pentallic frieze or temple front. We gaze upon this living naked embodiment of grace and decorum. We are enflamed by its beauty. We love it.

When we have exhausted the experiences of personal emotion, we gain from the statue the same glow of physical warmth and power.

The statue of Helios on the Olympic frieze, as the beautiful personality that once charmed us, acts as a go-between.

The youth is a link between men (let us say) and statues.

The statue is a link between the beauty of our human lovers and the gods.

The statue enflames us. Its beauty is a charm or definite talisman.

Our minds can go no further. The human imagination is capable of no further expression of beauty than the carved owl of Athene, the archaic, marble serpent, the arrogant selfish head of the Acropolis Apollo.

No individual has created beauty like this. No country or individual ever will.

But the Hellene did not throw down his chisel and rest in self-complacent admiration.

His work began when his work was finished.

The priest at Delphi, the initiate, even the more advanced worshiper, began his work where the artist ceased his labour.

The statue was like a ledge of rock, from which a great bird steps as he spreads his wings.

The mind, the intellect, like the bird rests for a moment, in the contemplation or worship of that Beauty.

The mind grips the statue as the bird grips the rock-ledge. It would convince itself that this is its final resting place.

The mind, in its effort to disregard the truth, has built up through the centuries, a mass of polyglot literature explanatory of Grecian myth and culture.

But the time has come for men and women of intelligence to build up a new standard, a new approach to Hellenic literature and art.

Let daemons possess us! Let us terrify like Erynnes, the whole tribe of academic Grecians!

Because (I state it inspired and calm and daemonaical) they know nothing!

III

It was in Helios' heart to break, in Athene's not to be broken.

So Delphi and Athens stood, existent, gaining power, gaining strength, through inter-dependence of hatred.

But this hatred was clear, defined, removed from any hint of personal intrusion, intellectual, abstract.

If Athene's citadel broke, Helios' temple crumbled. If Helios yielded to her, Athene herself was undone.

Delphi and Athens were thus allied forever.

Delphi, the serpent, the destructive heat, Delphi the devastatingly subtle seat of oracles, Delphi whose centre of religion was a centre of political intrigue, Delphi the lie, the inspiration, the music, found in Hellas, in the world, one equal: Athene.

Athene with silver line between eye-brow and ridge of helmet could look with all the concentrated power of her eyes and leave unscathed no God in the world but one: Phoebus of Delphi.

The olive, turned from sombre gray to trembling silver by the wind, sweeping from the snows of Pentellicus, the imperishable silver of her helmet, the serpent whose belly shone silver as she lured him by her daemonaic power to lift his head from the black grass; the white silver of the olive leaf, the white belly of the serpent were as her guarded eyes.

To Helios alone could she open wide their splendour.

He hated her because she stood unconquerable: he loved her as an equal.

IV

We cannot approach her direct, so abstract, so cold, so beautiful.

We approach her, if at all, through the medium of the Mysteries and through the intercession of other Gods.

At the foot of the Acropolis, as a lover, waiting at the feet of his Beloved, is the theatre of Dionysius.

The Greek Drama, the outgrowth of the worship of Dionysius, is a means of approach to Athene.

The greatest Athenians of the greatest period were initiates of the Eleusinian mysteries. Those great mysteries were protected by the Love of Athene.

The Love of Athene is symbolized by the arch of wings, for Demeter by the cavern or grot in the earth, and for Phoebus by the very essential male power. Love for Athene is the surrender to neither, the merging and welding of both, the conquering in herself of each element, so that the two merge in the softness and tenderness of the mother and the creative power and passion of the male. In her hand is the symbol of this double conquest and double power, the winged Nike.

The winged Nike, the white sea-gull, the imperturbable soft Owl, the owl, whose great eyes search the night, the mind, the dark places of ignorance.

Athene, the maiden, Parthanos, is doubly passionate.

Ariadne

(*From a lost play*)

ARIADNE   You have beaten me with swords
    but not with words,
    and I, my lord, am thankful:

    you have flayed me with an ox-thong,
    not a kiss,
    and I, my lord, am grateful:

you really were a panther, a wild-cat,
who tore me limb from limb;
my thanks for that.

I

Heaven shod, heaven sandalled and heaven found,
the long waves break,
the under-tone
comes back again,
furthering the message—
you were never dead—
I am still living—
listen to the sea,
break on the pebbles,
listen to the pine,
wait for the chant of sea-gulls
or the line
of swaying kestrels,
they will write my words,
heaven sandalled, heaven found, heaven shod:

you were no man, being God,
yet you were men,
the manifold armies and the shattered host;
you were the ghost
rising at night-fall
and the silver dawn
found you, my lover,
heaven-sandalled, and heaven-bound
waiting to leave the cities
where the ground
ran mingled blood of armies
you were those seas
of blood that ran, that ran across the sand,
O pitiful shattered land—

O land of beauty and of memory
O land of hosts
and hosts of singing voices;
land of the sated ghosts
that left being tired of blood-shed,
O bright coast
O lofting pinnacle,
Hymmetus, Lycabettus like a shell
through which the sun shines
crimson or pale opal,
O beautiful white land,
olives and wild anemone and violet
mingled among the shale,
and purple wings
of little winter-butterflies
say, here Psyche, the soul, lies.

II

Here is the intricate offering of my loom,
lady,
to hang from pillars
in the room,
dedicate to your altar;
here is bloom
of wide white roses
showing where Love trod,
and here is God,
set round about with stars,
and here is Mars,
lordly to save the Hero
bred of war;
here, near the floor,
is pattern of wild pansies
and a child;

Lady,
bend near;
your sweet cold hands have banished
heinous fear,

your cloak was wide,
your helmet and your spear
ready to save,
ready to extirpate
a woman
banished by an island monster;
the child and she were set afloat to drift
but there was light about the little boat,
a chest
flung on the water;
these are the Dioscuri
hovering near;

There was no god
in all the circling host
who had forsaken
the outcast and lost;
your infinite loveliness,
O violet-crowned,
comes first;
but see,
the others found
gifts,
old portents and old worship
drew them near;
Mars with his spear,
weary of battle
said, I will protect;
Hermes said,
magic never shall be dead;
the exquisite holiness of the sea-born
laid
offering,
white lilies
lilies that were red;
Eros spread wings
about a child's small bed;

See,
I am weaving here;
the colours glow
with blue, sea-blue and violet;
I have dipped deep my thread
it will not fade,
I have long practised stitch and counter-stitch;
the frame is firm;
the pattern clear but spaced
with subtlety
and symbol
those will know,
who have faced at the last
the ultimate,
ultimate fear;

You stand beyond me
at the temple gate,
and know not fear nor hate,
for there, emblazoned on your aegis rim,
is image of all evil,
no cruel whim
can strike beyond your cruelty
when you care to strike,
and none may dare
to counter you who know
when to withhold and when to deal the blow;
and you will strike
those whom you will and where
you will
who have defamed your holiest inner shrine;
that is your care,
this mine—

only to weave
to make the pattern clear,
the woven tale
to lay upon your altar,

to hang from pillar
to exquisite
wrought pillar,
so that men stop,
astonished
at its colour,
its gods
outlined with delicate woven contour,
men stop—men speak—men stare—
there must be real gods
see, the painted gods—
how fair!

The Shepherd

I'll shake the bees
from the thyme-heads for you,
and gather mint,
bound with coarse strands of grasses,
I'll tempt the marshes for the mirrored iris,
and break the thorn-bough's blossom.

I'll bring white violets
in a moss-lined basket,
and with young fern
I'll bind the pale narcissus,
I'll search the rocks
for the frail rock-cistus
and the rare violets.

O Hyacinth of the swamp-lands,
Blue lily of the marshes,
How could I know,
Being but a silly shepherd,
That you would mock at me?

But you will mourn
when the white fire flickers
out of my face
and leaves me staring, mortal;
you will be sorry
that you took their rose-leaves,
scorning my golden crocuses.

O Hyacinth of the swamp-lands,
blue lily of the marshes,
across the fields
I watch the white stars darken;
the day comes and the
white stars dim
and lessen
and the lights fade in the city:
so in the city do they dim your beauty;
only the fields have kept it and the singing
of goat-boys who must follow
to my piping.

At Croton

O take my gift
and do not count the cost;
hope not for over-gain
nor over-fear stark loss;
take my white hands
and when you clasp
the wrist with steel,
think if you will
how subtle and how real
the wrist of this was
or that other one,
Ianthe or Myrtle,
now both are gone.

Veils to my eyes?
nay, do not be afraid
that they will dart forth
serpents of appeal,
nay, do not cringe nor feel
that they are over-sweet
(being over-wise)
for this light game
of take and break and yield.

Come,
let us thank some god,
some common friend,
of light enchantment
and of light appeal,
let us stand straight
nor kneel
(foreknowledge in our eyes),
for gods thus feel
light changes, light annoy;
remember
they had slight and simple ways
sometimes,
slight, simple-hearted, suave,
imperious joys.

Antipater of Sidon

Where, Corinth, charm incarnate, are your shrines?
Your citadel? Your towered wall? Your line
Of noble women? Your ancient treasure?
And that ten thousand of your people lost?

War wreaked on you his hideous ravishment;
We, we alone, Nereids inviolate,
Remain to weep, with the sea-birds to chant:
Corinth is lost, Corinth is desolate.

Gift

Ardent
yet chill and formal,
how I ache
to tempt a chisel
as a sculptor, take
this one,
replacing this and this and this
for some defect
of point, of blade, of hilt;

in answer to my thwarted fingers, make
as from the clear edge of some glacier-drift,
a slim amphora,
a most gracious vase;

instead of ranging
from your shoulders' straight
clear line, uninterrupted stretch
of snow, with light
of some dawn-cloud on it,
I'd calm my hands
against this priceless thing,
chisel it, circumscribe
set pattern, formal-wise,
inset with stiff acanthus leaves and bays;

and where some boulder
shelves out in some place
where ice curves back

like sea-waves with the crest
of each green ripple
frozen marble wise,
under that rock that holds
the first swift kiss
of the spring-sun's white, incandescent breath,
I'd seek
you flowers:
(ah flowers
that sweetly fall and rest
softly and smoothly
on an icy bed,
the cyclamen white and red,
how sweet, how fiery,
lovers could only know,
bled in some ice of fire,
or fire of snow);

so I might set
about the Parian throat,
delicate tendrils
of the scented host,
slight fronds
with iridescent shell-like grace,
smooth like the alabaster,
thin and rare.

Psyche

"Love drove her to Hell."

Cythera's pearl were dim,
had I not won from him
this ruby, cut of fire;
my quivering lamp were dark,
but for its spark to light
the alabaster white shell
with his life and power.

The pearl were cold and dark
had I not won the spark
of love's intensest flame;
men speaking name no name
to tell the King I hold,
lord not of lands nor gold.

His kiss no poets tell;
Persephone in hell
might best describe his look,
and yet the flowers she lost,
lilies and myrtle tossed
by Aetna's fire-scarred rim,
were nothing to the few
iris and single blue
violets my starved hands took
when he invited me
to taste eternity.

You count your lover fair,
your bride or your bride-groom,
yet you would shun the room
where their enchantments are;
if I could prove how I
met ecstasy you'd choose
the very beggar's rod,
with poets sing or die.

If I could sing this god,
Persephone in Hell
would lift her quivering lids
and smile, the mysteries hid,
escaping all the years
alike both priest and cynic
would smilingly prevail;
dead men would start and move
toward me to learn of love.

Child Poems

[1] Dedication

When everything was over
and I didn't care
and I was alone
and there had been war,
and that thing (my soul)
was a lost star
or a lost boat
adrift, without rudder
or sail or sternsman,
then,

when my soul was a star,
a cloud
(there had been war)
had blacked out,
when there was no one to care,
just at that moment
you said
"a girl?
how old?"
I said
"not a year."

I could see the thing
with its black head
but there wasn't a tear left
and the scar of my wound
was hard;
you cut across,
prodded the thing
mal-healed,
re-opened it
with your knife-twist,

"you'd better send it
to India
to me,"
(we were on the sea)
and I was set free.

Someone wanted the thing,
not yet a year old
and the wound seared
with its iron scar
(you know of that war)
re-opened and bled;
the tears I shed
weren't bitter things,
so ice-floes in spring
touched by the sun,
show colour of flowers,
not roses,
not myrrh,
nor the fiery spire
of Ajax' flower,
but these
(hardly fit for the god you are)
daisies,
hearts-ease.

[2] If Your Eyes Had Been Blue

If your eyes had been blue,
I would have tricked up
tinsel wings,
gilt belt,
silver amulets,
necklet and bracelets,
made an idol,
hieratic:

I would have bartered
and slaved,
lied,
haggled
and stolen,
cheated and died for you:

if your eyes had been grey,
I would have worshiped
and prayed,
pondered and wrought,
worked out the chart of the stars
and of life for you,
made some mystical bargain
with thought:

love-of-love eyes—
they aren't that;
O what you might have been,
sacrosanct for desire,
or had you been wise
with mantle of steel
to protect me
and with grey eyes;

but. . .
you are problem and rune,
you are mystery;
writ on a stone;
you are myrrh-flower
from the incense land;
you are intricate tune;
endangering spark;
I don't understand the ways of you,
nor why
your eyes should be dark.

[3] Grown Up

"When I grow up
we will have boys."

"Darling, who?"

"Why I and you."

"How many?"

"Two."

"Boys? Whatever will you *do*
with them?"

"O, I'll buy things for them,
freed them."

"*Feed* them."

"Freed them apples,
put them to bed,
put out the light."

"You must grow up yourself first,
learn,
teach *them* to read."

"But mama,
you have such pretty hair,
curled,
Io has a mother too."

"O—oh?"

"Only with straight hair,
not like you."

[4] Dream

"I tell you it couldn't have been;
you couldn't have a dream
until you're ten."

"But I had
a five year old one—
it's always the same."

"What?"

"The dream."

"People don't dream
until they're ten."

"But *I* had one."

"You don't even know
what a dream is;
how did it come?"

"It didn't come,
it *was* there."

"Where?"

"In my eyes,
here."

"You made it up,
you were awake."

"No, asleep,
it was a picture—"

"you made up
any one could tell *that*—"

"no, no it was real—
a kitten and his cat."

[5] No

"See, I put them
all in a row,
the bowl of pebbles,
the bowl of shells,
the clay sheep,
the dolls;

now you *will* lie quiet?
now you *will* go to sleep?"

"My-mama, no."

"See,
I turn the lamp very low,
there's no sound anywhere,
no cricket,
bird-chirp,
mouse-creep,
nor ferret,
nor owl;
everything's quiet;

Well, *take* the boy doll;
the other?
well, *there* you are.

now see;
if I promise
to ask Rhoda for you
and Io
with *their* dolls
and your other doll
(don't press it so close
those wood dolls are so dangerous)
then—
(well, take off its dress—)

346

you promise me
you will go to sleep,
say, yes dear mam,
(now a kiss)"

"My-mama, no."

[6] Socratic

"They cut it in squares,
sometimes it comes
in little jars—"

"O—?"

"Under the trees—"
"Where?"

"By his *sheep*-pen."

"Whose?"

"The man
who brings eggs:
he put it
in a basket with moss."

"What?"

"Why,
the little jar."

"What for?"

"Why,
to carry it over—"

"Over where?"

"The field to Io's house."

"Then?"

"*Her* mother took it out
of the moss,
opened it—"

"What?"

"The little jar."

"And then?"

"We each *had* some."

"What?"

"Why the thing
in the little jar
they got
from the straw huts."

"What huts?"

"Why,
the little huts
under the apple-trees,
where they live—"

"Who live?"

"Why,
the *bees*."

Projector

Light takes new attribute
and yet his old
glory
enchants;
not this,
not this, they say,
lord as he was of the hieratic dance,
of poetry
and majesty
and pomp,
master of shrines and gateways
and of doors,
of markets
and the cross-road
and the street;
not this,
they say;
but we say otherwise
and greet
light
in new attribute,
insidious fire;
light reasserts
his power
reclaims the lost;
in a new blaze of splendour
calls the host
to reassemble
and to readjust
all severings
and differings of thought,
all strife and strident bickering
and rest;
O fair and blest,
he strides forth young and pitiful and strong,
a king of blazing splendour and of gold,

and all the evil
and the tyrannous wrong
that beauty suffered
finds its champion,
light
who is god
and song.

He left the place they built him
and the halls,
he strode so simply forth,
they knew him not;
no man deceived him,
no,
nor ever will,
with meagre counterfeit
of ancient rite,
he knows all hearts
and all imagining
of plot
and counterplot
and mimicry,
this measuring of beauty with a rod,
no formula
could hold him
and no threat
recall him
who is god.

Yet he returns,
O unrecorded grace,
over
and under
and through us
and about;
the stage is set now
for his mighty rays;

light,
light that batters gloom,
the Pythian
lifts up a fair head
in a lowly place,
he shows his splendour
in a little room;
he says to us,
be glad
and laugh,
be gay;
I have returned
though in an evil day
you crouched despairingly
who had no shrine;
we had no temple and no temple fire
for all these said
and mouthed
and said again;
beauty is an endighter
and is power
of city
and of soldiery
and might,
beauty is city
and the state
and dour duty,
beauty is this and this and this dull thing,
forgetting who was king.

Yet still he moves
alert,
invidious,
this serpent creeping
and this shaft of light,

his arrows slay
and still his footsteps
dart
gold
in the market-place;
vision returns
and with new vision
fresh
hope
to the impotent;
tired feet that never knew a hill-slope
tread
fabulous mountain sides;
worn
dusty feet
sink in soft drift of pine
needles
and anodyne
of balm and fir and myrtle-trees
and cones
drift across weary brows
and the sea-foam
marks the sea-path
where no sea ever comes;
islands arise where never islands were,
crowned with the sacred palm
or odorous cedar;
waves sparkle and delight
the weary eyes
that never saw the sun fall in the sea
nor the bright Pleiads rise.

Projector II

(*Chang*)

1

This is his gift;
light,
light that sears and breaks
us
from old doubts
and fears
and lassitudes;
this is his gift;
light,
light
that fascinates;
no bird
gazes more avidly
at Pythian snake
than we at this

vision of streams and path-ways
and small lakes;
streams,
cataracts
and valleys
and great forests;
our souls are merged with quietness
or stirred
by tidal-wave
or earth quake;

we sleep and are awake,
we dream and are not here;
our spirits walk elsewhere
with shadow-folk
and ghost-beast,

we speak a shadow-speech,
we tread a shadow-rock,
we lie along ghost-grass
in ghost shade
of the hillock;

with marvellous creatures rise
from shadow-stream
and sea-tide;
with wondrous creatures leap
from tree to tree
or creep
sinuous
along
the river-bed
and freshet;
blest
with rare suppleness
we bound
aloft
rapturously,
or rest
beside the river-head
and lap
waters
of holiness.

2

This is his gift;
light,
light
a wave
that sweeps
us
from old fears
and powers
and disenchantments;
this is his gift,

light
bearing us aloft,
enthusiastic,
into realms of magic;
old forms dispersed
take fresh
shapes
out of nothingness;
light
renders us spell-bound,
enchants us
and astounds;

delight
strikes at dark portals,
opens gates;
the dark breeds
mortal
and mortal-child,
bird,
insect
and rare serpent;
it gives
shape
upon numberless shape
to spring and bear upon us,
writhe
and rear
with anger
or surprise;
light
from his bounty
proffers exquisite things,
quivering of day-light,
rush of delicate wings,
exotic flower
and reed
and underbrush,
tenuous fern
and bush.

For such is his rare power;
he snares us in a net
of light
on woven
fair light;
so has the sun-god won us;
he knots the light to light,
he casts the thing afar,
he draws us to his altar;
we worship who no more
see star in Grecian water;
we worship
who may want
to sip Castalia's fount
in vain
and without hope;
he turns our pain to bliss;
we pass into a space
of intermediate life;

neophyte,
neophyte
your being is my grace
(he says)
your life, my life;
I catch you in my net
of light on over-light;
you are not any more,
being one with snake and bear,
with leopard
and with panther;
you have no life who taste
all-life
with bear and lynx;
evoe
to the car
of Linnaeus,
my brother.

You are myself being free
as bird
or humming-bee;
you are myself
being drawn
like any bee
along
a ray of gilded light;
as bee to out-rayed gold
so you to this;
behold
myself who starts the shout
evoe;
up and sing
evoe;
up and make
evoe's echo break
forth
on the listening air;
evoe,
you shall be
myself
being one with me
in love of lynx and pard
and bear
and prowling panther;

I am the god who trod
Parnassus;
with a nod,
I struck the monster down;
so here,
so in this town
of later day and mood,
I dare the Pythian,
slay direst Dark again;

here in this holy wood,
behold,
behold how good
is man's inventiveness;
I say behold and praise
myself
who struck the spark
that made the soul awake;
I who bade man create
form
from the formless dark.

5

Your souls upon the screen
live lives that might have been,
live lives that ever are;
(evoe
to the car
of god-king Dionysus)
evoe
to the feast;
I and my brother lure
your souls
from lesser matter,
I and my brother
greet
your souls;
on fragile feet
we raise a living thing
we draw it to the screen
of light on light on light;
day passes,
you are here;
to-morrow,
you are other;
the moment makes you great,
evoe makes you taste
pure ecstasy;

358

the snake
crawls from his leafy nest,
so you,
you to my breast
I call your spirit here,
I light you like a star,
I hail you as a child,
I claim you as a lover.

Other Sea-Cities

1

Other sea-cities have faltered,
and striven with the tide,
other sea-cities have struggled
and died:

other sea-walls
were stricken
and the pride of galleys broken,
only you, remained, beautiful,
O sea-bride!

2

Other sea-cities fell
though they built patiently and well,
other sea-cities wrought
intricate details
from rare rock,
stolen from inland,
set great lumps of lapis
above altars
and placed lamps
of alabaster or agate
before god's feet or goddess:

other sea-cities,
named Beauty
their mistress;

other sea-cities
poured oil and from vine-vats
distilled nectar as delicate;
other sea-cities
placed bright torches
on door-posts,
kept alight by the sea-port
the fire to that Spirit,
the Sea, that insistent
remained ever imminent,
threat and resistant,
the ultimate Mother:

other sea-cities,
prayed, chanted
and worshipped.

3

But other sea-cities fell,
Ah, great Tyre,
ah, bright sea-wall!

ah plunder of sea-depth,
pearl, rose-pearl, and the sea-quartz,
ah purple of sea-fish,
deep-purple and violet
that stained king's robes
like a sun-set;

ah sea-light, that touched marble,
till it quivered like live flesh,
ah city, ah intimate
dwelling of pleasure,
ah, prey of disaster!

What kept you, inviolate?
Sea-lover, Sea-mistress,
Sea-mother, Sea-daughter?

What spell through the ages
did your priests set upon you?
did your singers lay on you?
did your prophets bestow you?
why should you last and they go?
why should you stand and they fall?

other sea-cities flung roses
and chanted to the tide,
other sea-cities inter-married
with tribes-men
that their treasure be bountiful,
but other sea-cities knew no secret
to keep back
the slow sand-flow
the swift sea-rush,
knew no power against weather,
the storm wind from the bleak north,
the rain-wind from the cold west,
other sea-cities faced east, west and north, south,
you only controlled them,
alone wrought enchantment,
so they fondled, like charmed beasts,
the thongs of your sandal!

Other sea-cities knew day-fall
and night-fall,
knew change of each season,
marked each hour as it passed
by each high tower,
like a sun-dial;

other sea-cities marked
contour of high wall,
marked aspect of port-gate,
or town-gate or temple
with shadow as wonderful;

outlined, as a clear scroll
may mark contour of parapet
defence-tower and intricate
under-ground labyrinth;

other sea-cities sent helms-men
and brave men,
to islands
and inland;
had women as beautiful;

(were their women
as beautiful?)

their mines offered silver,
their pillars were wonderful,
wrought with as fine thought;

(were they wrought
with as fine thought?)

and laughter—
everywhere, there was laughter;

a boy with a fish-net,
a girl with a hamper
of lampreys,
the long days,
scented with tamarisk,
the long nights
sweet with the aloes,
the fruit piled in baskets,
the merchants with fresh scents
from Arabia,
from Cos,

the wind when it rose high
would open a shutter,
a girl in a blue veil
would push it,
and rain print
her garment upon her,
till she stood, blue
like lapis,
slaves drag from the harbour:

did these love sea-beauty less
than you,
mistress,
O sea-blest?

6

Their blue was as sea-blue,
their purple as purple,
indigo was indigo,
violet, violet,
and red ran its riot,
like the open red pomegranate;

they knew all the gamut
of glass
that took your name;
you reaped fame from their fame;
crystal,
white-gold
or ash-gold,
amethyst,
or fire amethyst,
gem, salt-water, clear air;

her craftsmen wrought marvels,
sea-creatures,
sea-bubbles;

amber caught light
like the sea-weed
a-wash on the sea-stair,
but men
naming such ware,
speak of you
not of rich Tyre.

7

What blessed you
that you sit,
sedately—no harlot—
a witness
as years pass,
to beauty?

we climb slowly
your sea-stair,
weave thought
as for bright hair,
fingers fashion
a chaplet:

but despair,
find no tribute;
for sea-purple,
sea-violet:
with what flowers can we match it?
marble goddess,
with what rose?

8

Tell city,
your secret:

for others built beautifully and well,
but fell
to lie
like a bleached hull;

364

other sea-cities have faltered
and striven with the tide,
other sea-cities have struggled
and died:

other sea-hulks
were stricken, riven
and the pride of galleys
broken,
not one beside you,
remained, beautiful,
O, Sea-Bride.

A Dead Priestess Speaks

Contents

[As prepared by H.D.]

A Dead Priestess Speaks
Electra-Orestes
Calypso
In Our Town
Delphi
Dodona
Sigil
Priest
Master [Magician]

A Dead Priestess Speaks

I

I was not pure,
nor brought
purity to cope
with the world's lost hope,
nor was I insolent;

I went my own way,
quiet and still by day,
advised my neighbour
on the little crop
that faded in the sudden heat,
or brought my seedlings
where hers fell too late
to catch the first
still summer-dew
or late rain-fall of autumn;

I never shone
with glory
among women,
and with men,
I stood apart,
smiling;
they thought me good;

far, far, far
in the wild-wood,
they would have found me other
had they found

me, whom no man yet found,
only the forest-god
of the wet moss,
of the deep underground,
or of the dry rock
parching to the moon;

at noon,
I folded hands; when my hands
lifted up
a moment from the distaff,

I spoke of luck
that got our Arton's son
dictatorship
in a far city;

when I left my room,
it was to tilt a water-jar or fill
a wine-jar with fresh vintage,
not too ripe;

I gave encouragement
and sought,
do you like this pattern
of the helm
of Jason's boat (a new one)
with the olive?

I smiled,
I waited,
I was circumspect;

O never, never, never write that I
missed life or loving;

when the loom
of the three spinning Sisters stops,
and she,
the middle spinner, pauses,
while the last
one with the shears,
cuts off the living thread,
then They may read
the pattern
though you may not,

I, being dead.

II

I laughed not overmuch,
nor sang nor cried;
they said, I might have had,
one year,
the prize, the archon offered
for an epitaph
to a dead soldier;

when I left my room
and saw the sunlight
long upon the grass
and knew that day was over,
the night near,

I scratched the tablet-wax
with a small broom
I made of myrtle from the stunted bush
that grows beside our harbour,

for I looked over the sea-wall
to the further sea—
dark, dark and purple;

no one could write, after his *wine-dark sea*,
an epitaph of glory and of spears;

I watched the years go on
like sun on grass,
and shadow across sunlight,

till they said,
O—you remember? trumpets,
the fire, the shout, the glory of the war?

I answered circumspectly,
claiming no
virtue
that helped the wounded
and no fire
that sung of battle ended,

then they said,
ah she is modest, she is purposeful,
and nominated for the Herald's place,
one
Delia of Miletus.

III

I walked sedately at the head of things,
who yet had wings they saw not;
had they seen,
they would have counted me as one of those
old women who were young when I was young,
who wore bright saffron vestments;

I wore white,
as fitting the high-priestess;

ah, at night—
I had my secret thought, my secret way,
I had my secret song,
who sang by day,
the holy metres that the matrons sang,
sung only by those dedicate to life
of civic virtue
and of civic good;

I knew the poor,
I knew the hideous death they die,
when famine lays its bleak hand on the door;
I knew the rich,
sated with merriment,
who yet are sad,
and I was ever glad,
and circumspect
who never knew their life,
nor poor nor rich,
nor entered into strife,
when the new archon spoke of a new war.

IV

Ah, there was fire—
it caught the light
from the wild-olive when it ceased to yield
a proper fruit,
being wild and small and dear
to me at least,
who bit the acrid berries;

I could have eaten ash-leaves
or wild-oak,
I could have grubbed for acorns like a boar,
or like a wild-goat
bitten into bark,

I could have pecked the bay-tree
like a bird,
winter-green berry
or the berried branch
of the wild-oleander;

tasting leaf and root,
I thought at times of poison,
hoped that I
might lie deep in the tangle,
tasting the hemlock
blossom,
and so die;

but I came home,
and the last archon saw
me reach the door, at dawn;

I did not even care what he might say;

he might have said,
Delia of Miletus is a whore,
she wanders in the open street at night;

how is it
I, who do not care, who did not,
was to him as a mother or a bride,
who was but Delia of Miletus
run wild;
he paused, he stood aside;

I waited for the crowd to mutter filth
and stone me from the altar,
but the new archon cried,
fresh honour to Miletus,
to Delia of Miletus who has found
a new brew of bay,

a new liniment of winter-green
and ripe oak-leaf
and berry of wild-olive
that will stay
the after-ravages of the plague
they brought here from Abydos.

V

Honour came to me,
though I sought it not;
I died at mid-day, sleeping;

they did not see the reach of purple-wing
that lifted me out of the little room,
they did not see drift of the purple-fire
that turned the spring-fire
into winter gloom;

they could not see that Spirit
in the day,
that turned the day to ashes,
though the sun
shone straight into the window.

I left the lintel swept,
the wine in jars,
placed
in a row as fitting;
all was neat,
no ash was left upon the hearth,
a few sprays of wild-crocus filled the cup
with the design, copied from one I wove,
once long ago,
of Jason at the helm
with frame of the wild-olive;

they cried aloud,
woe,
woe,
aie,
aie:
they said,
Delia,
Delia,
the high-priestess
here, lies dead.

VI

Would they have given me that simple white
pure slab of untouched marble,
had they known
had my wide wings sprung wide,

how my heart cried,
O, I was never pure nor wise nor good,
I never made a song that told of war,
I was not rich,
I was not very poor,
I stood unsmiling or I smiled
to match
the company about me;

how was it I,
who walked so circumspectly, yet was caught
in the arms of an angry lover,
who said,
late,

late,
I waited too long for you, Delia,
I will devour you,
love you into flame,

O late
my love,
my bride,
Delia of Miletus.

VII

They carved upon the stone
that I was good,
they scattered ashes that were only
ash of bone
and fibre,
burnt by wood,
gathered for ceremonial,
long instituted by the head of kings,
the high-priest from Arcadia;

they spoke of honours,
the line I drew with weaving,
the fine thread,
they told of liniments, I steeped in oil
to heal the burns of those washed here ashore,
when that old ship took light from a pine-torch,
dropped by a drunken sailor:

they told of how I wandered, risking life,
in the cool woods
to cull those herbs,
in this or that
sharp crescent-light;
or the full light
of moon.

From *Electra-Orestes*

1

ELECTRA   To love, one must slay,
how could I stay?
to love, one must be slain,
then, how could I remain,
waiting, watching in the cold,
while the rain
fell,
and I thought of rhododendron
fold on fold,
the rose and purple and dark-rose
of her garments;

her clothes
were purple,
her way,
toward an open temple,
mine toward a closed
portico;
the sea beat high
and the Aegean rose,
the wave and the sea-wave and the salt-wave
of the Aegean rose
to beat down the portal;
no one knows
what I myself did not,
how the soul grows,
how it wakes
and breaks
walls,
how, within the closed walled stone,
it throws
rays and buds and leaf-rays
and knows
it will die
if the stones lie much longer
across the lintel and between the shafts
of the epistyle;

no one knows
what I myself did not know,
that the soul grows in the dark
and outside one waits in the rain,
seeing her change from purple to dark-rose
again,
seeing her choose
the reds and the sea-blues,
knowing the sting of her rose-of-Cos
scent in my brain,
hating and longing and still;

O God,
if only someone would tell the child
how it loves—
but time goes,
no one knows
until it is too late
and the high-dead lie in state,
the heart—
the heart—
the heart—
how it thrives on hate.

2

He marked the pattern of the sky,
but I
saw not the passing of the Wain,
saw not the Plough,
saw no bright Dragon
nor the Water-snake,
saw not the great nor small Dog
nor the Bees,
saw not Orion nor the Pleiades,
saw not the glittering row
of that one's belt,
saw not star-angle nor star-tilt
of that sword-hilt;

he traced the Archer
on one summer night;
light from the terrace,
faded out star-flight
of doves,
we moved
out toward the lion-portal
through the grove
of myrtles;
one cypress
made a column
like black smoke from incense;
Agamemnon spoke:
the Sickle shines in winter
and the Maiden with the wheat-spike head
rules in the dead
heat of the summer;
a stream ran small and terrible and shrill;
it was so still;

the stream ran from the oak-copse
and returned and ran
back into shadow.

3

CHOROS   *Lovers may come and go,*
there was the memory of blood,
the low call,
(tread not here
where wine is spilled,
red,
red
on marble:
O, beware,
you who would know
later fulfilment:)

there was one cry
defilement:
one dull blow;
let no one say
the lustral vases will wash clean,
demean not your fair mind
with lies.

4

ELECTRA   No one knows,
the heart of a child,
how it grows
until it is too late,
no one knows hate
but worse,
too late,
too, too late
no one knows
love:
when she came
there was the whole earth in flame,
every hill,
every bush
must blush
rose
rose
rose,
O rhododendron-name,
mother;

no one knows the colour of a flower
till it is broken,
no one knows the inner-inner petal of a
    rose
till the purple
is torn open;
no one knew
Clytemnestra:

381

but—
too late,
too late,
too late,
too late,
Electra.

5

CHOROS   Never let it be said,
they are dead,
the high-dead,
never let it be sung
never be told;
O never, never say
they are gone;
they will live
till the isles sink,
they will live
till the stars drift
cold ash
in the track of the day;

while fire seeps in the rock
of Cos
and the Sporades,
they will live:
they will live
till the distant seas
cover the jagged rock
of Skyros;
the Cyclades
will crumble to dust
before these
high names burnt on the soul;
they are stamped on the soul of man
like the mark
of the herdsmen in iron
on the flank of the living sheep;

we are sheep in a herd of sheep,
but Clytemnestra, Electra and Death
are burnt like star-names in the sky,
like the names of the isles of the sea
Naxos and the Cyclades.

6

ORESTES   She is dead:
rend your veil,
cover your head,
kneel, O my sister;

let your tears fall,
but she does not feel,
and I do not feel,
she is dead:
her garments swathe her,
cover her, purple on red
and murex-red
where she bled;
the gold blossom hammered with rose-gold
and the old chains
on her bosom
do not rise,
do not glow
when she breathes,
nor change colour;
she does not move,
no light
can strike any more
from her sandal;
she will tread
no still hall,
running to answer her dead,
for her dead
will not call;

she is alone,
let your tears fall;
purple,
purple,
purple
are the bright folds,
torn in the struggle,
and her gown
is so beautiful,
soft, pleated and wonderful,
and her breasts under her gown
are cold,
for a flower has grown,
murex-red
on the red gown,
where my insatiate sword
went home;

kneel, O my sister,
call to Zeus and our father,
but I do not feel.

ORESTES   Now I see all horror, now I see all terror; this
is what the sun-god asked. He said "strike" and
he struck me; when I struck Clytemnestra, I
struck myself. I cut right through myself, and I
am nothing but the cold metal, I am cold, the
sword, I don't feel anything at all. But on one
side, there is a purple rose-garden and there is a
hum of many bees and there is one bright streak
of sunlight and there is my mother's red robe.
On one side, there is a rose and that shower of
gold-bees that falls down around me. They lie
and creep in the light on the pavement. On the
other side, there is a chasm and bat-wings and
the horrible whistling of those wings. There are
bat-wings and the horrible, horrible gaping
fissure. But I don't feel anything.

384

ELECTRA   Take my hand.

CHOROS   They stand
            like statues
            by a temple-gate.

ORESTES   It is too late. I have found you too late. You
            can't be a lover to me. I should like to love you.
            I used to see you, just you, staggering a little,
            drunken. That was the Pythian, she was a sort
            of sister. She said, I will find the answer.

ELECTRA   I was the sister, I was the priestess, I was alone.

ORESTES   No, you were never alone. You had my father.
            You had protection.

ELECTRA   Mother had him.

ORESTES   But you saw him.

ELECTRA   I saw *them.*

CHOROS   *They are fair,*
            they are tall,
            they stand twin-statues
            by a city-wall.

ORESTES   Stand up, stand up, O Electra, don't fall.

ELECTRA   Why should I stand while Clytemnestra lies?

ORESTES   Are you less than the priestess?

ELECTRA   I had Agamemnon for a father—you mere
            God.

ORESTES   Stop—I had Helios.

ELECTRA	You weep, you weep for the sun—an Image.
ORESTES	He loved me, he spoke through the Pythian—
ELECTRA	Imagination.
ORESTES	—you devil.
ELECTRA	Only Electra.
ORESTES	Why have you turned evil?
ELECTRA	No one knows,
	the heart of a child,
	how it grows,
	until it is too late,
	no one knows hate
	but worse,
	too late,
	too, too late,
	no one knows
	love:
	when she came
	there was the whole earth in flame,
	every hill,
	every bush
	must blush
	rose
	rose
	rose,
	O rhododendron-name,
	mother;
	no one knows the colour of a flower
	till it is broken,
	no one knows the inner-inner petal of a
	rose
	till the purple
	is torn open;

no one knew
Clytemnestra:

but—
too late,
too late,
too late,
too late,
Electra.

ORESTES   It was you who said, slay.

ELECTRA   Long ago—yesterday.

ORESTES   But now—the shadows have not moved.

ELECTRA   There are no shadows where the whole is black.

ORESTES   Would you take back the deed, take back the
sword?

ELECTRA   Only the—word.

ORESTES   The word was God.

ELECTRA   Who is to say whether the word was daemon,
God or devil?

ORESTES   The priests know and the priestess in the shrine.

ELECTRA   The Pythian who was drunk-with-god like
wine—

ORESTES   Aye,
aye,
aye,
aye,
aye
the Pythian.

ELECTRA   Un-sexed,
            inhuman,
            doomed.

ORESTES   She had God,
            she had God,
            and the whole sky for home.

ELECTRA   You loved this travesty
            of love.

ORESTES   And you loved
            love-for-man
            and love-for-woman.

CHOROS   *Out on the sea*
            the ships toil grievously,
            soon they will come,
            finding that they have lost
            Clytemnestra
            and home;

            in from the sea,
            the wind calls hideously,
            woe for the children's fate,
            woe for a palace rent,
            woe, woe for these who spent
            life-blood
            in hate.

Calypso

I

CALYPSO   Clumsy futility, drown yourself—
(*perceiving*   did I ask you to this rock-shelf,
the long-wandering did I lure you here?
Odysseus, clamber- did I call, far and near,
ing ashore)   *come, come Odysseus,*

388

you, you, you alone
are the unmatchable mate,
my own?
sea-nymph may sing;
I didn't say anything
even to the air;
I was alone,
bound hair,
unbound
and let it fall,
wound in no fillet nor any pearl
nor coral,
only nodded
peaceful things;
I asked no wings
to lift me to mid-heaven,
to drop me to earth;
I was alone
now
my beautiful peace has gone;

did I ask you here?
O laugh, most intimate waters,
little cove
and the answering ripples
of the spring
that sends clear water to the salt,
tell me,
did I whisper to you ought
that would work a charm?
did I, unwittingly,
invoke some swallow
to fly low,
to beat into the hollow
of those great eyes,
stupid as an ox,
wide with surprise?
did I? did I?
I am priestess, occult, nymph
    and goddess,

then what was my fault?
there must have been fault
    somewhere,
in the wind,
in the air,
some counter-trick
to mock magic,
some counter-smile
some malign goddess
to smile awry,

O see, Calypso, poor girl,
is caught at last;

O oaf, O ass,
O any slow, plodding and silly
    animal,
O man,
I am amused to think you may
    fall;
here where I feel
maiden-hair,
where I clutch the root of the
    sea-bay,
where I slide a thin foot along
a crack,
you will slip;
you are heavy,
great oaf,
walrus,
whale, clumsy on land,
clumsy with your great arms
    with an oar
at sea;
you have no wit in the air,
you are fit only to clamber
to climb, then to fall;
then to fall;

you will slide clumsy
unto the sand.

ODYSSEUS

On land, I know my way
as well as by sea,
she who is light as a bird,
who shouts wilful words
back to me,
shall know,
Odysseus is at home;
witness O land,
O rock,
O little fern that is torn here,
where my hand
fondles the rock,
to set back the torn root,
O shoot of bay-tree, here
a hand tore
a leaf,
leaf is scattered,
a shredded branch
lies below on the shore
making a letter;
I lean forward to read—alpha? it
    must be—
well begin then—
climb higher—

what letter did the branch make?
omega—the end?
a snake, wound to a cypher,
nothing, nothing for you
O land-lover,
but to follow;
Odysseus,
climb higher!

CALYPSO

Idiot;
did he think he could reach the
    ledge?

391

why, already he leans over the
    edge;
he is dizzy,
he will fall—
shout, shout O sea-gulls,
large pickings for the wrasse,
    the eel;
we eat Odysseus, the land-walrus
to-morrow with parsley
and bean-sauce—
eat,
that's what I could do;
eat fruit—
drink deep from crystal bowl—

ODYSSEUS

Where has she flown?
ah, a wild-plum branch has
    caught—
what?
the gilt clasp of a sandal?
vanity for a nymph—
a nymph is a woman—

CALYPSO
(*below in
the cave*)

What is that?

ODYSSEUS

Ah, I see,
a narrow track concealed,
and not too carefully.

CALYPSO

Isn't he drowned yet?

ODYSSEUS
(*peers
down*)

There she is under the ground.

CALYPSO
(*in the
cave*)

Now I am free;
no one can find,
no one can follow—

| ODYSSEUS | —but me. |

| CALYPSO | Vision of obscene force
what brought you here?
away—
evil goddesses of the west,
I will counter-provoke the
     elements—
will flood your shallow sands
     with sea-water—
my father— |

| ODYSSEUS | Your father? |

| CALYPSO | A king, a god—
owner of ocean— |

| ODYSSEUS
(*clasps her*) | All men are fathers,
kings and gods— |

| CALYPSO | Too soon—O hound—
beast of an insensitive pack—
you can not take me that way— |

| ODYSSEUS | A nymph is a woman. |

| CALYPSO | No human to weep
like your Greek— |

| ODYSSEUS | Laugh then. |

| CALYPSO | Not at the command of men. |

| ODYSSEUS | You will do as I say—
why did you wear sandals like a
     woman,
if you are not human? |

| CALYPSO | I am half of the air—
the rocks hurt my feet— |

ODYSSEUS
(*drops her*)

Beware—
you will moan soon
that you are not all woman.

CALYPSO
(*her hair
spread on
his chest.
He sleeps*)

What did he say?
O you gods— O you gods—
he shall never get away.

II

CALYPSO
(*on land*)

O you clouds,
here is my song;
man is clumsy and evil,
a devil.

O you sand,
this is my command,
drown all men in slow breathless
    suffocation—
then they may understand.

O you winds,
beat his sails flat,
shift a wave sideways
that he suffocate.

O you waves,
run counter to his oars,
waft him to blistering shores,
where he may die of thirst.

O you skies,
send rain
to wash salt from my eyes,

and witness all earth and heaven,
it was of my heart-blood
his sails were woven;

394

witness, river and sea and land;
you, you must hear me—
man is a devil,
man will not understand.

ODYSSEUS
(*on the sea*)

She gave me fresh water in an
    earth-jar,
strange fruits
to quench thirst,
a golden zither
to work magic on the water;

she gave me wine in a cup
and white wine in a crystal shell;
she gave me water and salt,
wrapped in a palm leaf
and palm-dates:

she gave me wool and a pelt of
    fur,
she gave me a pelt of silver-fox,
and a brown soft skin of a bear,

she gave me an ivory comb for
    my hair,
she washed brine and mud from
    my body,
and cool hands
held balm
for a rust-wound;

she gave me water
and fruit in a basket,
and shallow
baskets of pulse and grain, and
    a ball
of hemp
for mending the sail;

395

she gave me a willow basket
for letting into the shallows
for eels;

she gave me peace in her cave.

CALYPSO (*from land*)	He has gone, he has forgotten; he took my lute and my shell of crystal— he never looked back—
ODYSSEUS (*on the sea*)	She gave me a wooden flute, and a mantle, she wove of this wool—
CALYPSO (*from land*)	—for man is a brute and a fool.

In Our Town

Menexeus (*addresses a chance acquaintance, in the long-shoremen's inn, before the Egilian breakwater*):

I

True, the walls fell,
we had neither much beauty nor fame,
so when the hosts came,
we withstood them,
no more;

the horde pushed behind and before,
the gates weren't worth bashing down,
nor the gold-lions,
their cover
of old-gold;

(they'll stand by the market,
when his fine-goods are forfeit;)

true, we didn't go out of our way to stop them,
true, the walls fell,
but my grandfather
found a new trick of an angle;

we were a little out of the pulse of things,
we haven't much of a name,
provincial, he called us,
and other things still worse,
but my sister
discovered a new chord
to the harp-frame.

II

She was married to that Theban,
she could have turned a knife in his heart any day,
but she didn't,
she went quietly
her way;

he was patrician,
he spoke much of his connection;
my father was pounding away,
his hands
thick with white dust,
clotted with wet clay;

he had an idea of establishing a new architrave,
I didn't understand,
I was no artisan,
I spell from dictation,
sub-clerk to this kinsman,
whom you know,
her husband;

I am competent,
engrossed in a new bill of lading,
suggest this or that,
you know how I speak to him,
"why not apples in the hold of the *Naiad*,
who touches to-morrow
a near island,
or dried grapes?"

III

I calculate the number of the ships in the bay,
I say,
"so much grain,
so much wheat,
so many miles to Cos,
if this wind holds,
so many hours on,
then back in the autumn";

I watch the cycle of the stars,
now red Mars,
now the storm-Hyades,
I know the swarm of gold-bees,
can calculate
stress and weight;

I enumerate the possible action of the small-tide
and the great drag-under
at the Needles,
can discuss freight,
intricate detail
of foreign and nicked coin,
debased coinage,
and the recurring problem
of the silver and gold-weight;

I am after all,
a Greek,
though no Theban,

in his sense,
nor patrician;
we are, here, lamentably out of date;
my father still holds to the Doric kymation.

IV

We will wait;
I hear my sister singing by the lion-gate;
she thinks no one goes there;
she hasn't much to fear,
no one can understand anyhow,
her metre's too intricate;

she sings of blue-prows,
she sings of black prows,
she sings of a sword so white,
so luminous, that its own light
alone must slay;
she sings of a sword, a sword, a sword,
and I creep away;

I mustn't listen to this;

I slip back to the house,
"O," I say, quietly
(you know my manner
with this kinsman,
our brother)
"you know, you better recall the *Thetis*,
the Dragon, in the sky last night,
bore no good omen
to that ship."

V

She hates,
O, how she hates;
I say,
"you will be alone next week;

remember,
he visits the run of the small-ports;
what is there for you to do, but wait?
for me
but to calculate
the rise of the Kids,
the depth off the bay,
the stress of timber?

what is there to say
to that patrician, our brother,
who yet stands on good terms
with the merchants?"

of course there is always chance,
and maybe—I could calculate—

after all,
there is stress and over-stress,
there is weight and over-weight;
there are the good Needles
the twin-rocks,
there is the beach
and the break of surf;
or a word to a sailor.

VI

What,
you are that sailor?
well, could we do better than
another goblet of wine-of-Cos?

Delphi

Now I know
there is no before
nor after,
that all escape lies in the perfect
        contour;
now I know that the tale of his lust
is lies,
his allure has outwitted the flesh,
his lust
is pure-lust of the eyes
for beauty
in tangible things;
his words
fly with wings;

now I know
that all who have spoken ill,
who imperil
and threaten the god,
are holding their souls to a mirror,
light threatens, is active, is gone,
so it is with a song;

are you strong?
he is strong;
are you weak?
he prevails—but not you
to question
his power when you falter,
the blame is your own;
he knows not remorse nor repents,
he remains

faultless and perfect and whole;
he is;

you may burn,
you may curse,
you may threaten,
you may pour out red-gold on his
    altar,
he comes to no call,
not to magic
nor reason;

his word
is withdrawn,
hieratic,
authentic,
a king's,
yet all may receive it;
he turns at a whim,
who answers no threat,
no call of the flute,
no drum-beat of the drum;
you may bargain
and threaten,
the prophet
is distant and mute;

yet one day
he will speak
through a child or a thrush
or a stray in the market;
he will touch
with the arm of a herdsman
your arm,
he will brush
with the lips of a brother
your lips;
you will flame into song,

that no merchant can buy,
that no priest can cajole;
he is here,
he is gone.

I foreswore red wine
and the white,
I was whole,
I foreswore lover and love,
all delight
must come
I had said,
of the soul;
I waited impassioned,
alone and alert
in the night;
did he come?

I foreswore child and my home;
I said,
I will walk,
to his most distant wood
for his laurel;
I wandered alone;
I said,
on the height, I will find
      him;
I said,
he will come with the red
first pure light of the sun;

I read volume and tome
of old magic,
I made sign and cross-sign;
he must answer old magic;
he must know the old symbol,
I swear I will find him,
I will bind
his power in a faggot,
a tree,
a stone,
or a bush or a jar
of well-water,

403

I went far
to old pilgrim-sites
for that water;

I entreated the grove and the spring,
the bay-tree in flower,
I was wise on my way,
they said I was wise,
I was steeped in their lore,
I entreated his love,
I prayed him each hour;
I was sterile
and barren
and songless.

I came back:
he opened my door.

HIS RIDDLE   In his power then
a toad,
or a flower,
I asked,
does it wither?
does he rise in the clod,
does he die?
his riddle is painful,
his coming too facile,
if I serve him,
I lie
for years,
a field fallow
then furrows of rye, of wheat and of
        barley,
spring up,
all too early;

the wheat-ear
and the poppy,
nod, one with the lily,
iris
and anemone;

404

when my days are lonely,
he shuns me,
when busy,
he crowds through the throng
of my friends and my guests,
remember your vows, he says,
you are priest:

if I kneel at a shrine,
he says,
song is wine.

HIS ECSTASY   He is yours,
he is mine,
if we quarrel to hold him,
he goes;
his the red-lily,
the white-rose;
if you struggle to whet
your stylus,
if you hurry to melt
scented wax
for your tablets,
he knows
no pity;

you will write in the city
of fir-trees and loam,
in the fields
you will sing of the market;
you will be
among prophets,
a satyr;
when the note of the flute
calls to dance,
you will walk
drunk but not
with that mixed wine;
his tune is his own;
in his, not in your time,
ecstasy will betray you;

if he cares,
he will flay;
if he loves,
he will slay you.

Dodona

1

THE PEOPLE   God of the people,
INVOKE GOD   no clod is too base for your thought,
who made all will not cripple

the mind with injunction;
we pray you, immortal,
before you, are humble,

accepting your symbol,
the rod and the oak-bough,
the fire and the altar,

the bowl and the pillar,
the oil-vat and its savour,
the wine-jar and its flavour.

2

You are rich,
you are keen,
the ills of the world
and strange tongues
sweep between
you and us,
king and devote:

we come from afar,
we await,
we implore,
we hide and attend,
we are lost,
without friend,
loving your word the more;

we fear while we wait,
will you speak,
will you heal?
shall we creep,
shall we kneel?
shall we stand
with palms spread?

shall we bring white or red wine,
shall we bake brown or white bread?

3

THE PRIESTS
ANSWER

You have taken away the terror from
    the sun,
you have given new light to the day:

not ours,
not ours,
the gift,
ours but to sing and pray;
not to us
the inestimable choice is given,
god? man?
not ours to choose
earth or heaven;

yet each
has a soul
like a flame, you say;
each may purge the dross,
sweep earth,

burn myrtle and grass,
bid last day depart
and next day
show new radiance
over us;

you choose the earth;
our choice is clear,
we may share
your choice,
declare
meaning and rhythm and grace
in each daily act;
defeat the tale of man fallen,
we may cheat,
in your name,
the beast.

4

THE HIGH-
PRIESTESS
SPEAKS

Here am I, your daughter,
Zeus, provider,
I bring millet in a basket,
white-grain;

I am late
but come again,
after long absence;

I have lain
with strange lovers;

each one was your
power and steadiness
that grew luminous;

trust that failed
was forgotten,

evil has no part
in the white-lily,
set in marble whorls
upon your altar;

what lily unfurls
regardless of your light?

to what child
are you pitiless?

5

Turn to me,
O just witness
of all earth;

I said,
I am cursed,
Hyades brought tears,
Pleiades, misadventure;

bright tress of Aldebaran,
distress;

Hermes upset
any shelter,
pavilion in laurel,
portal, I had built,

as if for a mere jest;
but this sadness was all false;

eternal,
inscrutable,
you wait,
all-father;

you swear by the portal,
not one daughter
is lost;

here is food,
here, white lilies,
here, grain in a basket.

6

ZEUS SPEAKS
THROUGH THE
ORACLE

Know that my kiss
alone
will not satiate;

now, part of your mother,
initiate,
command grain
to spring fresh;

feed again
those who wronged you;

pay no trick on the trickster,
outwit brain
with your brain;

constant,
eternal,
mindful of the lost,
even as your father;

luminous,
unfearful;

high-priestess,
your fervour,
shall banish
all evil.

7

THE PRIESTESS
ANSWERS

O white bull,
now Europa
binds blossoming petal;

(ineffable fragrance,
your breath is more fragrant
than rose,
than pomegranate:)

I stand by your portal,
a white pillar,
luminous.

Sigil

VIII

There is no sign-post to say
the future is there,
the past lies the other way,
there is no lock, no key;

there is no bell on the door,
there is no door-mat before
the wide-open door:

there is no "he and me,"
there is no "you and she,"
there is no "it must be";

there is one mystery, "take, eat,"
I have found the clue,
there is no old nor new:

wine, bread, grape and sweet
honey; Galilee, Delphi, to-day.

IX

You'll go on, talking away,
you'll say all you've got to say,
if not now,
another day:

I'll listen, I'll hear,
all that I want to hear,
if not this,
next year.

X

Let me be
a splinter in your side
or a bride,

eventually,
I will go
from the red,
red,
red fire-lily,
back
to the snow.

XI

If you take the moon in your hands
and turn it round
(heavy, slightly tarnished platter)
you're there;

if you pull dry sea-weed from the sand
and turn it round
and wonder at the underside's bright amber,
your eyes

look out as they did here,
(you don't remember)
when my soul turned round,

perceiving the other-side of everything,
mullein-leaf, dog-wood leaf, moth-wing
and dandelion-seed under the ground.

XII

Are these ashes in my hand
or a wand
to conjure a butterfly

out of a nest,
a dragon-fly
out of a leaf,

a moon-flower
from a flower husk,

or fire-flies
from a thicket?

XIII

I could say,
red,
red,
red rose-petal
is my inheritance to-day,

but I would keep the rock-pool
still
and cool;

I could cry,
it's my right,
I've earned this,
I've waited eternity,

but I would rather see
other things rising,

frond,
sea-weed,
tentacles
(that might otherwise not uncurl)
move free.

XIV

Now let the cycle sweep us here and there,
we will not struggle,
somewhere,
under a forest-ledge,
a wild white-pear
will blossom;

somewhere,
under an edge of rock,
a sea will open;
slice of the tide-shelf
will show in coral, yourself,
in conch-shell,
myself;

somewhere,
over a field-hedge,
a wild bird
will lift up wild, wild throat,
and that song heard,
will stifle out this note
and this song note.

XV

So if you love me,
love me everywhere,
blind to all argument
or phantasy,
claim the one signet;

truly in the sky,
God marked me to be his,
scrawled, "I, I, I
alone can comprehend

this subtlety":
a song is very simple
or is bound
with inter-woven complicated sound;

one undertakes
the song's integrity,
another all the filament
wound round

chord and discord,
the quarter-note and whole
run of iambic
or of coryamb:

"no one can grasp,"
(God wrote)
"nor understand
the two, insolvent,
only he and you";

shall we two witness
that his writ is wise
or shall we rise,

wing-tip to purple wing,
create new earth,
new skies?

XVI

But it won't be that way,
I'm sane,
normal again;

I'm sane,
normal as when
we last sat in this room
with other people who spoke
pleasant speakable things;

though
you lifted your brow
as a sun-parched branch to the rain,
and I lifted my soul
as from the northern gloom,
an ice-flower to the sun,
they didn't know

how
my heart woke
to a range and measure
of song
I hadn't known;

as yours spoke through your eyes,
I recalled
a trivial little joke we had,
lest the others see
how the walls stretched out
to desert and sand,
the Symplegedes
and the sea.

XVII

Time breaks the barrier,
we are on a reef,
wave lengthens on to sand,
sand keeps wave-beat

furrowed in its heart,
so keep print of my hand;
you are the sea-surge,
lift me from the land,

416

let me be swept out in you,
let me slake the last,
last ultimate thirst;
I am you;

you are cursed;
men have cursed God,
let me be no more man,
God has cursed man,

let me go out and sink
into the ultimate sleep;
take me,
let your hand

gather my throat,
flower from that land
we both have loved,
have lost;

O wand of ebony, keep away the night,
O ivory wand,
bring back the ultimate light
on Delphic headland;

take me,
O ultimate breath,
O master-lyrist,
beat my wild heart to death.

XVIII

Are we unfathomable night
with the new moon
to give it depth
and carry vision further,
or are we rather stupid,
marred with feeling?

417

will we gain all things,
being over-fearful,
or will we lose the clue,
miss out the sense
of all the scrawled script,
being over-careful?

is each one's reticence
the other's food,
or is this mood
sheer poison to the other?

how do I know
what pledge you gave your God,
how do you know
who is my Lord
and Lover?

XIX

"I love you,"
spoken in rhapsodic metre,
leaves me cold:

I have a horror
of finality,
I would rather
hazard a guess,
wonder whether
either of us
could for a moment
endure the other,
after the first fine flavour
of irony
had worn off.

Priest

I

Now you are a priest,
and she is dead,
you said,
"she was gay;
she suffered too much,
but she laughed";
you say,
"she alone gave me prescience
and knowledge,
let me see God";
you say,
not hesitant,
but taut
and too eager to say,
"she went her way,
she was perfect,"
you say it too starkly,
you need not shout,
I hear, I am near;

maybe,
there is truth in what you say,
you are sincere
and strong
and know what you think,
(O, long, long was my way,
long, long was the path
I took,
many, many years,
seasons, moons, noons,
winter, summer,
all day
with a song,
a scimitar);
you say,
"she gave me everything."

419

II

Plentiful is your praise
for a woman who is dead,
while one lifts a proud head,
stalwart as the moon,
not to be killed
even by the most luminous sun-ray,
(you may see her at high-noon);
stubborn as moon-ray,
stubborn as steel,
stubborn as that platinum-disc
in the full day,
when the sun rides high
and flings gold arrow on gold arrow,
beauty to betray all,
all
but one
whom even he
may not slay;

stubborn as the crescent-moon
at dawn
or evening,
set like a knife
to separate night from day,
stubborn as the knife-blade of the moon
that tells winter from summer,
that decides the birth
even of the sun,
stubborn to live,
stubborn to brood,
stubborn to find
all secrets
from herb, sand, steel, rock;
mill
to grind grain from sand;
remorseless tide
none may withstand;

stubborn,
stubborn to continue,
repel,
attract,
command,
obey,
so that, at last,
even you meet an equal;
stubborn,
stubborn the love
that is burnt through
and burnt out
and burnt away.

III

She is dead,
but there is beauty,
a white rose;

you might have made her beautiful to me,
not taken her away,
you might have said,
"O my sister,
you wielder of arrows,
you,
you might have stayed
sickness;
my sister
culler of wild-herbs,
you might have cured madness;
sister,
my equal,
a woman
and human,
you might have gained,
have prevailed
with your magic of mountains,
where even I quailed
before darkness":

you might have given me to her,
have given her to me,
but you failed;
"she alone," you said,
"was true,"
and you lied;
as the moon draws the tide,
as the sun draws the day,
you knew you lied,
saying she alone
understood.

IV

But you will not say you lie,
and I,
I will not die,
and you will not praise me that I live,
nor give signification,
nor recognition,
nor any sort of sign,
nor hail me
who wear
a breast-plate,
difficult to bear,
radium,
with radium on my thighs,
and greaves
of white luminous power,
white as a knife
that eats through me,
rapture
like fire
that is and is not
that sort of thing
you would mistake,
in your innate stupidity,
for desire;

you will not see
that desire begets
love,
until it all flames
into one concise
and metallic blaze,
radium
and platinum
running like quicksilver,
never quiet
yet static,
love that you in your small way,
(your will, set to my will)
mistake;

and I say
tacitly,
"yes, love her,"
only I say tacitly,
"take, take, take,"
yet you in your stupidity
don't differentiate,
don't say, "this is terrible
and beautiful
and near to God,"

no,
you prefer a woman under the earth,
you heap roses above a grave;
a woman under the earth
is safe,
a woman dead
is beloved;
it's all neat,
but God is not neat,
He runs the fire in the dew,
the cob-web,
the newt's tongue,
the owl's ear,

the delicate flick
of a lizard's tail,
a swan's song
and a song's heart-break
and the wind asleep,
and the wind awake,

God is in mind;
but you say,
"she was simple,
she was true,"
tacitly you say,
we are through
with all that;

but you don't really know what you mean,
won't differentiate
between God in a swan-beak
and God in a fin-flick
under lake,
and God asleep
and God awake.

V

So you follow God in your way
and I say
ironically,
"go your way,"
you wake, you sleep,
you pour wine,
in a silver cup;
you say,
"God is in wheat,"
and to punctuate the manifest beauty
of God born again,
you rise early to praise
God in the red-grape.

But you will not be human;
I say, "yes,
love a woman
who is dead,"
I say,
"remember her frail head
remember her night and day,"
but you will not meet me, half-way,
you will not say,
"I see something that is intrinsically terrible,
and I honour you."

You will not love,
you will not honour,
you will obey,
only what you think you hear (or do hear),
God is waiting;
"my life," you said, "is a preparation for
God who is waiting";
and I think,
God forgive him,
God forgive him what he says,
pity him, O God,
pity him,
we do not wait for you,
you are here.

VII

You will not say,
"O reflector of beauty,
you are not beauty,
but you give back that beauty,
that ray,
that is beauty, a red rose,"

you will not say, "O terrible, terrible, that beauty,"
but you turn,
you flee,
(clever man,
how clever
to know
danger);

there is danger;
worship beauty
that is dead,
don't stop, do not turn,
do not say,
"O reflector of beauty
you are not beauty,
but you gave back beauty,
that ray,
that is beauty, a red rose";

God
who knows all, knows why you will not say,
"I do not love you,
but to-day,
you gave back the world to me,
the moon-ray
at dawn, that draws the sun
up, out of the dark
and home,
Lord of the Day."

VIII

You come late;
you say,
"we are old";

cold, cold, is the hand
that would draw you back,
cold, cold is death
but we are not old;

cold is life,
with a radium-heat more cold,
beautiful
(you are right)
and terrible,
(you are right)
life is more terrible than death,
but we are not old;

cold, cold is your breath,
cold is your face and your heart,
but not so cold
as the love that is radium,
that is my heart,
that has been my heart,
not so cold as the arrow, madness
that would slay
us
who forsake life, desire,
not so cold as my love
that is burnished to withstand
even your fire.

IX

She is dead,
but there is beauty,
a red rose;

she was luminous and pale
(so I infer)
like phosphorescence
on north-seas,
when the day is over;
she had no lover
but you,
who could not love her,
nor woo her
with a fervour
equal to his,

whose kiss
stings and stills;
your kiss was stale, satiate and pale
beside his,
who commands battles,
who kills
when the battle delays,
with plentiful
invention,
plague,
horror,
terror,
fever,
aye,
even fervour;

yet Death and I were equal;
I have walked with like fever, with like fervour,
but
I,
I did not die.

X

Love is no easy thing
to define,
you take plummet and line
and say,
you touch depth,
(all right,
all right,)
you measure that love,
it was so many hopes, so many fears,
nights, days;
but I say,
"there is no measure to the thing I knew
that took me out-of-time,"
how measure the years?

my hopes, my fears
were measureless,
five minutes?
five days?
(fifteen to be exact,
exactly fifteen years, almost to the day).

XI

I can not tell you what you say,
I can not take tablet and wax
and make words to fit
space on a tablet,
and make words to fit
any rhyme;
I can not measure that Love,
it was timeless;

it was mighty and took me up out of earth,
out of years;
you lay roses on earth,
on a small mound,
but earth was left behind,
I couldn't even measure that earth,
I don't know where I went;
somewhere, out-of-time.

XII

I listen to you talk,
I reply,
"yes—
death—how sad—your loss."
I hesitate, there is pause and counter-pause
and there is the moment we let lie,
(that last remark for instance,
to take up, turn it like glass to
the light,
let it reflect your life—
her life.)

I see you together,
I see you apart;
no, I don't see anything,
for your words,
spoken like a king
(at one with love, the earth, loss, death)
don't count,

your words don't mean anything.

XIII

And you are a stranger,
my lover—
(thank God, we never did love,
that would have broken the charm
wrought harm,
made that day potent,
this day sad),
thank God you never kissed my hand,
thank God you were separate, apart
from any other;
there was no other
but you;
I laugh . . .
you could never escape . . .
you and she . . .
and the others . . .

maybe you loved her,
but you could never escape,
for all your taut frame,
your valour,
your kind of honour,
spotless devotion and all that;
whatever you did with her, said, I know was tinged
with the wine-lees of the past.

430

XIV

"We go in opposite directions,"
you said,
as I waited for you to go,
(why did you say it then?)
"so we meet in the end."
(O, we meet in the end!)

You waited until the good-bye was through,
formal and yet gay,
as fitted two,
meeting after those years,
(my memory does not sear,
I do not seek God by an altar,
he was so near);
you waited for me to turn,
then you said,
in that voice
that throbs and burns,
that voice that was so conventionally
steady all through,
"we meet in the end."

O, my friend,
where is your wisdom?
the end is the beginning;
O, my priest,
where is your robe?
the beginning, the end.

Magician [Master]

1

There is no man can take,
there is no pool can slake,

ultimately I am alone;
ultimately I am done;

I say,
take colour;
break white into red,
into blue
into violet
into green;
I say,
take each separately,
the white will slay;

pray constantly,
give me green, Artemis,
red, Ares,
blue, Aphrodite, true lover,
or rose;
I say, look at the lawns,
how the spray
of clematis makes gold or the ray
of the delphinium
violet;
I say,
worship each separate;
no man can endure
your intolerable radium;

white,
radiant,
pure;
who are you?
we are unsure;
give us back the old gods,
to make your plight
tolerable;

pull out the nails,
fling them aside,

432

any old boat,
left at high-tide,
(you yourself would admit)
has iron as pliable;

burn the thorn;
thorn burns;
how it crackles;
you yourself would be the first to seek
dried weed by some high-sand
to make the land
liveable;

you yourself;
would be the first to scrap
the old trophies
for new.

2

We have crawled back into the womb;
you command?
be born again,
be born,
be born;
the sand
turns gold ripple and the blue
under-side of the wrasse
glints radium-violet as it leaps;
the dolphin leaves a new track,
the bird cuts new wing-beat,
the fox burrows,
begets;
the rabbit,
the ferret,
the weasel,
the stoat and the newt
have nests;
you said,
the foxes have holes,

you yourself none,
do you ask us
to creep in the earth?

too long, too long,
O my Lord,
have we crept,
too long, too long, O my King
have we slept,
too long have we slain,
too long have we wept.

3

What is fire upon rain?
colour;
what is dew upon grass?
odour;
what are you upon us?
fragrance of honey-locust.

What man is cursed?
he without lover;
what woman is blasphemous?
she who, under cover of your cloak,
casts love out.

Your cloak hides the sinner,
your cloak shields the lover,
colour of wine,
cyclamen,
red rhododendron.

4

Salt, salt the kiss
of beauty where Love is,
salt, salt the refrain,
beat, beat again,
say again,

again,
Beauty,
our King
is slain;

beautiful the hands,
beautiful the feet,
the thighs beautiful;

O is it right,
is it meet?
we have dared too long to worship
an idol,
to worship drab sack-cloth,
to worship dead candles;
light the candles, sing;
tear down every effigy, for none has granted
him beauty;

too long,
too long in the dark,
the sea howls,
and the wind,
a shark rises
to tear
teeth, jaws; revels in horrors;
too long, too long,
have we propitiated the terror in the sea,
forgotten its beauty.

5

I instil rest;
there is no faith and no hope
without sleep;
the poppy-seed is alive to wake
you to another world,
take:

take the poppy-seed,
one grain has more worth than fields of ripe grain or
    barley,

no yield of a thousand and thousand measure,
baskets piled up and pressed down,
no measure running over, can yield
such treasure;

He said,
consider the flower of the field;

did he specify
blue or red?

6

Too long we prayed
God in the thunder,
wonderful though he be
and our father;

too long, too long in the rain,
cowering lest he strike again;

showering peril,
disclosing our evil;

He was right, we knew;
so we fled
him in rocks,
cowered from the Power overhead,
ate grass like the ox;

we will submit;
yes, we bled,
cut ourselves to propitiate
his wrath;

for we asked,
what, what awaits us,
once dead?

we never heard the Magician
we never, never heard what he said.

7

We expected some gesture,
some actor-logic,
some turn of the head,
he spoke simply;
we had followed the priest and the answering word
of the people;

to this,
was no answer;

we expected some threat or some promise,
some disclosure,
we were not as these others;

but he spoke to the rabble;
dead,
dead,
dead were our ears
that heard not, yet heard.

8

A basket,
a fish
or fish net,
the knot of the cord
that fastens the boat,
the oar
or the rudder,
the board or the sail-cloth,

437

the wind as it lifts sand and grass,
the grass
and the flower in the grass;

the grape,
the grape-leaf,
the half-opened tendril,
the red grape, the white grape, the blue grape,
the size of the wood-vine stock,
its roots in the earth,
its bark and its contour,
the shape of the olive,
the goat,
the kid and the lamb,
the sheep,
the shepherd,
his wood-pipe,
his hound,
the wild-bird,
the bird untrapped,
the bird sold in the market;

the laying of fish on the embers,
the taste of the fish,
the feel of the texture of bread,
the round and the half-loaf,
the grain of a petal,
the rain-bow and the rain;

he named these things simply;
sat down at our table,
stood,
named salt,
called to a friend;

he named herbs and simples,
what garnish?
a fine taste,
he called for some ripe wine;

peeled a plum,
remembered the brass bowl
lest he stain
our host's towel;

was courteous,
not over-righteous;
why—
a girl came where he sat,
flung a rose from a basket,
and one broke
a fine box
of Cyprian ivory,
(or alabaster)
a rare scent.

9

He liked jewels,
the fine feel of white pearls;
he would lift a pearl from a tray,
flatter an Ethiopian merchant
on his taste;
lift crystal from Syria,
to the light;

he would see worlds in a crystal
and while we waited for a camel
or a fine Roman's litter
to crowd past,
he would tell of the whorl of whorl of light
that was infinity to be seen in glass,

or a shell
or a bead
or a pearl.

The Dancer

I

I came far,
you came far,
both from strange cities,
I from the west,
you from the east;

but distance can not mar
nor deter
meeting, when fire meets
ice or ice
fire;

which is which?
either is either;
you are a witch,
you rise out of nowhere,
the boards you tread on,
are transferred
to Asia Minor;

you come from some walled town,
you bring its sorcery with you;
I am a priestess,
I am a priest;
you are a priest,
you are a priestess;
I am a devote of Hecate,
crouched by a deep jar
that contains herb,
pulse and white-bean,
red-bean and unknown small leek-stalk and grass blade;

I worship nature,
you are nature.

I worship art;
I am now from the city
of thinkers, of wisdom-makers,
and I watch as one come from afar
in a silver robe;

I carry no wine-jar;

I watch intent,
as one outside with whom is the answer;
intelligence alert,
I am here to report,
to say this is
or is not
God;

I am perfectly aware,
perfectly cold;

a girl clutches her lover's wrist,
I do not care,
(I am perfectly aware of what you are doing,
of what seeds you are sowing)
I know what this youth thinks,
what nerve throbs in that old man,
how that wan soldier
back from the last war,
feels healing, electric, in a clear bar,
where an arm should be;

nothing is hidden
from me;

if you make one false move,
I will slay you;
I hate and have no fear,
you can not betray me,

you can not betray us,
not the Sun,
who is your Lord;

for you are abstract,
making no mistake,
slurring no word
in the rhythm you make,
the poem,
writ in the air.

III

Fair,
fair,
fair,
do we deserve beauty?
pure,
pure
fire,
do we dare
follow desire
where you show
perfection?

loveliest,
O strong,
ember
burns in ice,
snow folds over ember;
fire flashes through clear ice,
pattern frozen is red-rose,
rhododendrons bend under full snow,
yet each flower retains colour;

the rhododendrons are in flower
and snow covers
the flame heat
of purple,
of crimson,

of dark-blue,
of pale-blue,
of white
crystal
calyx;

miracle,
miracle of beauty returned to us,
the sun
born in a woman.

IV

We are more than human,
following your flame,
O woman;

we are more than fire,
following your controlled
vibrance;

we are more than ice,
listening to the slow
beat of our hearts,
like under-current of sap in a flowering tree,
covered with late snow;

we are more than we know.

V

Give us the strength to follow,
the power to hallow
beauty;

you are wind in a stark tree,
you are the stark tree unbent,
you are a strung bow,
you are an arrow,
another arrow;

your feet fling their arrows,
your twin arrows,
you then pulse into one flame;
O luminous,
your feet melt into folded wing,
to mer-maid's tail;

O love in the circle
of opening,
of closing,
of opening;

you are every colour of butterfly,
now in a frail robe, you are a white butterfly;
burning with white fervour,
you are moon-flower,
seen in water.

VI

You are every flower,
I can not stop to name;
nor do I claim
precedence among the harp-players;
my song-note falters;

I claim no precedence among the flute-players,
for I could not maintain
presence enough to stand,
there at your feet
with the rest,
making that music;

I can not name
the Doric nor the Ionic
measure,
nor claim greatness;
I have gained
no laurel
at Delphi;

444

but he,
your Father,
burning sun-lover
has yet had his jest,
has said, among all these
there is one voice,
one councillor;

listen,
Rhodocleia,

he says;

"dance for the world is dead,
dance for you are my mistress,
you are my stylus,
you write in the air with this foot,
with that foot,
with this arrow;
your flung hand
is that pointed arrow,
your taut frame
is one arrow,
my message;

you are my arrow,
my flame;
I have sent you into the world;
beside you,
men may name
no other;
you will never die;

nor this one,
whom you see not,
sitting, sullen and silent,
this poet."

VII

O let us never meet, my love,
let us never clasp hands
as man and woman,
as woman and man,
as woman and woman,
as man and man;

O let us never speak, my love,
let us never utter
words less than my heart-beat,
words less than your throbbing feet;

white cygnet,
black missel-thrush,

let us never crush
breast to breast,
let us never rush
purple to purple fire,
wide flowers,
crushed under the glory
of god in the whirl-wind,
of god in the torrent;

O chaste Aphrodite,

let us be wild and free,
let us retain integrity,
intensity,
taut as the bow,
the Pythian strings
to slay sorrow.

VIII

There is much to know
and little time,
O bright arrow;

446

there are many to heal
and few to feel
the majesty
of our King;

there is little to know
and all eternity,
O my sister;

there is no hurry,
no haste,
no waste,
only leisure;

infinite leisure
to proclaim
harmony,
our Master.

IX

So haste not,
bright meteor;

waste not strength,
O fair planet,
singing-sister;

move delicate strength,
pause,
never-weary pallor;

gather blue corn-flowers,
bind poppies in your hair,
O Priestess;

teach men
that the sun-disk
is bearable,
and his ardour;

447

dare further,
stare with me
into the face of Death,
and say,
Love is stronger.

X

Rhodocleia,
rhododendron,
sway, pause, turn again;

rhododendron,
O wide rose,
open, quiver, pause
and close;

rhododendron,
O strong tree,
sway and bend
and speak to me;

utter words
that I may
take
wax
and cut upon my tablets

words to make men pause
and cry
rhododendron
to the sky;

words that men may pause
and kneel,
broken
by this pulse we feel;

rhododendron,
laurel-tree,
sway, pause,
answer me;

you who fled your Lord and Sire,
till he pulsed to such desire
that no woman ever
could

after,
bear his sacred brood;

only singing fools and deft
trees
might speak
his prophecies.

XI

Rhododendron,
O wild-wood,
let no serpent
with drawn hood,
enter,
know the world we know;

rhododendron,
O white snow,
let no mortal ever know
mysteries
within the fold
of purple
and of rose
and gold
cluster
of this sacred tree;

449

rhododendron,
swear to me,
by his mountain,
by his stream,
none shall mar
the Pythian dream.

XII

We will build an altar here,
swear by wood, by hill, by star,
swear by wind, by curve of bay
where his leaping dolphins lay,

singing to the priests, *on high
build the altar
let life die,
but his song shall never die.*

XIII

Leap as sea-fish
from the water,
toss your arms as fins,
dive under;
where the flute-note
sings of men,
leaving home
and following dream,

bid men follow
as we follow;

as the harp-note tells of steel,
strung to bear immortal peril,
(pleasure such as gods may feel)
bid men feel
as we feel.

450

The Master

I

He was very beautiful,
the old man,
and I knew wisdom,
I found measureless truth
in his words,
his command
was final;

(how did he understand?)

when I travelled to Miletus
to get wisdom,
I left all else behind,
I fasted,
I worked late,
rose early;
whether I wore simple garments
or intricate
nothing was lost,
each vestment had meaning,
"every gesture is wisdom,"
he taught;
"nothing is lost,"
he said;
I went late to bed
or early,
I caught the dream
and rose dreaming,
and we wrought philosophy on the dream content,
I was content;

nothing was lost
for God is all
and the dream is God;
only to us,

to us
is small wisdom,
but great enough
to know God everywhere;

O he was fair,
even when I flung his words in his teeth,
he said,
"I will soon be dead
I must learn from the young";

his tyranny was absolute,
for I had to love him then,
I had to recognise that he was beyond all-men,
nearer to God
(he was so old)
I had to claim
pardon,
which he granted
with his old head
so wise,
so beautiful
with his mouth so young
and his eyes—

O God,
let there be some surprise in heaven for him,
for no one but you could devise
anything suitable
for him,
so beautiful.

II

I don't know what to suggest,
I can hardly suggest things to God
who with a nod
says, "rise Olympos,
sink into the sea,

O Pelion,
Ossa,
be still";

I do not know what to say to God,
for the hills
answer his nod,
and the sea
when he tells his daughter,
white Mother
of green
leaves
and green rills
and silver,
to still
tempest
or send peace
and surcease of peril
when a mountain has spit fire:

I did not know how to differentiate
between volcanic desire,
anemones like embers
and purple fire
of violets
like red heat,
and the cold
silver
of her feet:

I had two loves separate;
God who loves all mountains,
alone knew why
and understood
and told the old man
to explain

the impossible,

which he did.

453

III

What can God give the old man,
who made this possible?

for a woman
breathes fire
and is cold,
a woman sheds snow from ankles
and is warm;
white heat
melts into snow-flake
and violets
turn to pure amethysts,
water-clear:

no,
I did not falter,
I saw the whole miracle,
I knew that the old man made this tenable,
but how could he have foreseen
the impossible?

how could he have known
how each gesture of this dancer
would be hieratic?
words were scrawled on papyrus,
words were written most carefully,
each word was separate
yet each word led to another word,
and the whole made a rhythm
in the air,
till now unguessed at,
unknown.

IV

I was angry at the old man,
I wanted an answer,
a neat answer,

when I argued and said, "well, tell me,
you will soon be dead,
the secret lies with you,"
he said,
"you are a poet";

I do not wish to be treated like a child, a weakling,
so I said,
(I was angry)
"you can not last forever,
the fire of wisdom dies with you,
I have travelled far to Miletus,
you can not stay long now with us,
I came for an answer";

I was angry with the old man
with his talk of the man-strength,
I was angry with his mystery, his mysteries,
I argued till day-break;

O, it was late,
and God will forgive me, my anger,
but I could not accept it.

I could not accept from wisdom
what love taught,
woman is perfect.

V

She is a woman,
yet beyond woman,
yet in woman,
her feet are the delicate pulse of the narcissus bud,
pushing from earth
(ah, where is your man-strength?)
her arms are the waving of the young
male,
tentative,

reaching out
that first evening
alone in a forest;

she is woman,
her thighs are frail yet strong,
she leaps from rock to rock
(it was only a small circle for her dance)

and the hills dance,

she conjures the hills;
"rhododendrons
awake,"
her feet
pulse,
the rhododendrons
wake
there is purple flower
between her marble, her birch-tree white
thighs,
or there is a red flower,

there is a rose flower
parted wide,
as her limbs fling wide in dance
ecstatic
Aphrodite,
there is a frail lavender flower
hidden in grass;

O God, what is it,
this flower
that in itself had power over the whole earth?
for she needs no man,
herself
is that dart and pulse of the male,
hands, feet, thighs,
herself perfect.

VI

Let the old man lie in the earth
(he has troubled men's thought long enough)
let the old man die,
let the old man be of the earth
he is earth,
Father,
O beloved
you are the earth,
he is the earth, Saturn, wisdom,
rock, (O his bones are hard, he is strong, that old man)
let him create a new earth,
and from the rocks of this re-birth
the whole world
must suffer,
only we
who are free,

may foretell,
may prophesy,
he,
(it is he the old man
who will bring a new world to birth)
it is he,
it is he
who already has formed a new earth.

VII

He will trouble the thoughts of men
yet for many an aeon,
they will travel far and wide,
they will discuss all his written words,
his pen will be sacred
they will build a temple
and keep all his sacred writings safe,
and men will come
and men will quarrel
but he will be safe;

they will found temples in his name,
his fame
will be so great
that anyone who has known him
will also be hailed as master,
seer,
interpreter;

only I,
I will escape.

VIII

And it was he himself, he who set me free
to prophesy,

he did not say
"stay,
my disciple,"
he did not say,
"write,
each word I say is sacred,"
he did not say, "teach"
he did not say,
"heal
or seal
documents in my name,"

no,
he was rather casual,
"we won't argue about that"
(he said)
"you are a poet."

IX

So I went forth
blinded a little with the sort of terrible tears
that won't fall;

I said good-bye
and saw his old head
as he turned,
as he left the room
leaving me alone
with all his old trophies,
the marbles, the vases, the stone Sphynx,
the old, old jars from Egypt;
he left me alone with these things
and his old back was bowed;

O God,
those tears didn't come,
how could they?
I went away,
I said,
"I won't have this tyranny
of an old man
he is too old,
I will die,
if I love him;

I can not love him
he is too near
too precious to God."

X

But one does not forget him
who makes all things feasible,
one does not forgive him
who makes God-in-all
possible,
for that is unbearable.

XI

Now can I bear even God,
for a woman's laughter
prophesies
happiness:

(not man, not men,
only one, the old man,
sacred to God);

no man will be present in those mysteries,
yet all men will kneel,
no man will be potent,
important,
yet all men will feel
what it is to be a woman,
will yearn,
burn,
turn from easy pleasure
to hardship
of the spirit,

men will see how long they have been blind,
poor men
poor man-kind
how long
how long
this thought of the man-pulse has tricked them,
has weakened them,
shall see woman,
perfect.

XII

And they did;
I was not the only one that cried
madly,
madly,
we were together,
we were one;

we were together
we were one;
sun-worshippers,

we flung
as one voice
our cry
Rhodocleia;

Rhodocleia,
near to the sun,
we did not say
"pity us,"
we did not say, "look at us,"
we cried,
"O heart of the sun
rhododendron,
Rhodocleia,
we are unworthy your beauty,

you are near beauty the sun,
you are that Lord become woman."

The Poet

I

There were sea-horses and mer-men
and a flat tide-shelf,
there was a sand-dune,
turned moon-ward,
and a trail of wet weed
beyond it,
another of weed,
burnt another colour,
and scattered seed-pods
from the sea-weed;

461

there was a singing snail,
(does a snail sing?)
a sort of tenuous wail
that was not the wind
nor that one gull,
perched on the half-buried
keel,
nor was it any part of translatable sound,
it might have been, of course,
another sort of reed-bird,
further inland;

inland, there was a pond,
filled with water-lilies;
they opened in fresh-water
but the sea was so near,
one was afraid some inland tide,
some sudden squall,
would sweep up,
sweep in,
over the fresh-water pond,
down the lilies;

that is why I am afraid;
I look at you,
I think of your song,
I see the long trail of your coming,
(your nerves are almost gone)
your song is the wail
of something intangible
that I almost
but not-quite feel.

II

But you are my brother,
it is an odd thing that we meet here;
there is this year
and that year,

my lover,
your lover,
there is death
and the dead past:

but you were not living at all,
and I was half-living,
so where the years blight these others,
we, who were not of the years,
have escaped,
we got nowhere;

they were all going somewhere;

I know you now at this moment, when you turn
and thank me ironically,
(everything you say is ironical)
for the flagon I offer,
(you will have no more white wine);

you are over-temperate in all things;
(is inspiration to be tempered?)
almost, as you pause,
in reply to some extravagance
on my part,
I believe that I have failed,
because I got out of the husk that was my husk,

and was butterfly;

O snail,
I know that you are singing;
your husk is a skull,
your song is an echo,
your song is infinite as the sea,
your song is nothing,
your song is the high-tide that washed away the old
    boat-keel,

the wet weed,
the dry weed,
the seed-pods scattered,
but not you;

you are true
to your self, being true
to the irony
of your shell.

III

Yes,
it is dangerous to get out,
and you shall not fail;
but it is also
dangerous to stay in,
unless one is a snail:

a butterfly has antennae,
is moral
and ironical too.

IV

And your shell is a temple,
I see it at night-fall;
your small coptic temple
is left inland,
in spite of wind,
not yet buried
in sand-storm;

your shell is a temple,
its windows are amber;

you smile
and a candle is set somewhere
on an altar;

everyone has heard of the small coptic temple,
but who knows you,
who dwell there?

V

No,
I don't pretend, in a way, to understand,
nor know you,
nor even see you;

I say,
"I don't grasp his philosophy,
and I don't understand,"

but I put out a hand, touch a cold door,
(we have both come from so far);
I touch something imperishable;
I think,
why should he stay there?
why should he guard a shrine so alone,
so apart,
on a path that leads nowhere?

he is keeping a candle burning in a shrine
where nobody comes,
there must be some mystery
in the air
about him,

he couldn't live alone in the desert,
without vision to comfort him,

there must be voices somewhere.

VI

I am almost afraid to sit on this stone,
a little apart,
(hoping you won't know I am here)

465

I am almost afraid to look up at the windows,
to watch for that still flame;

I am almost afraid to speak,
certainly won't cry out, "hail,"
or "farewell" or the things people do shout:

I am almost afraid to think to myself,
why,
he is there.

Orestes Theme

ORESTES   Not God,
           not God
           with the pine-crowned rod,
           not God with the sickle,
           not God,
           not God
           to betray with a nod
           youth into battle,
           not God
           with wine,
           nor death,
           nor hate for a cry,
           but God with a song;

           late,
           late to answer,
           long, long to make amend,
           and what does he send?
           murder;
           I ask and I pray,
           I beg, I beseech, I implore,
           and what does he say?

slay;
slay, slay your mother,
slay her beloved,
slay love;
O, God,
O, my lover,
why did I follow
a song?

ELECTRA   Fair days are over,
is there yet terror to come?
men, men, my brother,
will slay us,
men will lift stones,
obeying the writ of their altar,
to drive us from home,
there is no island
no city,
no rock in the sea
for us;
if we flee,
the order will follow before us,
if we stay,
they will close like the net,
from the hills,
from the coves of the bay;
from the wood,
from the field, they will come;

Orestes, fly first,
there is shelter
there is hope
in the song.

ORESTES   How can I go,
O my sister,
and leave you to death?
mine was the sword, mine, mine the
      command,
is God-the-sun cursed?

ELECTRA I am older,
a woman;
Agamemnon stood by the throne
while the priests
chanted paeon,
and wonder
fell on us,
a prince had been born;
I remember the throne,
I remember the serpent of bronze
on his arm
and the bronze and gold circlet, his crown;
in my thought I can touch and remember;
God, God,
he is gone:

but Orestes
in that child,
in that prince (I remember),
he lives yet;
while you live,
he lives,
while you breathe,
he breathes
with your breath.

ORESTES You are maiden,
no woman,
you are slender and faultless and rare,
you are child of my father,
how could I leave you,
be gone,
while they break you
and slay you?
love does not ask it,
nor song.

Two Poems for Christmas, 1937

[1] Star by Day

We don't have to know,
only to be:
let go the jumble of worn words,
reason and vanity;

a star, a bird, an ox,
straw in a bin,
a reasonable dash of salt,
the price of sin:

where other err,
I have done worse than they;
they had not seen, I saw
that Star by day:

they groped to find the Sun,
I shot past heaven's centrifugal heaven,
to find
the ultimate Sun that makes our own sun, blind:

peace in the Pleiades,
that central hearth,
radium
to our earth:

fear not: that ultimate Star is frail,
only a flake of snow,
whirled in His breath;
be still and know,

flaked from His wings,
the stars and ultimate suns
fall softly on our hands,
His will being done

by children who call in joy
from the window-pane,
"it's snow, it's snow, it's snow,"
but snow is rain,

tears (blessed are they)
whose fears, drawn back to cloud,
fall, to blot out all ill;
O star-spun shroud,

fall softly on all of us;
I have done worse than they,
they had not seen, I saw
that Star by day.

[2] Wooden Animal

You think a wooden animal
is a simple thing;
it's not,
it's more important,
I believe,
than Sirius
or Algol
or Saturn's starry ring;

the beginning and the end
is there, is here;
between, our fingers strive to weave,
but bright threads tear,

and dark and knotted
block the delicate woof,
and we forget the pattern
and this proof

that God is here;
what woodman carved this square?
this bullock's painted feet
stand beside Apis, Ra;

470

where wave and Nile wave meet,
Upper and Lower Kingdom will declare
God's in this wooden toy,
no less

than where
great Taurus ploughs his course,
with ruby eye
on jewelled Archer
and the glittering Bear.

Fragments from Temple of the Sun

SATURN

I

Re-place me in the firmament,
nor fear
prophets of war;

let prayer
be fire:

admire,
re-light,
relate,
regain:

champion:

conspire,
stare down,
man-fear,
man-made,
pliable,
insecure:

invoke
my Star:

let eyes
take fire,
kindle the brain:

that will remain
(splinters of fire)
though the rose
fade:

cold is desire,
cold
(being old):

but rock-crystal
will yet
concentrate,
re-direct:

re-assemble my ray:

let the Scythe sweep
let Death's fever
I reap:

fields of gold,
gold
ripe wheat.

II

My promise is sweet,
sure,
unlike Love's
and the lovers:

I pledge
and I keep
faith:

you will sleep:

I, the last ring of fire,
the last of the seven,
bring reality:

beyond dream of heaven,
(severing the earth-chord)
I command you,
go rest:

poor child,
great the breast,
small you
from frail stalk:

one seed,
but at-one
with eternity:

one grain,
but my gain.

ZEUS-PROVIDER

I

Your daughters,
Zeus, provider,
bring millet in baskets,
white grain:

we are late
but come again,
after long absence:

we have lain
with strange lovers:

473

each was you,
power, steadiness
grew luminous:

man's trust failed,
was forgotten;
evil had no part
in the white-lily,
marble whorl,
on your altar:

what lily unfurls,
regardless of your light?

to what child
are you pitiless?

II

We said,
we are cursed,
Hyades brought tears,
Pleiades, misadventure:

bright tress of Aldebaran,
distress:

Hermes upset
any shelter,
pavilion in laurel,
portal, we had built:

as if for some cruel jest;
but this sadness was all false:

eternal,
inscrutable,
you wait,
all-father:

you swear by your portal,
not one daughter,
not one child
is lost:

here is millet,
here, lilies,
here, grain in a basket.

III

We go forth,
initiate,
we command grain
to spring fresh:

we feed again
those who wronged you:

we pay no trick on the trickster,
but outwit brain
with your brain:

we are constant,
eternal,
mindful of the lost,
even as our-father:

luminous,
unfearful;
high-priestesses,
our fervour
shall banish
all evil.

Archer

Fall the deep curtains,
delicate the weave,
fair the thread:

clear the colours,
apple-leaf green,
ox-heart blood-red:

rare the texture,
woven from wild ram,
sea-bred horned sheep:

the stallion and his mare,
unbridled, with arrow-pattern,
are worked on

the blue cloth
before the door
of religion and inspiration:

the scorpion, snake and hawk
are gold-patterned
as on a king's pall.

Scribe

Wildly dissimilar
yet actuated by the same fear,
the hippopotamus and the wild-deer
hide by the same river.

Strangely disparate
yet compelled by the same hunger,
the cobra and the turtle-dove
meet in the palm-grove.

476

Body and Soul

I

Why wait for Death to mow?
why wait for Death to sow
us in the ground?

precipitate the event
and in a row, plant
almond, olive, apple,

for by these fruits alone
shall we be known.

II

And see the bleak sky
dimmed as in a mirror,
and under-water furl
your under-nourished limbs
into a lily-shape
held to a lily-centre:

O be content;
be small, a lily-bud
or spread at will
your limbs, your feet, your hands,
peninsulas and islands
to your body's continent.

III

You are even a world,
a planet,

and pass from history
and the day's event
to myth and phantasy,

with the Cloud-man
or the Mer-man or the Angel
who spills rain
and snow and hail.

IV

Thou hast been slain
the nightingales wail;
the nightingales cry again
thou hast been slain:

red-coral knows thy pain,
the sponge, dredged from the red-coral reef,
witnessed thy agony
and told thy grief.

V

O do not grieve
for a torn earth
barren fields burnt forests

cracked riven volcano-broken
hill-slopes islands shrunken
mountains lost

O do not grieve
leave the stricken broken cities
give over prayer

for earthquake shaken
broken husks of old fair river-ways
dykes fallen

against fire flood famine
your prayers your fears are useless
leave this to us

do not waste with the fever
of distrust; terror subdued
is yet terror

terror submerged may yet break
the soul-dykes
flood drown.

London
1940

Erige Cor Tuum Ad Me In Caelum

I

Lift up your eyes on high,
under the sky—
indeed?
watch planets swerve and lend
lustre to partner-planet,
as they serve
magnetic stress and turn
subservient to your hands,
your will that guides
majestic cycle of obedient tides?

lift up our eyes to you?
no, God, we stare and stare,
upon a nearer thing
that greets us here,
Death, violent and near.

II

The alchemy and mystery is this,
no cross to kiss,

479

but a cross pointing on a compass-face,
east, west, south, north;

the secret of the ages is revealed,
the book un-sealed,
the fisherman entangled in his nets
felled where he waded
for the evening catch,
the house-door
swinging on the broken latch,
the woman with her basket on the quay,
shading her eyes to see,
if the last boat
is the last,
the house-dog lost,
the little hen escaped,
the precious hay-rick scattered,
and the empty cage,
the book of life is open,
turn and read:

the linnet pecking at the wasted seed,
is holy ghost,
the weed
broken by iron axle,
is the flower
magicians bartered for.

Ecce Sponsus

III

The lonely heart,
the broken vow
have no place now;

the great take precedence of none,
where widow, wife
and maid are one,

virgins about a bride
whose Lord is theirs or ours,
unspecified.

IV

Men's thoughts fling
living wires overhead,
the swallow wings there—dead.

Have men's words speeding
through the wind more worth,
than this bird
flung to earth?

V

Let Love sway free,
bound with no nails,
nor broken, joint and knee;

let Love step down,
open the clasped hands,
forfeit the thorny crown,

retrieve the garment
that was whole,
body and spirit one, spirit and soul.

London
July, 1940

481

Ancient Wisdom Speaks

For April 14, 1943

I

Where you are,
your cloak is blue as the robes
the priests of Tibet wear:

where you are,
you stare and stare at a mountain
and a picture of a mountain in the water:

and when the river is half frozen over,
still you stand,
snow on your sleeve and hood:

still you stand waiting,
not forgetting;
where were we now

if you had not said over and over,
as you watched the snow
slide down the runnels

and become, below on the slopes,
blossom of apple, quince and the wild-pear,
repeatedly, this prayer:

remember these (you said)
who when the earth-quake shook their city,
when angry blast and fire

broke open their frail door,
did not forget
beauty.

II

O—what a picture of a mountain!
in our desolation,
four times, four seasons

marched up from the valley,
each with its retinue and panoply,
each climbed the mountain slowly:

though the mountain changed its colour
as the seasons came and went,
she did not alter.

III

Her cloak is very old
yet blue as the blue-poppy,
blue as the flax in flower:

and not an hour passed
in our torment
but she thought of us:

she did not change,
the mountain changed from gold to violet,
as the sun rose and set:

she knew our fear,
and yet she did not falter
nor cast herself in anguish by the river:

but she stood,
the sun on her hair
or the snow on her blue hood:

winter and summer,
summer and winter
. . . again . . . again . . .

never forgetting
but remembering
our peculiar desolation:

I will stand here, she said to the mountain,
that even you must start awake, aware
that beauty can endure:

her cloak is very, very old
and blue. . . .

IV

O do not weep, she says,
for ages past I was
and I endure;

sand-castles and sand-cities
on the shore,
built carefully
with towers and gates,
patiently set about
with wall and moat,
have crumbled,
Nineveh, Tyre:

O do not weep, she says,
but let the fire burn out;
for having dared the flame,
endured the pyre,
your ashes,
sainted ones,
your chastened hearts,
your empty frames,
your very bones
still serve
to praise my name.

R.A.F.

I

He said, I'm just out of hospital,
but I'm still flying.

I answered, *of course,*
angry, prescient, knowing

what fire lay behind his wide stare,
what fury of desire

impelled him,
pretending not to notice

his stammer
and that now, in his agony to express himself

his speech failed
altogether,

and his eyes seemed to gather
in their white-heat,

all the fires of the wind,
fire of sleet,

snow like white-fire pellets,
congealed radium, planets

like snow-flakes:
and I thought,

the sun
is only a round platform

for his feet
to rest upon.

II

So I knew his name,
the coming-one

from a far star,
I knew he would come again,

though I did not know
he would come so soon;

he stood by my desk
in my room

where I write this;
he did not wear

his blue tunic with the wings,
nor his cap with the crown;

his flying-helmet,
and his cumbersome trappings

were unfamiliar,
like a deep-sea diver.

III

I had said,
I want to thank you,

he had said,
for what?

I had said,
it is very difficult

to say what I want,
I mean—I want

personally to thank you
for what you have done;

he had said,
I did nothing,

it was the others;
I went on,

for a moment infected with his stammer
but persistent,

I will think of you
when they come over,

I mean—I understand—I know—
I was there the whole time

in the Battle
of Britain.

IV

He came again,
he did not speak;

I thought; he stands by my desk
in the dark,

he is emissary,
maybe he will speak later,

(does he still stammer?)
I remembered

how I had thought
this field, that meadow

is branded for eternity
(whatever becomes of our earth)

with the mark
of the new cross,

the flying shadow
of high wings,

moving
over the grass.

V

Fortunately, there was no time
for lesser intimacy

than this—
instantaneous flash,

recognition, premonition, vision;
fortunately, there was no time,

for the two-edged drawn-swords
of our two separate twin-beings

to dull; no danger of rust;
the Archangel's own fine blade

so neatly divided us,
in the beginning.

VI

He was huddled
in the opposite corner,

bare-headed, curiously slumped forward
as if he were about to fall over;

the compartment was crowded,
I was facing forward;

I said, put your feet up here
and I wedged myself tighter

and dozed off in the roar
and the train rumble.

VII

In the train jolt
our knees brushed

and he murmured, sorry:
he was there;

I knew in the half-daze,
in the drug and drift,

the hypnotic sway
of the train, that we were very near;

we could not have been nearer,
and my mind winged away;

our minds are winged,
though our feet are clay.

VIII

True, I had travelled the world over,
but I had found no beauty, no wonder

to equal the cliff-edge,
the line of a river

we had just passed,
no picture nor colour in glass

to equal the fervour
of sea-blue, emerald, violet,

the stone-walls, prehistoric circles
and dolmens

that I had just left
in Cornwall.

IX

True, we are cold, shivering,
and we ponder on many things,

waiting for the war to be over;
and I wonder,

has he come for me?
is this my particular winged messenger?

or was it tact,
a code of behaviour,

was it only a sort of politeness,
did he "drop in," as it were,

to explain
why he had not come sooner?

X

My thoughts in the train,
rushed forward, backward,

I was in the lush tall grass
by the burning beeches,

I followed the avenue, out of Tregonning,
across the fields to the other house,

Trenoweth,
where friends were staying;

there was the camellia-bush,
the stone-basin with the tiny lilies

and the pink snails; I remembered
the Scilly Islands off the coast,

and other islands,
the isles of Greece

whose stone thresholds (nor Karnak)
were older

than the sun-circles I had just left;
I thought of Stonehenge,

I thought,
we will be saved yet.

XI

He could not know my thoughts,
but between us,

the shuttle sped,
passed back,

the invisible web,
bound us;

whatever we thought or said,
we were people who had crossed over,

we had already crashed,
we were already dead.

XII

If I dare recall
his last swift grave smile,

I award myself
some inch of ribbon

for valour,
such as he wore,

for I am stricken
as never before,

by the thought
of ineptitude, sloth, evil

that prosper,
while such as he fall.

London,
17th September, 1941

May 1943

I

You may say this is no poem
but I
will remember this hour
till I die:

the clock from the old bell-tower
says two
but the sun climbing the sky-clock
points noon,

492

exactly noon; May 14
says the calendar,
and the steps of William's orangery
at Kensington,
become the Venetian doge's water-stair:

exact perfection,
I am 56,
the may-trees blossom:

the wall-door under the chestnut-tree
that I nor anyone else ever saw open,
opens and lets out a carpenter:

he has his chisel,
I have my pencil:

he mends the broken window-frame of the orangery,
I mend a break in time.

II

Do you remember over there,
how a sparrow got caught
in the lily-roots
(fleur-de-lis or water-lily)
of King William IVth's water-trough,
in Dutch William's Dutch garden?

do you remember how you leapt
the fast-locked iron-gate,
and where no profane foot was ever set
(and only the head-gardener's
sacrosanct under-gardener's
favourites might potter)
you untangled the sparrow's foot
from the threads of the lily-root?

A canoe slips from under a rhododendron-bush,
or is it Danielli's gondola,
trailing its purple stuff?

the old clock ticks,
but I hear drop-drop of an older water-clock;
the leaves whisper,
or is it a card-game in the orangery?
bright ghosts?
is it sun-light or jets of the candle-points
on the unbroken window-panes?
here is one whole,
here is one nicely set with matchbox wood,
or varnished cardboard,
so the uneven squares make patch-work;
humanity returns
to this exquisite untidy place,
and oddly with humanity the fashionable ghosts
come back;

is it clock-tick?
is it the snip-snap of a snuff-box?
or a patch-box?
is it an older water-clock?
is it the delicate, only-just perceptible whisper
of the hour-glass?

is it a later fashionable hour-glass lady?
or merely a box-tree?
is it a lady in a hoop or is it a box-tree peacock?

this placard announces:
*The damage to this room is part of the
destruction caused by German incendiary bombs
dropped on Kensington Palace, 14 October, 1940;*

but enemy action has not driven away
the happy ghosts
somehow it has brought them back;

this is not a poem
only a day to remember,
I say the war is over . . .
the war is over . . .

IV

He said (last winter),
these people have the advantage over us,
and I was sorry, God knows I was sorry enough;
the burnt-red of Texas or the sun-burnt bronze
of his Arizona desert
had not had time to wear off,
and the rest of them stood in the rain,
a neat line waiting,
not saying anything,
but he barked from a young angry throat,
these people have the advantage:

so we did, so we had,
we shuffled along in the rain,
a dingy crowd
with fish-baskets, old rain-coats,
funny umbrellas, a motley host,
dim, undistinguished, water-rats
in the water,
land-rats in the gutter.

V

These people have the advantage over us,
did he speak for himself or for
the rest of the bronze giants?
I wanted to stop, slithered along,
web-footed, trying to work out in that moment,
whether it were better to stop, to speak,

but I was embarrassed by the neat row of them,
drawn up on the pavement,
and what would I say anyway?
I wanted to say I was sorry,
actually thinking of them,
not of us.

VI

I wanted to say I was sorry,
but why should I? but anyway
I did want to say I was sorry,
but how could I? who was I?
I wanted to say, yes, we're used to it,
we have the advantage,
you're new to it;
we've slithered so long in the rain,
prowled like cats in the dark,
like owls in the black-out,
look at us—anaemic, good-natured,
for a rat in the gutter's a rat in the gutter,
consider our fellowship,
look at each one of us,
we've grown alike, slithering,
slipping along with fish-baskets,
grey faces, fish-faces, frog gait,
we slop, we hop,
we're off to the bread-queue,
the meat-shop, the grocery,
an egg?—really madam—maybe to-morrow—
one here—one there—another one over there
is heroic (who'd know it?)
heroic? no bronze face—

no
    no
        no
what am I saying?

VII

It was Goldie, that was her vulgar name,
(one of these was her mother);
better move over,
the fire-man said, miss,
getting a bit hot, miss,
(*look out*

       look out

           wall!)
better run your little bus
around the other side,
cigarette miss?
he offered her a cigarette
because . . . he thought . . . for a minute . . .
he might push her out of it . . .
it's no use Frank, that's Goldie—
what of it? she's a kid,
she's too young—shut up,
all the kids are in it.

Goldie wouldn't move away,
she was told to stay.

VIII

Goldie had her picture
in a little exhibition,
Goldie was in the news
for half a second,
Goldie had her little job,
ambulance?

       mobile canteen?

             extra fire-girl?
I don't know,
I only just remember
the caption,
a line and a half,
below the newspaper photograph,
which said:

known as Goldie
because of her
fair
hair,
she was found sitting upright
at the wheel of her emergency car,
dead.

IX

Goldie was one of us,
we are one with Goldie;
Arizona desert,
Texas and Arkinsaw,
how could you know,
you did not see
what we saw:

Goldie was only one,
Goldie's all around us,
gutter-rats,
land-rats,
look at us,
slop flop,
stop hop,
past Arkinsaw, Kansas
drawn up on the pavement:

no one will tell you;
only I, one of you,
one of them,
know the rune,
only I can play the tune,
make the song,
tell the story
of Goldie:

Goldie made the words come true,
the sun never sets on . . .
anaemic faces in the line
waiting in the bread-queue.

498

X

The reason is:

rats leave the sinking ship
but we . . .
     we . . .
didn't leave,
so the ship
didn't sink,
and that's madness,
Lear's song,
that's Touchstone's forest-jest,
that's Swan of Avon logic:

the ship didn't sink
because
the rats knew
the timber true:

the ship-rats hop flop
along the pavement-deck a-wash,
O Kansas, O Arkinsaw,

Goldie wouldn't move away,
Goldie was told to stay.

XI

Frog faces,
frog lust,
frog bellies
in the dust,
till unexpected flame
gave you another name:

(there's the siren wail again,
May 15;
by the clock,
near 6,

that's 4
by the sun):

frog faces,
frog lust,
frog bellies
in the dust
of the Last Judgment Day:

when winter-fog is gone,
the frogs sit in the sun,
and now you can see
strawberry-leaves
on a crown,
a lion,
a unicorn:

now you can clearly see
what frogs in the sun
become:

salamanders in the flame,
heraldic wings surround the name
English from Englisc from
Engle, Angle
from the Angles who settled
in Briton.

XII

Now you can clearly see
why I sing this mystery
of Goldie, Angel in the sun,
of Goldie up with the fire-alarm,

now this stocking,
now the other shoe on,

of Goldie who ran and chaffed
the telephone-girl because she laughed
at Goldie lazy
but up with the gong:

sea-nymphs hourly ring his knell
(hers, rather—Goldie's—)
    ding
        dong
            bell.

XIII

Goldilocks, Goldilocks let down your hair,
for we have never seen anywhere
a thread so delicate, spun so fair:

Goldie in a tissue-paper frock
hunts for strawberries in the snow,
or was that another? anyhow

Goldie or Gretel in woollen socks
scatters bread-crumbs to show the way
through the dark forest, or did you say

a Saint with Halo beside a wheel
is set on an altar where people kneel,
to take their bread from a priest, instead

of Gretel who changed her crumbs
for pebbles? the pebbles lay like little shells
under green-boughs that swayed like water,

while over and through it swam sea-girls;
the youngest princess begged feet for fins,
Goldie, Gretel or Saint Catherine?

501

Christmas 1944

I

The stratosphere was once where angels were;
if we are dizzy and a little mad,
forgive us, we have had
experience of a world beyond our sphere,
there—where no angels are;

the angel host and choir
is driven further, higher,
or (so it seems to me) descended to our level,
to share our destiny;

we do not see the fire,
we do not even hear
the whirr and distant roar,
we have gone hence before

the sound manifests;
are we here? or there?
we do not know,
waiting from hour to hour,

hoping for what? dispersal
of our poor bodies' frame?
what do we hope for?
name remembered? faults forgot?

or do we hope to rise upward?
no—no—not to those skies;
rather we question here,
what do I love?

what have I left un-loved?
what image would I choose
had I one thing, as gift,
redeemed from dust and ash?

I ask, what would I take?
which doll clutch to my breast?
should some small tender ghost,
descended from the host

of cherubim and choirs, speak:
'look, they are all here,
all, all your loveliest treasures,
look and then choose—but *one*—

we have our journey now,
poor child—come.'

II

A Dresden girl and boy
held up the painted dial,
but I had quite forgot
I had that little clock;

I'll take the clock—but how?
why, it was broken, lost,
dismantled long ago;

but there's another treasure,
that slice of amber-rock,
a traveller once brought
me from the Baltic coast,

and with it (these are small)
the little painted swallow—
where are they? one, I left,
I know at a friend's house;

and there's that little cat
that lapped milk from my tray
at breakfast-time—but where?

at some hotel perhaps?
or staying with a friend?
or was it in a dream?

a small cat with grey fur;
perhaps you may remember?

it's true I lent or gave away the amber,
the swallow's somewhere else in someone's house,
the clock was long ago, dismantled, lost,
the cat was dream or memory or both;
but I'll take these—is it too much?

III

We are a little dizzy
and quite mad,
but we have had
strange visitations
from the stratosphere,
of angels drawn to earth
and nearer angels;

we think and feel and speak
like children lost,
for one Child too, was cast
at Christmas, from a house
of stone with wood for beam
and lintel and door-shaft;

go—go—there is no room
for you, in this our Inn:

to Him, the painted swallow,
to Him, the lump of amber,
to Him, the boy and girl
with roses and love-knots,
to Him, the little cat
to play beneath the Manger:

if we are dizzy
and a little mad,
forgive us, we have had
strange visitations
from the stratosphere.

TRILOGY

The Walls Do Not Fall

To Bryher

for Karnak 1923
from London 1942

[1]

An incident here and there,
and rails gone (for guns)
from your (and my) old town square:

mist and mist-grey, no colour,
still the Luxor bee, chick and hare
pursue unalterable purpose

in green, rose-red, lapis;
they continue to prophesy
from the stone papyrus:

there, as here, ruin opens
the tomb, the temple; enter,
there as here, there are no doors:

the shrine lies open to the sky,
the rain falls, here, there
sand drifts; eternity endures:

ruin everywhere, yet as the fallen roof
leaves the sealed room
open to the air,

so, through our desolation,
thoughts stir, inspiration stalks us
through gloom:

unaware, Spirit announces the Presence;
shivering overtakes us,
as of old, Samuel:

trembling at a known street-corner,
we know not nor are known;
the Pythian pronounces—we pass on

to another cellar, to another sliced wall
where poor utensils show
like rare objects in a museum;

Pompeii has nothing to teach us,
we know crack of volcanic fissure,
slow flow of terrible lava,

pressure on heart, lungs, the brain
about to burst its brittle case
(what the skull can endure!):

over us, Apocryphal fire,
under us, the earth sway, dip of a floor,
slope of a pavement

where men roll, drunk
with a new bewilderment,
sorcery, bedevilment:

the bone-frame was made for
no such shock knit within terror,
yet the skeleton stood up to it:

the flesh? it was melted away,
the heart burnt out, dead ember,
tendons, muscles shattered, outer husk dismembered,

yet the frame held:
we passed the flame: we wonder
what saved us? what for?

[2]

Evil was active in the land,
Good was impoverished and sad;

Ill promised adventure,
Good was smug and fat;

Dev-ill was after us,
tricked up like Jehovah;

Good was the tasteless pod,
stripped from the manna-beans, pulse, lentils:

they were angry when we were so hungry
for the nourishment, God;

they snatched off our amulets,
charms are not, they said, grace;

but gods always face two-ways,
so let us search the old highways

for the true-rune, the right-spell,
recover old values;

nor listen if they shout out,
your beauty, Isis, Aset or Astarte,

is a harlot; you are retrogressive,
zealot, hankering after old flesh-pots;

your heart, moreover,
is a dead canker,

511

they continue, and
your rhythm is the devil's hymn,

your stylus is dipped in corrosive sublimate,
how can you scratch out

indelible ink of the palimpsest
of past misadventure?

[3]

Let us, however, recover the Sceptre,
the rod of power:

it is crowned with the lily-head
or the lily-bud:

it is Caduceus; among the dying
it bears healing:

or evoking the dead,
it brings life to the living.

[4]

There is a spell, for instance,
in every sea-shell:

continuous, the sea-thrust
is powerless against coral,

bone, stone, marble
hewn from within by that craftsman,

the shell-fish:
oyster, clam, mollusc

is master-mason planning
the stone marvel:

512

yet that flabby, amorphous hermit
within, like the planet

senses the finite,
it limits its orbit

of being, its house,
temple, fane, shrine:

it unlocks the portals
at stated intervals:

prompted by hunger,
it opens to the tide-flow:

but infinity? no,
of nothing-too-much:

I sense my own limit,
my shell-jaws snap shut

at invasion of the limitless,
ocean-weight; infinite water

can not crack me, egg in egg-shell;
closed in, complete, immortal

full-circle, I know the pull
of the tide, the lull

as well as the moon;
the octopus-darkness

is powerless against
her cold immortality;

so I in my own way know
that the whale

can not digest me:
be firm in your own small, static, limited

orbit and the shark-jaws
of outer circumstance

will spit you forth:
be indigestible, hard, ungiving.

so that, living within,
you beget, self-out-of-self,

selfless,
that pearl-of-great-price.

[5]

When in the company of the gods,
I loved and was loved,

never was my mind stirred
to such rapture,

my heart moved
to such pleasure,

as now, to discover
over Love, a new Master:

His, the track in the sand
from a plum-tree in flower

to a half-open hut-door,
(or track would have been

but wind blows sand-prints from the sand,
whether seen or unseen):

His, the Genius in the jar
which the Fisherman finds,

He is Mage,
bringing myrrh.

[6]

In me (the worm) clearly
is no righteousness, but this—

persistence; I escaped spider-snare,
bird-claw, scavenger bird-beak,

clung to grass-blade,
the back of a leaf

when storm-wind
tore it from its stem;

I escaped, I explored
rose-thorn forest,

was rain-swept
down the valley of a leaf;

was deposited on grass,
where mast by jewelled mast

bore separate ravellings
of encrusted gem-stuff

of the mist
from each banner-staff:

unintimidated by multiplicity
of magnified beauty,

such as your gorgon-great
dull eye can not focus

515

nor compass, I profit
by every calamity;

I eat my way out of it;
gorged on vine-leaf and mulberry,

parasite, I find nourishment:
when you cry in disgust,

a worm on the leaf,
a worm in the dust,

a worm on the ear-of-wheat,
I am yet unrepentant,

for I know how the Lord God
is about to manifest, when I,

the industrious worm,
spin my own shroud.

[7]

Gods, goddesses
wear the winged head-dress

of horns, as the butterfly
antennae,

or the erect king-cobra crest
to show how the worm turns.

[8]

So we reveal our status
with twin-horns, disk, erect serpent,

though these or the double-plume or lotus
are, you now tell us, trivial

intellectual adornment;
poets are useless,

more than that,
we, authentic relic,

bearers of the secret wisdom,
living remnant

of the inner band
of the sanctuaries' initiate,

are not only 'non-utilitarian',
we are 'pathetic':

this is the new heresy;
but if you do not even understand what words say,

how can you expect to pass judgement
on what words conceal?

yet the ancient rubrics reveal that
we are back at the beginning:

you have a long way to go,
walk carefully, speak politely

to those who have done their worm-cycle,
for gods have been smashed before

and idols and their secret is stored
in man's very speech,

in the trivial or
the real dream; insignia

in the heron's crest,
the asp's back,

enigmas, rubrics promise as before,
protection for the scribe;

he takes precedence of the priest,
stands second only to the Pharoah.

[9]

Thoth, Hermes, the stylus,
the palette, the pen, the quill endure,

though our books are a floor
of smouldering ash under our feet;

though the burning of the books remains
the most perverse gesture

and the meanest
of man's mean nature,

yet give us, they still cry,
give us books,

folio, manuscript, old parchment
will do for cartridge cases;

irony is bitter truth
wrapped up in a little joke,

and Hatshepsut's name is still circled
with what they call the *cartouche.*

[10]

But we fight for life,
we fight, they say, for breath,

so what good are your scribblings?
this—we take them with us

beyond death; Mercury, Hermes, Thoth
invented the script, letters, palette;

the indicated flute or lyre-notes
on papyrus or parchment

are magic, indelibly stamped
on the atmosphere somewhere,

forever; remember, O Sword,
you are the younger brother, the latter-born,

your Triumph, however exultant,
must one day be over,

in the beginning
was the Word.

[11]

Without thought, invention,
you would not have been, O Sword,

without idea and the Word's mediation,
you would have remained

unmanifest in the dim dimension
where thought dwells,

and beyond thought and idea,
their begetter,

Dream,
Vision.

[12]

So, in our secretive, sly way,
we are proud and chary

of companionship with you others,
our betters, who seem to imply

that we will soon be swept aside,
crumpled rags, no good for banner-stuff,

no fit length for a bandage;
but when the shingles hissed

in the rain of incendiary,
other values were revealed to us,

other standards hallowed us;
strange texture, a wing covered us,

and though there was whirr and roar in the high air,
there was a Voice louder,

though its speech was lower
than a whisper.

[13]

The Presence was spectrum-blue,
ultimate blue ray,

rare as radium, as healing;
my old self, wrapped round me,

was shroud (I speak of myself individually
but I was surrounded by companions

in this mystery);
do you wonder we are proud,

aloof,
indifferent to your good and evil?

peril, strangely encountered, strangely endured,
marks us;

520

we know each other
by secret symbols,

though, remote, speechless,
we pass each other on the pavement,

at the turn of the stair;
though no word pass between us,

there is subtle appraisement;
even if we snarl a brief greeting

or do not speak at all,
we know our Name,

we nameless initiates,
born of one mother,

companions
of the flame.

[14]

Yet we, the latter-day twice-born,
have our bad moments when

dragging the forlorn
husk of self after us,

we are forced to confess to
malaise and embarrassment;

we pull at this dead shell,
struggle but we must wait

till the new Sun dries off
the old-body humours;

awkwardly, we drag this stale
old will, old volition, old habit

about with us;
we are these people,

wistful, ironical, wilful,
who have no part in

new-world reconstruction,
in the confederacy of labour,

the practical issues of art
and the cataloguing of utilities:

O, do not look up
into the air,

you who are occupied
in the bewildering

sand-heap maze
of present-day endeavour;

you will be, not so much frightened
as paralysed with inaction,

and anyhow,
we have not crawled so very far

up our individual grass-blade
toward our individual star.

[15]

Too old to be useful
(whether in years of experience,

we are the same lot)
not old enough to be dead,

we are the keepers of the secret,
the carriers, the spinners

of the rare intangible thread
that binds all humanity

to ancient wisdom,
to antiquity;

our joy is unique, to us,
grape, knife, cup, wheat

are symbols in eternity,
and every concrete object

has abstract value, is timeless
in the dream parallel

whose relative sigil has not changed
since Nineveh and Babel.

[16]

Ra, Osiris, *Amen* appeared
in a spacious, bare meeting-house;

he is the world-father,
father of past aeons,

present and future equally;
beardless, not at all like Jehovah,

he was upright, slender,
impressive at the Memnon monolith,

yet he was not out of place
but perfectly at home

in that eighteenth-century
simplicity and grace;

then I woke with a start
of wonder and asked myself,

523

but whose eyes are those eyes?
for the eyes (in the cold,

I marvel to remember)
were all one texture,

as if without pupil
or all pupil, dark

yet very clear with amber
shining . . .

[17]

. . . coals for the world's burning,
for we must go forward,

we are at the cross-roads,
the tide is turning;

it uncovers pebbles and shells,
beautiful yet static, empty

old thought, old convention;
let us go down to the sea,

gather dry sea-weed,
heap drift-wood,

let us light a new fire
and in the fragrance

of burnt salt and sea-incense
chant new paeans to the new Sun

of regeneration;
we have always worshipped Him,

we have always said,
forever and ever, Amen.

[18]

The Christos-image
is most difficult to disentangle

from its art-craft junk-shop
paint-and-plaster medieval jumble

of pain-worship and death-symbol,
that is why, I suppose, the Dream

deftly stage-managed the bare, clean
early colonial interior,

without stained-glass, picture,
image or colour,

for now it appears obvious
that *Amen* is our Christos.

[19]

He might even be the authentic Jew
stepped out from Velasquez;

those eye-lids in the Velasquez
are lowered over eyes

that open, would daze, bewilder
and stun us with the old sense of guilt

and fear, but the terror of those eyes
veiled in their agony is over;

I assure you that the eyes
of Velasquez' crucified

now look straight at you,
and they are amber and they are fire.

[20]

Now it appears very clear
that the Holy Ghost,

childhood's mysterious enigma,
is the Dream;

that way of inspiration
is always open,

and open to everyone;
it acts as go-between, interpreter,

it explains symbols of the past
in to-day's imagery,

it merges the distant future
with most distant antiquity,

states economically
in a simple dream-equation

the most profound philosophy,
discloses the alchemist's secret

and follows the Mage
in the desert.

[21]

Splintered the crystal of identity,
shattered the vessel of integrity,

till the Lord *Amen*,
paw-er of the ground,

bearer of the curled horns,
bellows from the horizon:

here am I, Amen-Ra,
Amen, Aries, the Ram;

time, time for you to begin a new spiral,
see—I toss you into the star-whirlpool;

till pitying, pitying,
snuffing the ground,

here am I, Amen-Ra whispers,
Amen, Aries, the Ram,

be cocoon, smothered in wool,
be Lamb, mothered again.

[22]

Now my right hand,
now my left hand

clutch your curled fleece;
take me home, take me home,

my voice wails from the ground;
take me home, Father:

pale as the worm in the grass,
yet I am a spark

struck by your hoof from a rock:
Amen, you are so warm,

hide me in your fleece,
crop me up with the new-grass;

let your teeth devour me,
let me be warm in your belly,

the sun-disk,
the re-born Sun.

[23]

Take me home
where canals

flow
between iris-banks:

where the heron
has her nest:

where the mantis
prays on the river-reed:

where the grasshopper says
Amen, Amen, Amen.

[24]

Or anywhere
where stars blaze through clear air,

where we may greet individually,
Sirius, Vega, Arcturus,

where these separate entities
are intimately concerned with us,

where each, with its particular attribute,
may be invoked

with accurate charm, spell, prayer,
which will reveal unquestionably,

whatever healing or inspirational essence
is necessary for whatever particular ill

the inquiring soul is heir to:
O stars, little jars of that indisputable

and absolute Healer, Apothecary,
wrought, faceted, jewelled

boxes, very precious, to hold further
unguent, myrrh, incense:

jasper, beryl, sapphire
that, as we draw them nearer

by prayer, spell,
litany, incantation,

will reveal their individual fragrance,
personal magnetic influence,

become, as they once were,
personified messengers,

healers, helpers
of the One, *Amen*, All-father.

[25]

Amen,
only just now,

my heart-shell
breaks open,

though long ago, the phoenix,
your *bennu* bird

dropped a grain,
as of scalding wax;

there was fragrance, burnt incense,
myrtle, aloes, cedar;

the Kingdom is a Tree
whose roots bind the heart-husk

529

to earth,
after the ultimate grain,

lodged in the heart-core,
has taken its nourishment.

[26]

What fruit is our store,
what flower?

what savour do we possess,
what particular healing-of-the-nations

is our leaf? is it balsomodendron,
herb-basil, or is ours

the spear and leaf-spire
of the palm?

are we born from island or oasis
or do we stand

fruit-less on the field-edge,
to spread

shade to the wheat-gatherers
in the noon-heat?

[27]

Is ours lotus-tree
from the lotus-grove,

magnolia's heavy, heady, sleepy
dream?

or pomegranate
whose name decorates sonnets,

but either acid or over-ripe,
perfect only for the moment?

of all the flowering of the wood,
are we wild-almond, winter-cherry?

or are we pine or fir,
sentinel, solitary?

or cypress,
arbutus-fragrant?

[28]

O Heart, small urn
of porphyry, agate or cornelian,

how imperceptibly the grain fell
between a heart-beat of pleasure

and a heart-beat of pain;
I do not know how it came

nor how long it had lain there,
nor can I say

how it escaped tempest
of passion and malice,

nor why it was not washed away
in flood of sorrow,

or dried up in the bleak drought
of bitter thought.

[29]

Grant us strength to endure
a little longer,

now the heart's alabaster
is broken;

we would feed forever
on the amber honey-comb

of your remembered greeting,
but the old-self,

still half at-home in the world,
cries out in anger,

I am hungry, the children cry for food
and flaming stones fall on them;

our awareness leaves us defenceless;
O, for your Presence

among the fishing-nets
by the beached boats on the lake-edge;

when, in the drift of wood-smoke,
will you say again, as you said,

the baked fish is ready,
here is the bread?

[30]

I heard Scorpion whet his knife,
I feared Archer (taut his bow),

Goat's horns were threat,
would climb high? then fall low;

across the abyss
the Waterman waited,

this is the age of the new dimension,
dare, seek, seek further, dare more,

here is the alchemist's key,
it unlocks secret doors,

the present goes a step further
toward fine distillation of emotion,

the elixir of life, the philosopher's stone
is yours if you surrender

sterile logic, trivial reason;
so mind dispersed, dared occult lore,

found secret doors unlocked,
floundered, was lost in sea-depth,

sub-conscious ocean where Fish
move two-ways, devour;

when identity in the depth,
would merge with the best,

octopus or shark rise
from the sea-floor:

illusion, reversion of old values,
oneness lost, madness.

[31]

Wistfulness, exaltation,
a pure core of burning cerebration,

jottings on a margin,
indecipherable palimpsest scribbled over

with too many contradictory emotions,
search for finite definition

of the infinite, stumbling toward
vague cosmic expression,

obvious sentiment,
folder round a spiritual bank-account,

with credit-loss too starkly indicated,
a riot of unpruned imagination,

jottings of psychic numerical equations,
runes, superstitions, evasions,

invasion of the over-soul into a cup
too brittle, a jar too circumscribed,

a little too porous to contain the out-flowing
of water-about-to-be-changed-to-wine

at the wedding; barren search,
arrogance, over-confidence, pitiful reticence,

boasting, intrusion of strained
inappropriate allusion,

illusion of lost-gods, daemons;
gambler with eternity,

initiate of the secret wisdom,
bride of the kingdom,

reversion of old values,
oneness lost, madness.

[32]

Depth of the sub-conscious spews forth
too many incongruent monsters

and fixed indigestible matter
such as shell, pearl; imagery

done to death; perilous ascent,
ridiculous descent; rhyme, jingle,

534

overworked assonance, nonsense,
juxtaposition of words for words' sake,

without meaning, undefined; imposition,
deception, indecisive weather-vane;

disagreeable, inconsequent syllables,
too malleable, too brittle,

over-sensitive, under-definitive,
clash of opposites, fight of emotion

and sterile invention—
you find all this?

conditioned to the discrimination
of the colours of the lunar rainbow

and the outer layers of the feathers
of the butterfly's antennae,

we were caught up by the tornado
and deposited on no pleasant ground,

but we found the angle of incidence
equals the angle of reflection;

separated from the wandering stars
and the habits of the lordly fixed ones,

we noted that even the erratic burnt-out comet
has its peculiar orbit.

[33]

Let us measure defeat
in terms of bread and meat,

and continents
in relative extent of wheat

535

fields; let us not teach
what we have learned badly

and not profited by;
let us not concoct

healing potions for the dead,
nor invent

new colours
for blind eyes.

[34]

We have seen how the most amiable,
under physical stress,

become wolves, jackals,
mongrel curs;

we know further that hunger
may make hyenas of the best of us;

let us, therefore (though we do not forget
Love, the Creator,

her chariot and white doves),
entreat Hest,

Aset, Isis, the great enchantress,
in her attribute of Serqet,

the original great-mother,
who drove

harnessed scorpions
before her.

Let us substitute
enchantment for sentiment,

re-dedicate our gifts
to spiritual realism,

scrape a palette,
point pen or brush,

prepare papyrus or parchment,
offer incense to Thoth,

the original Ancient-of-days,
Hermes-thrice-great,

let us entreat
that he, by his tau-cross,

invoke the true-magic,
lead us back to the one-truth,

let him (Wisdom),
in the light of what went before,

illuminate what came after,
re-vivify the eternal verity,

be ye wise
as asps, scorpions, *as serpents.*

[36]

In no wise is the pillar-of-fire
that went before

different from the pillar-of-fire
that comes after;

chasm, schism in consciousness
must be bridged over;

we are each, householder,
each with a treasure;

now is the time to re-value
our secret hoard

in the light of both past and future,
for whether

coins, gems, gold
beakers, platters,

or merely
talismans, records or parchments,

explicitly, we are told,
it contains

for every scribe
which is instructed,

things new
and old.

[37]

Thou shalt have none other gods but me;
not on the sea

shall we entreat Triton or Dolphin,
not on the land

shall we lift rapt face and clasp hands
before laurel or oak-tree,

not in the sky
shall we invoke separately

Orion or Sirius
or the followers of the Bear,

not in the higher air
of Algorab, Regulus or Deneb

shall we cry
for help—or shall we?

[38]

This search for historical parallels,
research into psychic affinities,

has been done to death before,
will be done again;

no comment can alter spiritual realities
(you say) or again,

what new light can you possibly
throw upon them?

my mind (yours),
your way of thought (mine),

each has its peculiar intricate map,
threads weave over and under

the jungle-growth
of biological aptitudes,

inherited tendencies,
the intellectual effort

of the whole race,
its tide and ebb;

but my mind (yours)
has its peculiar ego-centric

personal approach
to the eternal realities,

and differs from every other
in minute particulars,

as the vein-paths on any leaf
differ from those of every other leaf

in the forest, as every snow-flake
has its particular star, coral or prism shape.

[39]

We have had too much consecration,
too little affirmation,

too much: but this, this, this
has been proved heretical,

too little: I know, I feel
the meaning that words hide;

they are anagrams, cryptograms,
little boxes, conditioned

to hatch butterflies . . .

[40]

For example:
Osiris equates O-sir-is or O-Sire-is;

Osiris,
the star Sirius,

relates resurrection myth
and resurrection reality

through the ages;
plasterer, crude mason,

not too well equipped, my thought
would cover deplorable gaps

in time, reveal the regrettable chasm,
bridge that before-and-after schism,

(*before Abraham was I am*)
uncover cankerous growths

in present-day philosophy,
in an endeavour to make ready,

as it were, the patient for the Healer;
correlate faith with faith,

recover the secret of Isis,
which is: there was One

in the beginning, Creator,
Fosterer, Begetter, the Same-forever

in the papyrus-swamp
in the Judean meadow.

[41]

Sirius:
what mystery is this?

you are seed,
corn near the sand,
enclosed in black-lead,
ploughed land.

Sirius:
what mystery is this?

you are drowned
in the river;
the spring freshets
push open the water-gates.

Sirius:
what mystery is this?

where heat breaks and cracks
the sand-waste,
you are a mist
of snow: white, little flowers.

[42]

O, Sire, is this the path?
over sedge, over dune-grass,

silently
sledge-runners pass.

O, Sire, is this the waste?
unbelievably,

sand glistens like ice,
cold, cold;

drawn to the temple gate, O, Sire,
is this union at last?

[43]

Still the walls do not fall,
I do not know why;

there is zrr-hiss,
lightning in a not-known,

unregistered dimension;
we are powerless,

dust and powder fill our lungs
our bodies blunder

through doors twisted on hinges,
and the lintels slant

cross-wise;
we walk continually

on thin air
that thickens to a blind fog,

then step swiftly aside,
for even the air

is independable,
thick where it should be fine

and tenuous
where wings separate and open,

and the ether
is heavier than the floor,

and the floor sags
like a ship floundering;

we know no rule
of procedure,

we are voyagers, discoverers
of the not-known,

the unrecorded;
we have no map;

possibly we will reach haven,
heaven.

Tribute to the Angels

To Osbert Sitwell

. . . possibly we will reach haven,
heaven.

[1]

Hermes Trismegistus
is patron of alchemists;

his province is thought,
inventive, artful and curious;

his metal is quicksilver,
his clients, orators, thieves and poets;

steal then, O orator,
plunder, O poet,

take what the old-church
found in Mithra's tomb,

candle and script and bell,
take what the new-church spat upon

and broke and shattered;
collect the fragments of the splintered glass

and of your fire and breath,
melt down and integrate,

547

re-invoke, re-create
opal, onyx, obsidian,

now scattered in the shards
men tread upon.

[2]

Your walls do not fall, he said,
because your walls are made of jasper;

but not four-square, I thought,
another shape (octahedron?)

slipped into the place
reserved by rule and rite

for the *twelve foundations,*
for the *transparent glass,*

for *no need of the sun*
nor *moon to shine;*

for the vision as we see
or have seen or imagined it

or in the past invoked
or conjured up or had conjured

by another, was usurped;
I saw the shape

which might have been of jasper,
but it was not four-square.

[3]

I John saw. I testify;
if any man shall add

548

God shall add unto him the plagues,
but he that sat upon the throne said,

I make all things new.
I John saw. I testify,

but *I make all things new,*
said He of the seven stars,

he of the seventy-times-seven
passionate, bitter wrongs,

He of the seventy-times-seven
bitter, unending wars.

[4]

Not in our time, O Lord,
the plowshare for the sword,

not in our time, the knife,
sated with life-blood and life,

to trim the barren vine;
no grape-leaf for the thorn,

no vine-flower for the crown;
not in our time, O King,

the voice to quell the re-gathering,
thundering storm.

[5]

Nay—*peace be still*—
lovest thou not Azrael,

the last and greatest, Death?
lovest not the sun,

549

the first who giveth life,
Raphael? *lovest thou me?*

lover of sand and shell,
know who withdraws the veil,

holds back the tide and shapes
shells to the wave-shapes? Gabriel:

Raphael, Gabriel, Azrael,
three of seven—what is War

to Birth, to Change, to Death?
yet he, red-fire is one of seven fires,

judgement and will of God,
God's very breath—Uriel.

[6]

Never in Rome,
so many martyrs fell;

not in Jerusalem,
never in Thebes,

so many stood and watched
chariot-wheels turning,

saw with their very eyes,
the battle of the Titans,

saw Zeus' thunderbolts in action
and how from giant hands,

the lightning shattered earth
and splintered sky, nor fled

to hide in caves,
but with unbroken will,

with unbowed head, watched
and though unaware, worshipped

and knew not that they worshipped
and that they were

that which they worshipped,
had they known the fire

of strength, endurance, anger
in their hearts,

was part of that same fire
that in a candle on a candle-stick

or in a star,
is known as one of seven,

is named among the seven Angels,
Uriel.

[7]

To Uriel, no shrine, no temple
where the red-death fell,

no image by the city-gate,
no torch to shine across the water,

no new fane in the market-place:
the lane is empty but the levelled wall

is purple as with purple spread
upon an altar,

this is the flowering of the rood,
this is the flowering of the reed,

551

where, Uriel, we pause to give
thanks that we rise again from death and live.

[8]

Now polish the crucible
and in the bowl distill

a word most bitter, *marah*,
a word bitterer still, *mar*,

sea, brine, breaker, seducer,
giver of life, giver of tears;

now polish the crucible
and set the jet of flame

under, till *marah-mar*
are melted, fuse and join

and change and alter,
mer, mere, mère, mater, Maia, Mary,

Star of the Sea,
Mother.

[9]

Bitter, bitter jewel
in the heart of the bowl,

what is your colour?
what do you offer

to us who rebel?
what were we had you loved other?

what is this mother-father
to tear at our entrails?

552

what is this unsatisfied duality
which you can not satisfy?

[10]

In the field-furrow
the rain-water

showed splintered edge
as of a broken mirror,

and in the glass
as in a polished spear,

glowed the star Hesperus,
white, far and luminous,

incandescent and near,
Venus, Aphrodite, Astarte,

star of the east,
star of the west,

Phosphorus at sun-rise,
Hesperus at sun-set.

[11]

O swiftly, re-light the flame
before the substance cool,

for suddenly we saw your name
desecrated; knaves and fools

have done you impious wrong,
Venus, for venery stands for impurity

and Venus as desire
is venereous, lascivious,

while the very root of the word shrieks
like a mandrake when foul witches pull

its stem at midnight,
and rare mandragora itself

is full, they say, of poison,
food for the witches' den.

[12]

Swiftly re-light the flame,
Aphrodite, holy name,

Astarte, hull and spar
of wrecked ships lost your star,

forgot the light at dusk,
forgot the prayer at dawn;

return, O holiest one,
Venus whose name is kin

to venerate,
venerator.

[13]

"What is the jewel colour?"
green-white, opalescent,

with under-layer of changing blue,
with rose-vein; a white agate

with a pulse uncooled that beats yet,
faint blue-violet;

it lives, it breathes,
it gives off—fragrance?

554

I do not know what it gives,
a vibration that we can not name

for there is no name for it;
my patron said, "name it";

I said, I can not name it,
there is no name;

he said,
"invent it."

[14]

I can not invent it,
I said it was agate,

I said it lived, it gave—
fragrance—was near enough

to explain that quality
for which there is no name;

I do not want to name it,
I want to watch its faint

heart-beat, pulse-beat
as it quivers, I do not want

to talk about it,
I want to minimize thought,

concentrate on it
till I shrink,

dematerialize
and am drawn into it.

15

Annael—this was another voice,
hardly a voice, a breath, a whisper,

and I remembered bell-notes,
Azrael, Gabriel, Raphael,

as when in Venice, one of the campanili
speaks and another answers,

until it seems the whole city (Venice-Venus)
will be covered with gold pollen shaken

from the bell-towers, lilies plundered
with the weight of massive bees . . .

Annael—and I remembered the sea-shell
and I remembered the empty lane

and I thought again of people,
daring the blinding rage

of the lightning, and I thought,
there is no shrine, no temple

in the city for that other, *Uriel,*
and I knew his companion,

companion of the fire-to-endure
was another fire, another candle,

was another of seven,
named among the seven Angels,

Annael,
peace of God.

[17]

So we hail them together,
one to contrast the other,

two of the seven Spirits,
set before God

as lamps on the high-altar,
for one must inexorably

take fire from the other
as spring from winter,

and surely never, never
was a spring more bountiful

than this; never, never
was a season more beautiful,

richer in leaf and colour;
tell me, in what other place

will you find the may flowering
mulberry and rose-purple?

tell me, in what other city
will you find the may-tree

so delicate, green-white, opalescent
like our jewel in the crucible?

[18]

For Uriel, no temple
but everywhere,

the outer precincts and the squares
are fragrant;

the festival opens as before
with the dove's murmuring;

for Uriel, no temple
but Love's sacred groves,

withered in Thebes and Tyre,
flower elsewhere.

[19]

We see her visible and actual,
beauty incarnate,

as no high-priest of Astoroth
could compel her

with incense
and potent spell;

we asked for no sign
but she gave a sign unto us;

sealed with the seal of death,
we thought not to entreat her

but prepared us for burial;
then she set a charred tree before us,

burnt and stricken to the heart;
was it may-tree or apple?

[20]

Invisible, indivisible Spirit,
how is it you come so near,

how is it that we dare
approach the high-altar?

we crossed the charred portico,
passed through a frame—doorless—

entered a shrine; like a ghost,
we entered a house through a wall;

then still not knowing
whether (like the wall)

we were there or not-there,
we saw the tree flowering;

it was an ordinary tree
in an old garden-square.

[21]

This is no rune nor riddle,
it is happening everywhere;

what I mean is—it is so simple
yet no trick of the pen or brush

could capture that impression;
music could do nothing with it,

nothing whatever; what I mean is—
but you have seen for yourself

that burnt-out wood crumbling . . .
you have seen for yourself.

[22]

A new sensation
is not granted to everyone,

not to everyone everywhere,
but to us here, a new sensation

strikes paralysing,
strikes dumb,

strikes the senses numb,
sets the nerves quivering;

I am sure you see
what I mean;

it was an old tree
such as we see everywhere,

anywhere here—and some barrel staves
and some bricks

and an edge of the wall
uncovered and the naked ugliness

and then . . . music? O, what I meant
by music when I said music, was—

music sets up ladders,
it makes us invisible,

it sets us apart,
it lets us escape;

but from the visible
there is no escape;

there is no escape from the spear
that pierces the heart.

[23]

We are part of it;
we admit the transubstantiation,

not God merely in bread
but God in the other-half of the tree

that looked dead—
did I bow my head?

did I weep? my eyes saw,
it was not a dream

yet it was vision,
it was a sign,

it was *the Angel which redeemed me,*
it was the Holy Ghost—

a half-burnt-out apple-tree
blossoming;

this is the flowering of the rood,
this is the flowering of the wood,

where Annael, we pause to give
thanks that we rise again from death and live.

[24]

Every hour, every moment
has its specific attendant Spirit;

the clock-hand, minute by minute,
ticks round its prescribed orbit;

but this curious mechanical perfection
should not separate but relate rather,

our life, this temporary eclipse
to that other . . .

[25]

. . . of the *no need*
of the moon to shine in it,

for it was ticking minute by minute
(the clock at my bed-head,

with its dim, luminous disc)
when the Lady knocked;

I was talking casually
with friends in the other room,

when we saw the outer hall
grow lighter—then we saw where the door was,

there was no door
(this was a dream, of course),

and she was standing there,
actually, at the turn of the stair.

[26]

One of us said, how odd,
she is actually standing there,

I wonder what brought her?
another of us said,

have we some power between us,
we three together,

that acts as a sort of magnet,
that attracts the super-natural?

(yet it was all natural enough,
we agreed);

I do not know what I said
or if I said anything,

for before I had time to speak,
I realized I had been dreaming,

that I lay awake now on my bed,
that the luminous light

was the phosphorescent face
of my little clock

and the faint knocking
was the clock ticking.

[27]

And yet in some very subtle way,
she was there more than ever,

as if she had miraculously
related herself to time here,

which is no easy trick, difficult
even for the experienced stranger,

of whom we must *be not forgetful*
for *some have entertained angels unawares.*

[28]

I had been thinking of Gabriel,
of the moon-cycle, of the moon-shell,

of the moon-crescent
and the moon at full:

I had been thinking of Gabriel,
the moon-regent, the Angel,

and I had intended to recall him
in the sequence of candle and fire

and the law of the seven;
I had not forgotten

his special attribute
of annunciator; I had thought

to address him as I had the others,
Uriel, Annael;

how could I imagine
the Lady herself would come instead?

[29]

We have seen her
the world over,

Our Lady of the Goldfinch,
Our Lady of the Candelabra,

Our Lady of the Pomegranate,
Our Lady of the Chair;

we have seen her, an empress,
magnificent in pomp and grace,

and we have seen her
with a single flower

or a cluster of garden-pinks
in a glass beside her;

we have seen her snood
drawn over her hair,

or her face set in profile
with the blue hood and stars;

we have seen her head bowed down
with the weight of a domed crown,

or we have seen her, a wisp of a girl
trapped in a golden halo;

we have seen her with arrow, with doves
and a heart like a valentine;

we have seen her in fine silks imported
from all over the Levant,

and hung with pearls brought
from the city of Constantine;

we have seen her sleeve
of every imaginable shade

of damask and figured brocade;
it is true,

the painters did very well by her;
it is true, they missed never a line

of the suave turn of the head
or subtle shade of lowered eye-lid

or eye-lids half-raised; you find
her everywhere (or did find),

in cathedral, museum, cloister,
at the turn of the palace stair.

[30]

We see her hand in her lap,
smoothing the apple-green

or the apple-russet silk;
we see her hand at her throat,

fingering a talisman
brought by a crusader from Jerusalem;

we see her hand unknot a Syrian veil
or lay down a Venetian shawl

on a polished table that reflects
half a miniature broken column;

we see her stare past a mirror
through an open window,

where boat follows slow boat on the lagoon;
there are white flowers on the water.

[31]

But none of these, none of these
suggest her as I saw her,

though we approach possibly
something of her cool beneficence

in the gracious friendliness
of the marble sea-maids in Venice,

who climb the altar-stair
at *Santa Maria dei Miracoli*,

or we acclaim her in the name
of another in Vienna,

Maria von dem Schnee,
Our Lady of the Snow.

[32]

For I can say truthfully,
her veils were *white as snow,*

*so as no fuller on earth
can white them;* I can say

she looked beautiful, she looked lovely,
she was *clothed with a garment*

566

down to the foot, but it was not
girt about with a golden girdle,

there was no gold, no colour,
there was no gleam in the stuff

nor shadow of hem and seam,
as it fell to the floor; she bore

none of her usual attributes;
the Child was not with her.

[33]

Hermes took his attribute
of Leader-of-the-dead from Thoth

and the T-cross becomes caduceus;
the old-church makes its invocation

to Saint Michael and Our Lady
at the death-bed; Hermes Trismegistus

spears, with Saint Michael,
the darkness of ignorance,

casts the Old Dragon
into the abyss.

[34]

So Saint Michael,
regent of the planet Mercury,

is not absent
when we summon the other Angels,

another candle appears
on the high-altar,

it burns with a potent flame
but quivers

and quickens and darkens
and quickens again;

remember, it was Thoth
with a feather

who weighed the souls
of the dead.

[35]

So she must have been pleased with us,
who did not forgo our heritage

at the grave-edge;
she must have been pleased

with the straggling company of the brush and quill
who did not deny their birthright;

she must have been pleased with us,
for she looked so kindly at us

under her drift of veils,
and she carried a book.

[36]

Ah (you say), this is Holy Wisdom,
Santa Sophia, the SS of the *Sanctus Spiritus*,

so by facile reasoning, logically
the incarnate symbol of the Holy Ghost;

your Holy Ghost was an apple-tree
smouldering—or rather now bourgeoning

with flowers; the fruit of the Tree?
this is the new Eve who comes

clearly to return, to retrieve
what she lost the race,

given over to sin, to death;
she brings the Book of Life, obviously.

[37]

This is a symbol of beauty (you continue),
she is Our Lady universally,

I see her as you project her,
not out of place

flanked by Corinthian capitals,
or in a Coptic nave,

or frozen above the centre door
of a Gothic cathedral;

you have done very well by her
(to repeat your own phrase),

you have carved her tall and unmistakable,
a hieratic figure, the veiled Goddess,

whether of the seven delights,
whether of the seven spear-points.

[38]

O yes—you understand, I say,
this is all most satisfactory,

but she wasn't hieratic, she wasn't frozen,
she wasn't very tall;

she is the Vestal
from the days of Numa,

she carries over the cult
of the *Bona Dea,*

she carries a book but it is not
the tome of the ancient wisdom,

the pages, I imagine, are the blank pages
of the unwritten volume of the new;

all you say, is implicit,
all that and much more;

but she is not shut up in a cave
like a Sibyl; she is not

imprisoned in leaden bars
in a coloured window;

she is Psyche, the butterfly,
out of the cocoon.

[39]

But nearer than Guardian Angel
or good Daemon,

she is the counter-coin-side
of primitive terror;

she is not-fear, she is not-war,
but she is no symbolic figure

of peace, charity, chastity, goodness,
faith, hope, reward;

she is not Justice with eyes
blindfolded like Love's;

I grant you the dove's symbolic purity,
I grant you her face was innocent

and immaculate and her veils
like the Lamb's Bride,

but the Lamb was not with her,
either as Bridegroom or Child;

her attention is undivided,
we are her bridegroom and lamb;

her book is our book; written
or unwritten, its pages will reveal

a tale of a Fisherman,
a tale of a jar or jars,

the same—different—the same attributes,
different yet the same as before.

[40]

This is no rune nor symbol,
what I mean is—it is so simple

yet no trick of the pen or brush
could capture that impression;

what I wanted to indicate was
a new phase, a new distinction of colour;

I wanted to say, I did say
there was no sheen, no reflection,

no shadow; when I said white,
I did not mean sculptor's or painter's white,

nor porcelain; dim-white could
not suggest it, for when

571

is fresh-fallen snow (or snow
in the act of falling) dim?

yet even now, we stumble, we are lost—
what can we say?

she was not impalpable like a ghost,
she was not awe-inspiring like a Spirit,

she was not even over-whelming
like an Angel.

[41]

She carried a book, either to imply
she was one of us, with us,

or to suggest she was satisfied
with our purpose, a tribute to the Angels;

yet though the campanili spoke,
Gabriel, Azrael,

though the campanili answered,
Raphael, Uriel,

though a distant note over-water
chimed *Annael,* and *Michael*

was implicit from the beginning,
another, deep, un-named, resurging bell

answered, sounding through them all:
remember, where there was

no need of the moon to shine . . .
I saw no temple.

[42]

Some call that deep-deep bell
Zadkiel, the righteousness of God,

he is regent of Jupiter
or Zeus-pater or Theus-pater,

Theus, God; God-the-father, father-god
or the Angel god-father,

himself, heaven yet at home in a star
whose colour is amethyst,

whose candle burns deep-violet
with the others.

[43]

And the point in the spectrum
where all lights become one,

is white and white is not no-colour,
as we were told as children,

but all-colour;
where the flames mingle

and the wings meet, when we gain
the arc of perfection,

we are satisfied, we are happy,
we begin again;

I John saw. I testify
to rainbow feathers, to the span of heaven

and walls of colour,
the colonnades of jasper;

but when the jewel
melts in the crucible,

we find not ashes, not ash-of-rose,
not a tall vase and a staff of lilies,

not *vas spirituale*,
not *rosa mystica* even,

but a cluster of garden-pinks
or a face like a Christmas-rose.

This is the flowering of the rod,
this is the flowering of the burnt-out wood,

where, Zadkiel, we pause to give
thanks that we rise again from death and live.

London
May 17–31, 1944.

The Flowering of the Rod

To Norman Holmes Pearson

. . . pause to give
thanks that we rise again from death and live.

[1]

O the beautiful garment,
the beautiful raiment—

do not think of His face
or even His hands,

do not think how we will stand
before Him;

remember the snow
on Hermon;

do not look below
where the blue gentian

reflects geometric pattern
in the ice-floe;

do not be beguiled
by the geometry of perfection

for even now,
the terrible banner

darkens the bridge-head;
we have shown

that we could stand;
we have withstood

the anger, frustration,
bitter fire of destruction;

leave the smouldering cities below
(we have done all we could),

we have given until we have no more to give;
alas, it was pity, rather than love, we gave;

now having given all, let us leave all;
above all, let us leave pity

and mount higher
to love—resurrection.

[2]

I go where I love and where I am loved,
into the snow;

I go to the things I love
with no thought of duty or pity;

I go where I belong, inexorably,
as the rain that has lain long

in the furrow; I have given
or would have given

life to the grain;
but if it will not grow or ripen

with the rain of beauty,
the rain will return to the cloud;

578

the harvester sharpens his steel on the stone;
but this is not our field,

we have not sown this;
pitiless, pitiless, let us leave

The-place-of-a-skull
to those who have fashioned it.

[3]

In resurrection, there is confusion
if we start to argue; if we stand and stare,

we do not know where to go;
in resurrection, there is simple affirmation,

but do not delay to round up the others,
up and down the street; your going

in a moment like this, is the best proof
that you know the way;

does the first wild-goose stop to explain
to the others? no—he is off;

they follow or not
that is their affair;

does the first wild-goose care
whether the others follow or not?

I don't think so—he is so happy to be off—
he knows where he is going;

so we must be drawn or we must fly,
like the snow-geese of the Arctic circle,

to the Carolinas or to Florida,
or like those migratory flocks

who still (they say) hover
over the lost island, Atlantis;

seeking what we once knew,
we know ultimately we will find

happiness; *to-day shalt thou be
with me in Paradise.*

[4]

Blue-geese, white-geese, you may say,
yes, I know this duality, this double nostalgia;

I know the insatiable longing
in winter, for palm-shadow

and sand and burnt sea-drift;
but in the summer, as I watch

the wave till its edge of foam
touches the hot sand and instantly

vanishes like snow on the equator,
I would cry out, stay, stay;

then I remember delicate enduring frost
and its mid-winter dawn-pattern;

in the hot noon-sun, I think of the grey
opalescent winter-dawn; as the wave

burns on the shingle, I think,
you are less beautiful than frost;

but it is also true that I pray,
O, give me burning blue

and brittle burnt sea-weed
above the tide-line,

as I stand, still unsatisfied,
under the long shadow-on-snow of the pine.

[5]

Satisfied, unsatisfied,
satiated or numb with hunger,

this is the eternal urge,
this is the despair, the desire to equilibrate

the eternal variant;
you understand that insistent calling,

that demand of a given moment,
the will to enjoy, the will to live,

not merely the will to endure,
the will to flight, the will to achievement,

the will to rest after long flight;
but who knows the desperate urge

of those others—actual or perhaps now
mythical birds—who seek but find no rest

till they drop from the highest point of the spiral
or fall from the innermost centre of the ever-narrowing
       circle?

for they remember, they remember, as they sway and
       hover,
what once was—they remember, they remember—

they will not swerve—they have known bliss,
the fruit that satisfies—they have come back—

what if the islands are lost? what if the waters
cover the Hesperides? they would rather remember—

remember the golden apple-trees;
O, do not pity them, as you watch them drop one by
one,

for they fall exhausted, numb, blind
but in certain ecstasy,

for theirs is the hunger
for Paradise.

[6]

So I would rather drown, remembering—
than bask on tropic atolls

in the coral-seas; I would rather drown,
remembering—than rest on pine or fir-branch

where great stars pour down
their generating strength, Arcturus

or the sapphires of the Northern Crown;
I would rather beat in the wind, crying to these others:

yours is the more foolish circling,
yours is the senseless wheeling

round and round—yours has no reason—
I am seeking heaven;

yours has no vision,
I see what is beneath me, what is above me,

what men say is-not—I remember,
I remember, I remember—you have forgot:

you think, even before it is half-over,
that your cycle is at an end,

but you repeat your foolish circling—again, again,
        again;
again, the steel sharpened on the stone;

again, the pyramid of skulls;
I gave pity to the dead,

O blasphemy, pity is a stone for bread,
only love is holy and love's ecstasy

that turns and turns and turns about one centre,
reckless, regardless, blind to reality,

that knows the Islands of the Blest are there,
for *many waters can not quench love's fire.*

[7]

Yet resurrection is a sense of direction,
resurrection is a bee-line,

straight to the horde and plunder,
the treasure, the store-room,

the honeycomb;
resurrection is remuneration,

food, shelter, fragrance
of myrrh and balm.

[8]

I am so happy,
I am the first or the last

of a flock or a swarm;
I am *full of new wine*;

I am branded with a word,
I am burnt with wood,

583

drawn from glowing ember,
not cut, not marked with steel;

I am the first or the last to renounce
iron, steel, metal;

I have gone forward,
I have gone backward,

I have gone onward from bronze and iron,
into the Golden Age.

[9]

No poetic phantasy
but a biological reality,

a fact: I am an entity
like bird, insect, plant

or sea-plant cell;
I live; I am alive;

take care, do not know me,
deny me, do not recognise me,

shun me; for this reality
is infectious—ecstasy.

[10]

It is no madness to say
you will fall, you great cities,

(now the cities lie broken);
it is not tragedy, prophecy

from a frozen Priestess,
a lonely Pythoness

who chants, who sings
in broken hexameters,

doom, doom to city-gates,
to rulers, to kingdoms;

it is simple reckoning, algebraic,
it is geometry on the wing,

not patterned, a gentian
in an ice-mirror,

yet it is, if you like, a lily
folded like a pyramid,

a flower-cone,
not a heap of skulls;

it is a lily, if you will,
each petal, a kingdom, an aeon,

and it is the seed of a lily
that having flowered,

will flower again;
it is that smallest grain,

the least of all seeds
that grows branches

where the birds rest;
it is that flowering balm,

it is heal-all,
everlasting;

it is the greatest among herbs
and becometh a tree.

[11]

He was the first that flew
(the heavenly pointer)

but not content to leave
the scattered flock,

He journeys back and forth
between the poles of heaven and earth forever;

He was the first to wing
from that sad Tree,

but having flown, the Tree of Life
bears rose from thorn

and fragrant vine,
from barren wood;

He was the first to say,
not to the chosen few,

his faithful friends,
the wise and good,

but to an outcast and a vagabond,
to-day shalt thou be with me in Paradise.

[12]

So the first—it is written,
will be the twisted or the tortured individuals,

out of line, out of step with world so-called progress;
the first to receive the promise was a thief;

the first actually to witness His life-after-death,
was an unbalanced, neurotic woman,

who was naturally reviled for having left home
and not caring for house-work . . . or was that Mary of
    Bethany?

in any case—as to this other Mary
and what she did, everyone knows,

but it is not on record
exactly where and how she found the alabaster jar;

some say she took the house-money
or the poor-box money,

some say she had nothing with her,
neither purse nor script,

no gold-piece or silver
stamped with image of Caesar.

[13]

In any case, she struck an uncanny bargain
(or so some say) with an Arab,

a stranger in the market-place;
actually, he had a little booth of a house

set to the left, back of the market
as you pass through the lower-gate;

what he had, was not for sale; he was on his way
to a coronation and a funeral—a double affair—

what he had, his priceless, unobtainable-elsewhere
    myrrh
was for the double ceremony, a funeral and a throning;

his was not ordinary myrrh and incense
and anyway, it is not for sale, he said;

he drew aside his robe in a noble manner
but the un-maidenly woman did not take the hint;

she had seen nobility herself at first hand;
nothing impressed her, it was easy to see;

she simply didn't care whether he acclaimed
or snubbed her—or worse; what are insults?

she knew how to detach herself,
another unforgivable sin,

and when stones were hurled,
she simply wasn't there;

she wasn't there and then she appeared,
not a beautiful woman really—would you say?

certainly not pretty;
what struck the Arab was that she was unpredictable;

this had never happened before—a woman—
well yes—if anyone did, he knew the world—a lady

had not taken a hint, had not sidled gracefully
at a gesture of implied dismissal

and with no apparent offence really,
out of the door.

[14]

It was easy to see that he was not an ordinary merchant;
she saw that certainly—he was an ambassador;

there was hardly anyone you could trust
with this precious merchandise,

though the jars were sealed,
the fragrance got out somehow,

588

and the rumour was bruited about,
even if you yourself managed to keep out

of the ordinary haunts of the merchants;
some said, this distillation, this attar

lasted literally forever, had so lasted—
though no one could of course, actually know

what was or was-not in those alabaster boxes
of the Princesses of the Hyksos Kings,

there were unguent jars, certainly;
but who would open them?

they had charms wrought upon them,
there were sigils and painted figures on all the jars;

no one dismantled the tombs,
that would be wickedness—but this he knew,

his own people for centuries and centuries,
had whispered the secret of the sacred processes of
    distillation;

it was never written, not even in symbols, for this they
    knew—
no secret was safe with a woman.

[15]

She said, I have heard of you;
he bowed ironically and ironically murmured,

I have not had the pleasure,
his eyes now fixed on the half-open door;

she understood; this was his second rebuff
but deliberately, she shut the door;

589

she stood with her back against it;
planted there, she flung out her arms,

a further barrier,
and her scarf slipped to the floor;

her face was very pale,
her eyes darker and larger

than many whose luminous depth
had inspired some not-inconsiderable poets;

but eyes? he had known many women—
it was her hair—un-maidenly—

It was hardly decent of her to stand there,
unveiled, in the house of a stranger.

[16]

I am Mary, she said, of a tower-town,
or once it must have been towered

for Magdala is a tower;
Magdala stands on the shore;

I am Mary, she said, of Magdala,
I am Mary, a great tower;

through my will and my power,
Mary shall be myrrh;

I am Mary—O, there are Marys a-plenty,
(though I am Mara, bitter) I shall be Mary-myrrh;

I am that myrrh-tree of the gentiles,
the heathen; there are idolaters,

even in Phrygia and Cappadocia,
who kneel before mutilated images

and burn incense to the Mother of Mutilations,
to Attis-Adonis-Tammuz and his mother who was
     myrrh;

she was a stricken woman,
having borne a son in unhallowed fashion;

she wept bitterly till some heathen god
changed her to a myrrh-tree;

I am Mary, I will weep bitterly,
bitterly . . . bitterly.

[17]

But her voice was steady and her eyes were dry,
the room was small, hardly a room,

it was an alcove or a wide cupboard
with a closed door, a shaded window;

there was hardly any light from the window
but there seemed to be light somewhere,

as of moon-light on a lost river
or a sunken stream, seen in a dream

by a parched, dying man, lost in the desert . . .
or a mirage . . . it was her hair.

[18]

He who was unquestionably
master of caravans,

stooped to the floor;
he handed her her scarf;

it was unseemly that a woman
appear disordered, dishevelled;

591

it was unseemly that a woman
appear at all.

[19]

I am Mary, the incense-flower of the incense-tree,
myself worshipping, weeping, shall be changed to myrrh;

I am Mary, though melted away,
I shall be a tower . . . she said, Sir,

I have need, not of bread nor of wine,
nor of anything that you can offer me,

and demurely, she knotted her scarf
and turned to unfasten the door.

[20]

Some say she slipped out and got away,
some say he followed her and found her,

some say he never found her
but sent a messenger after her

with the alabaster jar;
some say he himself was a Magician,

a Chaldean, not an Arab at all,
and had seen the beginning and the end,

that he was Balthasar, Melchior,
or that other of Bethlehem;

some say he was masquerading,
was an Angel in disguise

and had really arranged this meeting
to conform to the predicted pattern

which he or Balthasar or another
had computed exactly from the stars;

some say it never happened,
some say it happens over and over;

some say he was an old lover
of Mary Magdalene and the gift of the myrrh

was in recognition of an old burnt-out
yet somehow suddenly renewed infatuation;

some say he was Abraham,
some say he was God.

[21]

Anyhow, it is exactly written,
the house was filled with the odour of the ointment;

that was a little later and this was not such a small
    house
and was maybe already fragrant with boughs and
    wreaths,

for this was a banquet, a festival;
it was all very gay and there was laughter,

but Judas Iscariot turned down his mouth,
he muttered Extravagant under his breath,

for the nard though not potent,
had that subtle, indefinable essence

that lasts longer and costs more;
Judas whispered to his neighbour

and then they all began talking about the poor;
but Mary, seated on the floor,

like a child at a party, paid no attention;
she was busy; she was deftly un-weaving

the long, carefully-braided tresses
of her extraordinary hair.

[22]

But Simon the host thought,
we must draw the line somewhere;

he had seen something like this
in a heathen picture

or a carved stone-portal entrance
to a forbidden sea-temple;

they called the creature,
depicted like this,

seated on the sea-shore
or on a rock, a Siren,

a maid-of-the-sea, a mermaid;
some said, this mermaid sang

and that a Siren-song was fatal
and wrecks followed the wake of such hair;

she was not invited,
he bent to whisper

into the ear of his Guest,
I do not know her.

[23]

There was always a crowd hanging about outside
any door his Guest happened to enter;

594

he did not wish to make a scene,
he would call someone quietly to eject her;

Simon though over-wrought and excited,
had kept careful count of his guests;

things had gone excellently till now,
but this was embarrassing;

she was actually kissing His feet;
He does not understand;

they call him a Master,
but Simon questioned:

*this man if he were a prophet, would have known
who and what manner of woman this is.*

[24]

Simon did not know but Balthasar
or Melchior could have told him,

or better still, Gaspar or Kaspar,
who, they say, brought the myrrh;

Simon wished to avoid a scene
but Kaspar knew the scene was unavoidable

and already written in a star
or a configuration of stars

that rarely happens, perhaps once
in a little over two thousand years.

[25]

Simon could say, yes,
she looked like a heathen

picture or carved idol
from a forbidden sea-temple;

and Simon might have heard
that this woman from the city,

was devil-ridden or had been;
but Kaspar might call

the devils *daemons,*
and might even name the seven

under his breath, for technically
Kaspar was a heathen;

he might whisper tenderly, those names
without fear of eternal damnation,

Isis, Astarte, Cyprus
and the other four;

he might re-name them,
Ge-meter, De-meter, earth-mother

or Venus
in a star.

[26]

But it is not fair to compare
Kaspar with Simon;

this Simon is not Simon Peter, of course,
this is not Simon Zelotes, the Canaanite

nor Simon of Cyrene
nor the later Simon, the sorcerer,

this Simon is Simon, the leper;
but Simon being one of the band,

we presume was healed of his plague,
healed in body, while the other,

the un-maidenly mermaid, Mary of Magdala
was healed of soul; out of her, the Master

had cast seven devils;
but Simon, though healed of body,

was not conditioned to know
that these very devils or *daemons*,

as Kaspar would have called them,
were now unalterably part of the picture;

they had entered separately or together
the fair maid, perhaps not wantonly,

but crossing the threshold
of this not un-lovely temple,

they intended perhaps to pay homage,
even as Kaspar had done,

and Melchior
and Balthasar.

[27]

And Kaspar (for of course, the merchant was Kaspar)
did not at first know her;

she was frail and slender, wearing no bracelet
or other ornament, and with her scarf

wound round her head, draping her shoulders,
she was impersonal, not a servant

sent on an errand, but, as it were,
a confidential friend, sent by some great lady;

597

she was discretion itself
in her dark robe and head-dress;

Kaspar did not recognise her
until her scarf slipped to the floor,

and then, not only did he recognise Mary
as the stars had told (Venus in the ascendant

or Venus in conjunction with Jupiter,
or whatever he called these wandering fires),

but when he saw the light on her hair
like moonlight on a lost river,

Kaspar
remembered.

[28]

And Kaspar heard
an echo of an echo in a shell,
            in her were forgiven
            the sins of the seven
            daemons cast out of her;

and Kaspar saw as in a mirror,
another head uncovered and two crowned,

one with a plain circlet, one with a circlet of gems
which even he could not name;

and Kaspar, master of caravans,
had known splendour such as few have known,

and seen jewels cut and un-cut that altered
like water at sun-rise and sun-set,

and blood-stones and sapphires;
we need no detailed statement of Kaspar's specific
        knowledge

598

nor inventory of his own possessions,
all we need to know is that Kaspar

knew more about precious stones than any other,
more even than Balthasar;

but his heart was filled with a more exalted ecstasy
than any valuer over a new tint of rose or smoke-grey

in an Indian opal or pearl; this was Kaspar
who saw as in a mirror,

one head uncrowned and then one with a plain head-
    band
and then one with a circlet of gems of an inimitable
    colour;

they were blue yet verging on purple,
yet very blue; if asked to describe them,

you would say they were blue stones
of a curious square cut and set so that the light

broke as if from within; the reflecting inner facets
seemed to cast incalculable angles of light,

this blue shot with violet;
how convey what he felt?

he saw as in a mirror, clearly, O very clearly,
a circlet of square-cut stones on the head of a lady,

and what he saw made his heart so glad
that it was as if he suffered,

his heart laboured so
with his ecstasy.

It was not solely because of beauty
though there was that too,

it was discovery, discovery that exalted him
for he knew the old tradition, the old, old legend,

his father had had from his grandfather
and his grandfather from his great-grandfather (and so
    on),

was true; this was never spoken about, not even
    whispered in secret;
the legend was contained in old signs and symbols,

and only the most painful application could decipher
    them,
and only the very-few could even attempt to do this,

after boy-hood and youth dedicated
to the rigorous sessions of concentration

and study of the theme and law
of time-relation and retention of memory;

but in the end, Kaspar, too, received the title Magian
(it is translated in the Script, *Wise Man*).

[30]

As he stooped for the scarf, he saw this,
and as he straightened, in that half-second,

he saw the fleck of light
like a flaw in the third jewel

to his right, in the second circlet,
a grain, a flaw or a speck of light,

and in that point or shadow,
was the whole secret of the mystery;

literally, as his hand just did-not touch her hand,
and as she drew the scarf toward her,

the speck, fleck, grain or seed
opened like a flower.

[31]

And the flower, thus contained
in the infinitely tiny grain or seed,

opened petal by petal, a circle,
and each petal was separate

yet still held, as it were,
by some force of attraction

to its dynamic centre;
and the circle went on widening

and would go on opening
he knew, to infinity;

but before he was lost,
out-of-time completely,

he saw the Islands of the Blest,
he saw the Hesperides,

he saw the circles and circles of islands
about the lost centre-island, Atlantis;

he saw what the sacrosanct legend
said still existed,

he saw the lands of the blest,
the promised lands, lost;

he, in that half-second, saw
the whole scope and plan

of our and his civilization on this,
his and our earth, before Adam.

[32]

And he saw it all as if enlarged under a sun-glass;
he saw it all in minute detail,

the cliffs, the wharves, the citadel,
he saw the ships and the sea-roads crossing

and all the rivers and bridges and dwelling-houses
and the terraces and the built-up inner gardens;

he saw the many pillars and the Hearth-stone
and the very fire on the Great-hearth,

and through it, there was a sound as of many waters,
rivers flowing and fountains and sea-waves washing the
        sea-rocks,

and though it was all on a very grand scale,
yet it was small and intimate,

Paradise
before Eve . . .

[33]

And he heard, as it were, the echo
of an echo in a shell,

words neither sung nor chanted
but stressed rhythmically;

the echoed syllables of this spell
conformed to the sound

602

of no word he had ever heard spoken,
and Kaspar was a great wanderer,

a renowned traveller;
but he understood the words

though the sound was other
than our ears are attuned to,

the tone was different
yet he understood it;

it translated itself
as it transmuted its message

through spiral upon spiral of the shell
of memory that yet connects us

with the drowned cities of pre-history;
Kaspar understood and his brain translated:

*Lilith born before Eve
and one born before Lilith,
and Eve; we three are forgiven,
we are three of the seven
daemons cast out of her.*

[34]

Then as he dropped his arm
in the second half-second,

his mind prompted him,
even as if his mind

must sharply differentiate,
clearly define the boundaries of beauty;

hedges and fences and fortresses
must defend the innermost secret,

even the hedges and fortresses of the mind;
so his mind thought,

though his spirit was elsewhere
and his body functioned, though himself,

he-himself was not there;
and his mind framed the thought,

the last inner defence
of a citadel, now lost,

> *it is unseemly that a woman*
> *appear disordered, dishevelled,*

> *it is unseemly that a woman*
> *appear at all.*

[35]

What he thought was the direct contradiction
of what he apprehended,

what he saw was a woman of discretion,
knotting a scarf,

and an unpredictable woman
sliding out of a door;

we do not know whether or not
he himself followed her

with the alabaster jar; all we know is,
the myrrh or the *spikenard, very costly*, was Kaspar's,

all we know is that it was all so very soon over,
the feasting, the laughter.

And the snow fell on Hermon,
the place of the Transfiguration,

and the snow fell on Hebron
where, last spring, the anemones grew,

whose scarlet and rose and red and blue,
He compared to a King's robes,

but *even Solomon,* He said,
was not arrayed like one of these;

and the snow fell on the almond-trees
and the mulberries were domed over

like a forester's hut or a shepherd's hut
on the slopes of Lebanon,

and the snow fell
silently . . . silently . . .

[37]

And as the snow fell on Hebron,
the desert blossomed as it had always done;

over-night, a million-million tiny plants
broke from the sand,

and a million-million little grass-stalks
each put out a tiny flower,

they were so small, you could hardly
visualize them separately,

so it came to be said,
snow falls on the desert;

it had happened before,
it would happen again.

[38]

And Kaspar grieved as always,
when a single twin of one of his many goats was lost—

such a tiny kid, not worth thinking about,
he was such a rich man, with numberless herds,
        cattle and sheep—

and he let the long-haired mountain-goats
return to the pasture earlier than usual,

for they chafed in their pens, sniffing the air
and the flowering-grass; and he himself watched all
        night

by his youngest white camel whose bearing was difficult,
and cherished the foal—it looked like a large white owl—

under his cloak and brought it to his tent
for shelter and warmth; that is how the legend got about

that Kaspar
was Abraham.

[39]

He was a very kind man
and he had numberless children,

but he was not Abraham come again;
he was the Magian Kaspar;

he said *I am Kaspar,*
for he had to hold on to something;

I am Kaspar, he said when a slender girl
holding a jar, asked deferentially

if she might lower it into his well;
I am Kaspar; if her head were veiled

and veiled it almost always would be,
he would remember, though never

for a moment did he quite forget
the turn of a wrist as it fastened a scarf,

the saffron-shape of the sandal,
the pleat of the robe, the fold of the garment

as Mary lifted the latch and the door half-parted,
and the door shut, and there was the flat door

at which he stared and stared,
as if the line of the wood, the rough edge

or the polished surface or plain,
were each significant, as if each scratch and mark

were hieroglyph, a parchment of incredible worth or a
    mariner's map.

[40]

And no one will ever know
whether the picture he saw clearly

as in a mirror was pre-determined
by his discipline and study

of old lore and by his innate capacity
for transcribing and translating

the difficult secret symbols,
no one will ever know how it happened

607

that in a second or a second and half a second,
he saw further, saw deeper, apprehended more

than anyone before or after him;
no one will ever know

whether it was a sort of spiritual optical-illusion,
or whether he looked down the deep deep-well

of the so-far unknown
depth of pre-history;

no one would ever know
if it could be proved mathematically

by demonstrated lines,
as an angle of light

reflected from a strand of a woman's hair,
reflected again or refracted

a certain other angle—
or perhaps it was a matter of vibration

that matched or caught an allied
or exactly opposite vibration

and created a sort of vacuum,
or rather a *point* in time—

he called it a fleck or flaw in a gem
of the crown that he saw

(or thought he saw) as in a mirror;
no one would know exactly

how it happened,
least of all Kaspar.

[41]

No one will know exactly how it came about,
but we are permitted to wonder

if it had possibly something to do
with the vow he had made—

well, it wasn't exactly a vow,
an idea, a wish, a whim, a premonition perhaps,

that premonition we all know,
this has happened before somewhere else,

or *this will happen again—where? when?*
for, as he placed his jar on the stable-floor,

he remembered old Azar . . . old Azar
had often told how, in the time of the sudden
        winter-rain,

after the memorable autumn-drought,
the trees were mortally torn,

when the sudden frost came;
but Azar died while Kaspar was still a lad,

and whether Azar's tale referred
to the year of the yield of myrrh,

distilled in this very jar,
or another—Kaspar could not remember;

but Kaspar thought, there were always two jars,
the two were always together,

why didn't I bring both?
or should I have chosen the other?

609

for Kaspar remembered old, old Azar muttering,
other days and better ways, and it was always maintained

that one jar was better than the other,
but he grumbled and shook his head,

no one can tell which is which,
now your great-grandfather is dead.

[42]

It was only a thought,
someday I will bring the other,

as he placed his jar
on the floor of the ox-stall;

Balthasar had offered the spikenard,
Melchior, the rings of gold;

they were both somewhat older than Kaspar
so he stood a little apart,

as if his gift were an after-thought,
not to be compared with theirs;

when Balthasar had pushed open the stable-door
or gate, a shepherd was standing there,

well—a sort of shepherd, an older man with a staff,
perhaps a sort of night-watchman;

as Balthasar hesitated, he said, Sir,
I am afraid there is no room at the Inn,

as if to save them the trouble of coming further,
inquiring perhaps as to bedding-down

their valuable beasts; but Balthasar
acknowledged the gentle courtesy of the man

610

and passed on; and Balthasar entered the ox-stall,
and Balthasar touched his forehead and his breast,

as he did at the High Priest's side
before the Holy-Presence-Manifest;

and Balthasar spoke the Great Word,
and Balthasar bowed, as if the weight of this honour

bent him down, as if over-come
by this overwhelming Grace,

and Balthasar stood aside
and Melchior took his place.

And Melchior made gesture with his hands
as if in a dance or play,

to show without speaking, his unworthiness,
to indicate that this, his gift, was symbolic,

worthless in itself (those weighty rings of gold),
and Melchior bent and kissed the earth, speechless,

for this was the ritual
of the second order of priests.

And Kaspar stood a little to one side
like an unimportant altar-servant,

and placed his gift
a little apart from the rest,

to show by inference
its unimportance in comparison;

and Kaspar stood,
he inclined his head only slightly,

as if to show,
out of respect to the others,

these older, exceedingly honoured ones,
that his part in this ritual

was almost negligible,
for the others had bowed low.

[43]

But she spoke so he looked at her,
she was shy and simple and young;

she said, Sir, it is a most beautiful fragrance,
as of all flowering things together;

but Kaspar knew the seal of the jar was unbroken.
he did not know whether she knew

the fragrance came from the bundle of myrrh
she held in her arms.

London
December 18–31, 1944.

Notes

Introduction

1. *Bid me to Live (A Madrigal)* (New York: Grove Press, 1960), p. 97. Reissued by Black Swan Books, Redding Ridge, Conn., 1983, with a memoir by Perdita Schaffner and an essay by John Walsh.

2. *Borderline: A Pool Film with Paul Robeson* (London: Mercury Press, 1930), p. 5. Astrid and Thorne, H.D. adds, "are specifically chosen to offset another borderline couple of more dominant integrity"—Pete and Adah (played by Paul and Eslanda Robeson), who "dwell on the cosmic racial borderline."

3. Ezra Pound, *Literary Essays*, ed. T. S. Eliot (Norfolk, Conn.: New Directions, 1954), pp. 3–4.

4. William Carlos Williams, *Autobiography* (New York: Random House, 1951 and New York: New Directions, 1967), p. 69.

5. I quote the translation by Edward Storer, which would have been well known to both H.D. and Aldington: Storer's translations from Sappho formed number 2 in *The Poets' Translation Series* published by *The Egoist*, 1916. Aldington's version of Anyte of Tegea was number 1 in this series; H.D.'s version of the choruses from *Iphigeneia* was number 3. In her numbering of the Sappho fragments H.D. is following the then standard arrangement of T. Bergk (*Poetae Lyrici Graeci*, 3 vols., Leipzig, 1882). H.D.'s "Fragment 41" is fragment 131 in the new Loeb Library edition, *Greek Lyric*, ed. David A. Campbell, vol. 1 (London: Heinemann, 1982).

6. H.D.'s "Fragment 40" in the translation of the new Loeb edition, where it appears as fragment 130; the editor notes that this is "perhaps followed immediately by 131"—H.D.'s "Fragment 41."

7. H.D.'s "Fragment 68" in the translation of the new Loeb edition, where it appears as fragment 55.

8. H.D. is referring to her long story, "Narthex," which appeared in *The Second American Caravan* (New York: Macaulay, 1928), pp. 225–84; and to her trilogy of fictions, *Palimpsest* (Paris: Contact Editions and Boston: Houghton Mifflin, 1926).

9. See also H.D.'s denial in a letter to Bryher (Jan. 16, 1935), written after she had been reading Frieda Lawrence's *Not I, But the Wind*. She says she "quite liked" the book, "but O how it makes my hair stand on end, and how grateful I am to Fish that I never slept with D.H.L.; it makes my hair stand on end—his talk of men being 'morphia' to her." ("Fish" being her way of referring to

Occult Powers.) It will be evident that I am disagreeing here with the view of the relationship between Lawrence and H.D. advanced by Janice Robinson in *H.D. The Life and Work of an American Poet* (Boston: Houghton Mifflin, 1982). But one should add that not all the evidence was available to Robinson when she wrote her book; and in any case her book has performed a service by being the first to stress the importance of the relationship to H.D. It was not, I think, nearly so important to Lawrence.

10. See Paul Delany, *D. H. Lawrence's Nightmare* (New York: Basic Books, 1978), p. 333, where the names of Esther Andrews and Hilda Aldington are restored from manuscript; they were deleted when Aldous Huxley edited Lawrence's *Letters* (London: Heinemann, 1932), pp. 422–23. The complete letter, written when Lawrence and Frieda were staying in the Aldington's flat in the autumn of 1917, is printed by Janice Robinson in her book (see above), pp. 107–8.

11. *Collected Letters of D. H. Lawrence*, ed. Harry T. Moore, 2 vols. (New York: Viking, 1962), p. 505; letter of March 1917.

12. *Tribute to Freud: Writing on the Wall, Advent*, Foreword by Norman Holmes Pearson, Introduction by Kenneth Fields (Boston: Godine, 1974), p. 134.

13. For a full account of the influence of Freudian thought upon H.D. see Susan Stanford Friedman, *Psyche Reborn: The Emergence of H.D.* (Bloomington: Indiana University Press, 1981).

14. I am grateful to Susan Friedman for calling my attention to this letter.

15. See H.D.'s letter to Bryher from London, June 5, 1932. Anny Ahlers had been trained as a ballet dancer and became *prima ballerina* at the Vienna State Opera. She died in 1933 at the age of 26, apparently a suicide: the death brought forth a poignant note by H.D. in a letter to Bryher from Vienna on March 19, 1933, at the time of her consultations with Freud. It is clear from a subsequent letter that H.D. identified herself in some respects with Ahlers. See her letter to Bryher from Vienna, March 25, 1933: "papa [Freud] seems to imply that I wanted all along in [unconscious] to be an actress, and that is one reason I am never satisfied with writing. . . . But it is apparently the artistic out-let for people like us, my dance and song turn in Corfu, was final and complete indication of what I wanted. You see now, why it upset me so about Anny A. She did actually walk out of a window though I didn't quite in Corfu." H.D. refers to Ahlers "and how I heard her sing" in *Tribute to Freud* (p. 186, under the date of March 25), and says she read about her death "in my usual café picture-paper." One can be sure that the Viennese account would have stressed her role as a dancer with the State Opera. For Ahlers' career see the obituary in the London *Times*, March 15, 1933, p. 16. In the poem the Dancer is treated as though she were alive, and so she is, as a symbol in H.D.'s mind.

Except for a few corrections and additions, we have followed the text of this volume, as representing the poet's final published version of these poems. Typescripts of many of her poems, with variant readings, and frequently with manuscript revisions in the author's hand, are included in the H.D. Collection (bequest of Norman Holmes Pearson) in the Yale Collection of American Literature, Beinecke Rare Book and Manuscript Library, Yale University. Only the most important of these variants are listed or discussed in the notes that follow.

In her volume of 1925 H.D. has brought together all the poems of her early books, but she has rearranged some of them to form the two sections that lie between *Sea Garden* (1916) and *Hymen* (1921), sections where she has also included some poems previously published only in periodicals, pamphlets, or anthologies. We have added the dates for all the sections. In the following notes the symbol *CP 1925* indicates this collected volume. The symbol BL indicates the above collection in the Beinecke Library. In compiling the present volume we have been constantly assisted by the valuable bibliography, "H.D.: A Preliminary Checklist," by Jackson R. Bryer and Pamela Roblyer, published in *Contemporary Literature* 10 (Autumn 1969) 632–75.

Sea Garden, 1916

"The Gift." Entitled "The Last Gift" in *Egoist* 3 (March 1916) 35.

"Loss." Stanza 6: "with slight lift of muscle and shoulder." The reading is "life" in 1916 and 1925; changed to "lift" by H.D. in her copy of *CP 1925* (in Beinecke Library).

"Orchard." In *Poetry* 1 (Jan. 1913) 121–22, the poem is entitled "Priapus / Keeper-of-Orchards."

"Acon." In *Poetry* 3 (Feb. 1914) 165, the poem bears the epigraph: "After Johannes Baptista Amaltheus." An extract from his poem "Acon" was translated by Richard Aldington in *Latin Poems of the Renaissance, The Poets' Translation Series,* No. 4, 1916.

The God, 1913–1917

This section does not represent a published volume, but was created by H.D. to include six early poems published in *Heliodora* (1924), along with other poems that had been excluded from her previous books. They originally appeared as follows:

"The God." "Adonis." *Egoist* 4 (Jan. 1917) 2–3.

"Pygmalion." *Egoist* 4 (Feb. 1917) 21.

"Eurydice." *Egoist* 4 (May 1917) 54–55.

All four of the above also appeared as H.D.'s contribution to

Amy Lowell's *Some Imagist Poets* (Boston: Houghton Mifflin, 1917).

"Oread." *Egoist* 1 (Feb. 1914) 55. Included in *Heliodora*.

"The Pool." "Moonrise." *Poetry* 5 (March 1915) 265–67. Included in *Heliodora*.

"Orion Dead." Entitled "Incantation" in *Egoist* 1 (Feb. 1914) 55, with the subheading "Artemis over the body of Orion." Included in *Heliodora* with new title and the subheading "Artemis speaks"; the subheading is omitted in *CP 1925*.

"Hermonax." *Poetry* 3 (Feb. 1914) 164. Included in *Heliodora*.

"Sitalkas." *New Freewoman* 1 (Sept. 1913) 114. Included in *Heliodora*.

"The Tribute." *Egoist* 3 (Nov. 1916) 165–67. Also privately printed: *The Tribute and Circe* (Cleveland: The Clerk's Private Press, 1917).

Translations, 1915–1920

Again, this section does not represent a published volume, but was arranged by H.D. to bring together her early translations. In *CP 1925* the table of contents groups these under the inaccurate heading "Choruses"; we have added the present title. They originally appeared as follows:

Choruses from *Iphigeneia in Aulis*. The first two choruses appeared in *Egoist* 2 (Nov. 1915) 171–72; the complete set appeared in *The Poets' Translation Series*, No. 3, issued by *The Egoist*, London, 1916; this was also privately printed (Cleveland: The Clerk's Private Press, 1916).

Choruses from *Hippolytus*. These were added to the choruses from *Iphigeneia* in the second set of the above translation series, No. 3, 1919.

"Odyssey." This appeared in *Heliodora*; it was written in 1920, according to the BL typescript.

Hymen, 1921

The dedication appears only in the first edition.

Dedicatory poem, "They said." In the BL typescripts this is entitled "Pallas" and "Daemon."

"Thetis." H.D. published only sections I and II in *Hymen*. Sections III and IV are here added from the complete poem as it exists in a BL typescript (other typescripts contain revisions).

"Hippolytus Temporizes." BL typescript contains many revisions in the author's hand.

"Fragment 113." The line "not so—" at the beginning of the second stanza has been restored from *Hymen*; it is omitted in *CP 1925* but seems essential to the parallelism of the stanzas.

"Phaedra." BL typescript contains many revisions in the author's hand.

"She Rebukes Hippolyta." BL typescript contains many revisions in the author's hand.

"Egypt." We have restored the dedication to Poe from *Hymen*; it is omitted in *CP 1925*.

Heliodora and Other Poems, 1924

"Wash of cold river." *CP 1925* uses these opening words as a title, but in *Heliodora* the poem stands as a dedication, untitled.

"Cassandra." For a drastically different version of this poem see *Rhythmus* 2 (June/July 1923) 48–49. Three BL typescripts are heavily revised.

Red Roses for Bronze, 1931

The text of the poems is based upon this volume. A note at the beginning explains: "The *Songs for Cyprus* were originally written for the play *Hippolytus Temporizes*, and appeared in that volume."

Uncollected and Unpublished Poems, 1912–1944

In the following notes the words "Text from BL typescript" indicate that the text of the poem has been taken from a typescript in the H.D. Collection of the Beinecke Library. Otherwise the text has been taken from the published version in the periodical or pamphlet listed.

"Epigram." *Poetry* 1 (Jan. 1913) 122.

"Late Spring." *Little Review* 2 (Jan./Feb. 1916) 1.

"Amaranth." "Eros." "Envy." These three poems were published according to H.D.'s revised typescript in *Contemporary Literature* 10 (Autumn 1969) 589–601. Our text here holds to the original, uncorrected typescript, except that we have followed the revised punctuation as much superior, and we have accepted a few alterations in places that do not affect the basic meaning of the poems. For the previous appearance of parts of these three poems in *Heliodora* (1924), see the Introduction.

The typescripts suggest two stages of revision. The first, done in pencil, consists of a relatively few verbal changes, along with a careful and effective revision of the punctuation throughout. The second stage is done in ink (sometimes covering the penciled revision) and in "Amaranth" is very extensive. Among the important revisions in this poem is the substitution of the name "Aphrodite" for "Andromeda" (I, stanza 5) and the cancellation of the name "Atthis" (II, stanza 1); these alterations are made in pencil and thus appear to represent an early stage of revision which might in some respects be regarded as an improvement, since these names from Sappho would puzzle most readers. It is in any case clear throughout the poem that the goddess being addressed as "shameless and radiant" (I, stanza 3) is Aphrodite, whose attributes are also applied to Aphrodite's followers.

Since the changes in ink for section III of "Amaranth" match almost exactly the version published in *Heliodora*, it seems right to assume that all the changes in ink were made with a view toward publication, and toward a consequent masking of the poem's original impulse. This is especially clear in the inked alterations of section IV of "Amaranth," where the masculine singular pronoun is consistently changed to the plural:

> Let them go forth radiant,
> let life rise in their breasts . . .
> life is theirs if they ask it,
> life is theirs if they take it,
> let them take beauty,
> their birth-right.

These revisions fit well with the changes made in the last two lines of section III, where "for" is changed to "and," while "his" is changed to "her," thus creating a quite different situation:

> I give you my praise for this:
> the love of my lover for his mistress.
>
> I give you my praise and this:
> the love of my lover for her mistress.

The original ending attempts a magnanimous gesture toward the male lover (see Introduction). But the inked revision changes the lover to female and gives, along with praise, something the Sapphic speaker cannot really give, since she no longer possesses it— her lover's love. A further change, disguising the original biographical element, is made in section V, where the word "too" is inked out in the line *"she too is my poet."* Then, after all these revisions, H.D. decided against publishing sections IV and V of "Amaranth" and in *Heliodora* reverted to the original "his" in the final line of section III.

"Eros." The typescript contains only revisions in pencil, none of them verbal.

"Envy." The typescript contains a few verbal revisions in pencil and in ink. In section II we have followed the inked reading: "with purple in the lift of locks" because the ink has made illegible what seems to be an important alteration in pencil.

"I said." Two typescripts are simply headed "To. W. B." [Winifred Bryher]. In the apparently final typescript which here provides the text, the date is given as "(Winter 1919)" with "Winter" canceled. Published in *Southern Review* 18 (Spring 1982) 344–47.

"Helios and Athene." Text from BL typescript, dated "Athens 1920" in a penciled notation by H.D. Published in *Iowa Review* 12 (Spring / Summer 1981) 150–54, with an essay by Adalaide Morris. We include this sequence of prose epigrams because of its importance for the understanding of H.D.'s use of Greek mythology.

"Ariadne." Text from BL typescript. Part I is typed on pages numbered 65 and 66, obviously adapted from a longer work.

"The Shepherd." Text from BL typescript. Dating uncertain: stylistically the poem seems quite early.

"At Croton." *Little Review* 9 (Spring 1923) 30–31.

"Antipater of Sidon." *Adelphi* 3 (June 1925) 64.

"Gift." "Psyche." *Transition* 4 (July 1927) 105–8.

"Child Poems." Listed in this order as a group of six poems in the typescripts. "Dedication," "If your eyes had been blue," (originally entitled "Girl"), and "Grown Up" are here printed from the typescripts. "Dream," "No," and "Socratic" were published under the title "Three Child-Songs" in *Transition* 4 (July 1927) 109–14; text is taken from the periodical.

"Projector." *Close Up* 1 (July 1927) 46–51.

"Projector II." *Close Up* 1 (Oct. 1927) 35–44. "Chang" indicates a dedication to Bryher; this was one of the names used for her in their circle.

"Other Sea-Cities." Text from BL typescript. Dating uncertain. As it stands the typescript indicates stages of revision: pages 1–3 are typed on larger paper; the following pages were originally numbered 2–4, and sections 6–8 were originally numbered II–IV. In section 2 lines 3–6 and 10 are marked for deletion, but we have retained the lines. For the misplacement of this poem among the typescripts see note on "The Dancer." Published in *Yale Review* 71 (Winter 1982) 165–71.

"A Dead Priestess Speaks." Text from BL typescript. For H.D.'s projected volume under this title see Introduction. Copper Canyon Press plans to print this poem with "Priest" in 1983.

"From *Electra-Orestes.*" Text from BL typescript. Parts 1, 2, 3 appeared in *Pagany* 3 (Spring 1932) 81–84; parts 4, 5, 6, and final "Choros" appeared in *Poetry* 45 (Dec. 1934) 135–39.

"Calypso." Text from BL typescript. Part II appeared in *Poetry* 52 (June 1938) 140–43, under the title "From Episode I"; also in *Wake* 10 (1951) 73–75, under the title "Caught." Included in *H.D.: Selected Poems* (New York: Grove Press, 1957), under the title "Callypso Speaks." "Callypso" is H.D.'s spelling of the name, perhaps with allusion to the Greek "kallos": "beauty." But this spelling has no authority in Greek.

"In Our Town." Text from *Life and Letters Today* 17 (Winter 1937) 59–62. The epigraph appears only in the published text.

"Delphi." Text from BL typescript. Parts 1, 2, and 4 appeared in *Poetry* 41 (March 1933) 320–25, under the title "Apollo at Delphi." Part 2 appeared in *Nine* 2 (May 1950) 111–12, and in *Wake* 9 (1950) 20–21. Complete poem appeared in *Poetry* 140 (Jan. 1982) 223–28. Typescripts give variant titles: "Song of Sun / Choros Sequence" (in pencil); "Sun God at Delphi" (canceled); "At Delphi." A "2" before "His presence" is here omitted.

"Dodona." Text from BL typescript. Published in *Southern Review* 18 (Spring 1982) 338–43. Sections 4, 5, and 6 appear, in a quite different version, as the poem "Zeus-Provider" in "Temple of the Sun."

"Sigil." Text from BL typescript. Section X appeared in *Wake* 10 (1951) 72–73; section XI in *New Republic* 65 (Jan. 21, 1931) 265; section XIV in *Virginia Quarterly Review* 28 (Spring 1952) 209; section XV in *Poetry* 52 (June 1938) 139–40; whole sequence (VIII–XIX) in *Antaeus* 44 (Winter 1982) 37–45. Sections XI and XIV also appeared in *Selected Poems*, the first under the title "The Moon in Your Hands." Typescript shows that sections XV–XIX were originally entitled "Sequence 1, 2, 3, 4, 5."

"Priest." Text from BL typescript. For the background of this poem see H.D.'s letter to George Plank quoted in the Introduction.

"Magician." Text from *Seed* 1 (Jan. 1933) 2–6. H.D. later changed the title to "Master," with matching change at end of section 6. The text here follows the published version, to avoid confusion with her poem about Freud.

"The Dancer." The text here follows the divisions of the typescript, which differ from those in the version published in *Life and Letters Today* 13 (Sept. 1935) 84–93. In section X, stanzas 7–8, we have followed the published reading: "answer me; / you who fled your Lord and Sire," instead of the reading of the typescript: "torture me; / as you fled your Lord and Sire." In the last stanza of section X we have followed the typescript reading "deft trees," instead of the published reading "delf trees"—but with some hesitation. "Delf," sometimes spelled "delph," is an archaic or dialect noun meaning "a cavity in the earth, a pit, a ditch." In the context of "prophecies" H.D. may be playing on the term "delphic."

In the typescripts the heading "Three Poems" is written at the top of the first page of "The Dancer"; the other two poems in the group must be "The Master" and "The Poet," since these two poems are signed with the same flourish of initials, and all three are typed upon the same paper. At some point in the handling of the typescripts "The Poet" became displaced so that "Other Sea-Cities" seemed to follow as the third poem. But the nature of all the typescripts concerned makes this impossible: see the note on "Other Sea-Cities."

"The Master." Text from BL typescript. Numbering skips from VII to IX: evidently an error. Published in *Feminist Studies* 7 (Fall 1981) 407–16, with an essay in interpretation by Rachel Blau DuPlessis and Susan Stanford Friedman.

"The Poet." Text from *Life and Letters Today* 13 (Dec. 1935) 80–83. This poem and "The Dancer" were printed together in San Francisco (Five Trees Press, 1975).

"Orestes Theme." Text from *Life and Letters Today* 17 (Winter 1937) 63–65. This may be based on Strauss's *Elektra*, which H.D. saw in Vienna, as she reports in a letter to Bryher of May 24, 1933: "I was terribly over-come. . . . I was terribly upset. . . . It was something that has almost changed my life." If so, this poem is later than "Electra-Orestes."

"Two Poems for Christmas, 1937." Text from *Life and Letters Today* 17 (Winter 1937) 70–72. Reprinted by the Ārif Press (Berkeley, Calif., 1971).

"Fragments from *Temple of the Sun*." Text from *Life and Letters Today* 21 (May 1939) 51–56. For another version of the poem "Zeus-Provider" see the note on "Dodona." The "fragments" were published as *Temple of the Sun* in a pamphlet issued by the Ārif Press, Berkeley, Calif., for Christmas, 1972, with a colophon stating that the poems "were written in 1936"—information apparently obtained from Norman Holmes Pearson.

"Archer." "Scribe." Texts from BL typescripts. Published in *Virginia Quarterly Review* 28 (Spring 1952) 210. Both poems are included in *Selected Poems*, with "Archer" bearing the title "Fair the Thread."

"Body and Soul." Text from BL typescript. Published in *Yale Review* 40 (Dec. 1950) 220–22. Included in *Selected Poems* under the title "Fire, Flood, and Olive-Tree."

"Erige Cor Tuum Ad Me In Caelum." Text from BL typescript. Section I appeared in *Life and Letters Today* 65 (June 1950) 191; section II in *Nation* 185 (Aug. 31, 1957) 94, under the title "The Revelation / 'Death, violent and near.'" Sections I and II appear in *Selected Poems* with the date "September 1940" under the title. "Ecce Sponsus," which, from the numbering, seems to be the second part of this whole sequence, is dated "July, 1940" in the typescript; that dating may apply only to the second part.

"Ancient Wisdom Speaks." Text from BL typescript. The first three parts appeared in *Times Literary Supplement* (May 8, 1943) 226, with the title "Ancient Wisdom Speaks to the Mountain." Section II appeared in *Wake* 10 (1951) 73.

"R.A.F." "May 1943." "Christmas 1944." These three poems (with "May 1943" placed first) were printed in 1950 in a pamphlet with the title *What Do I Love?* and the imprint: "Privately published by The Brendin Publishing Co., Ltd. at 430 Strand, London, W.C.2." Its origin is described by H.D. in a letter to Norman Holmes Pearson on October 15, 1950: "But Bryher and Robert [Herring] had a tiny book set up, as for a Xmas card for me to send out, just before L. and L. [*Life and Letters Today*] folded up and they could put things through with the printer. I am posting you a pre-Xmas copy; it is just three poems, I think you have them, a series that I call May 1943, another I call R.A.F., the third and last,

Christmas 1944. They hardly fit into any of the Trilogy sequences, but I like them and they do very well in this tiny book that I call "What do I love?" I have left the signature out, as I will sign the copies with Xmas greetings. I have 30 copies here; I think there are 50 altogether." Our text here is taken from this pamphlet. Most of "May 1943" appeared in *Poetry* 77 (Dec. 1950) 125–34, under the title "Last Winter"; sections II, III, and VIII were omitted, and the first section was placed last.

Trilogy: The Walls Do Not Fall, Tribute to the Angels, The Flowering of the Rod

The three parts were published as separate booklets by the Oxford University Press, London and New York, in 1944, 1945, and 1946. They were later brought together as *Trilogy*, with a Foreword by Norman Holmes Pearson (New York: New Directions, 1973). The texts here follow the first editions, except that the numbering of the sections has been changed from roman to arabic. Among the typescripts we find the following sections with the heading in H.D.'s hand: "Dec. 1944. / Deleted from: / The Rod."

XXVIII.

And Kaspar heard a song,
whether siren-song and un-holy,

whether mermaid-song or part of a story
not yet written, it was in any case,

part of history, it was the mystery
or part of the mystery of beauty.

XXIX.

It seemed to him he saw the throng
gently dismissed (there was always a crowd

about Him); it seemed to him he heard
the whispered *peace*

and saw how He sat alone with Mary
in a little room;

it seemed to him the room was very still
after the shrill cry, *woe, woe—aië, aië—*

wail for Adonis, and again and again
the softly spoken

peace—I say—
peace—be still.

XXX

True I must die, but wail no more, poor Spirit,
true I must suffer for alas, they know

not yet My Father; true I must pass the gate
of death, of Hell, but wail no more,

I come to comfort you (O, soon I come),
there I will save all beauty that has been,

there I shall create all beauty that shall be,
peace Spirit of Beauty that has been,

Peace, Aphrodite, peace Astarte, peace Cyprus,
peace, be still:

    peace Cybele whose worship on the hills,
    brought many from their weary toil,

    from the stale air of teeming cities;
    I who have loved the mountains, can I fail to see

    that mountain-worship is allied to Beauty?
    peace, Cybele, the hills have known me and shall know:

peace Maia, Gaia, Kore—you have known
peace more than many, many that shall come;

your orgies were not of the sword
your hedges border paradise,

the blood you shed was of the bull and ram,
not of your fellow-man . . .

XXXI.

This was never the word of the Master,
nor can we by any process of imagination

or inspiration ever re-capture his thought;
but this is an echo from a deep-sea shell

or a whisper of an echo
as it came to Kaspar,

when he saw the light on her hair . . .
a mirage . . . or moonlight on a lost river.

Index of Titles

Acon, 31
A Dead Princess Speaks, 369
Adonis, 47
After Troy, 168
All Mountains, 288
Amaranth, 310
Ancient Wisdom Speaks, 482
Antipater of Sidon, 337
Archer, 476
Ariadne, 330
At Baia, 128
At Croton, 336
At Eleusis, 179
At Ithaca, 163

Birds in Snow, 292
Body and Soul, 477

Calliope, 286
Calypso, 388
Cassandra, 169
Centaur Song, 158
Chance, 292
Chance Meeting, 231
Charioteer, 190
Child Poems, 341
Choros Sequence, 253
Choros Translations, 223
Christmas 1944, 502
Circe, 118
Cities, 39
Cuckoo Song, 122

Dedication, 341
Delphi, 401
Demeter, 111
Dodona, 406
Dream, 345

Ecce Sponsus, 480
Egypt, 140
Electra-Orestes, 378
Envy, 319
Epigram, 309
Epigrams, 172

Epitaph, 299
Erige Cor Tuum Ad Me In
    Caelum, 479
Eros, 315
Evadne, 132
Evening, 18
Eurydice, 51

Flute Song, 168
Fragment Forty, 173
Fragment Forty-one, 181
Fragment 113, 131
Fragment Sixty-eight, 187
Fragment Thirty-six, 165

Garden, 24
Gift, 338
Grown Up, 344

Halcyon, 270
Helen, 154
Heliodora, 151
Helios, 142
Helios and Athene, 326
Hermes of the Ways, 37
Hermonax, 57
Hippolytus, 85
Hippolytus Temporizes, 121
Holy Satyr, 148
Huntress, 23
Hyacinth, 201
Hymen, 101

If Your Eyes Had Been Blue,
    342
If You Will Let Me Sing, 222
In Our Town, 396
In the Rain, 215
Ion, 206
Iphigeneia in Aulis, 71
I Said, 322

Lais, 149
Late Spring, 309
Leda, 120

Lethe, 190
Let Zeus Record, 281
Loss, 21

Magician [Master], 431
May 1943, 492
Mid-day, 10
Moonrise, 56
Myrtle Bough, 245

Night, 33
No, 346
Nossis, 155

Odyssey, 93
Orchard, 28
Oread, 55
Orestes Theme, 466
Orion Dead, 56
Other Sea-Cities, 359

Pear Tree, 39
Phaedra, 135
Prayer, 141
Priest, 419
Prisoners, 33
Projector, 349
Projector II, 353
Psyche, 339
Pursuit, 11
Pygmalion, 48

R.A.F., 485
Red Roses for Bronze, 211

Scribe, 476
Sea-Choros, 237
Sea Gods, 29
Sea Heroes, 129
Sea Iris, 36
Sea Lily, 14
Sea Poppies, 21
Sea Rose, 5
Sea Violet, 25
*She Contrasts with Herself
  Hippolyta*, 136
Sheltered Garden, 19

She Rebukes Hippolyta, 138
Sigil, 294, 411
Simaetha, 115
Sitalkas, 58
Socratic, 347
Song, 133
Songs from Cyprus, 277
Star by Day, 469
Storm, 36

Telesila, 184
Temple of the Sun, 471
The Cliff Temple, 26
The Contest, 12
The Dancer, 440
The Flowering of the Rod, 575
The Gift, 15
The God, 45
The Helmsman, 5
The Islands, 124
The Look-out, 197
The Master, 451
The Mysteries, 300
The Poet, 461
The Pool, 56
The Shepherd, 335
The Shrine, 7
Thetis, 116, 159
The Tribute, 59
The Walls Do Not Fall, 507
The Wind Sleepers, 15
They said, 101
Toward the Piraeus, 175
Trance, 244
Tribute to the Angels, 545
Triplex, 291
*Two Poems for Christmas,
  1937*, 469

Wash of cold river, 147
We Two, 164
When I Am a Cup, 294
White Rose, 284
White World, 134
Why Have You Sought?, 133
Wine Bowl, 241
Wooden Animal, 470

Index of First Lines

Ah, bird, 122
All Greece hates, 154
Amber husk, 21
Am I blind alas, 181, 310
An incident here and there, 509
Ardent, 338
Are you alive?, 56
Are your rocks shelter for
  ships—, 7
(Artemis speaks), 56

Bear me to Dictaeus, 31
Better the wind, the sea, the
  salt, 197
Birds from Parnassus, 206

Can flame beget white steel—,
  136
Can we believe—by an effort,
  39
Chance says, 292
Clumsy futility, drown
  yourself—, 388
Come, blunt your spear with
  us, 23
Crash on crash of the sea, 129
Cythera's pearl were dim, 339

Daemon initiate, spirit, 85
Dark, 300
Drenched with purple, 115

Each of us like you, 47
Egypt had cheated us, 140

Fall the deep curtains, 476
From the closed garden, 102

Gather for festival, 277
Give me all mountains, 288
Give me your poppies, 253
God of the people, 406
Gods of the sea, 57
Great, bright portal, 26
Ground, 294

He and I sought together, 151
He had asked for immortal
  life, 159
Helios makes all things
  right:—, 142
Hermes Trismegistus, 547
He said, I'm just out of
  hospital, 485
He was very beautiful, 451
Hymen, O Hymen king, 169

I asked of your face, 45
I came far, 440
I crossed sand-hills, 71
I envy you your chance of
  death, 187, 319
If I might take a weight of
  bronze, 211
I first tasted under Apollo's
  lips, 132
If your eyes had been blue, 342
If you will let me sing, 222
I have had enough, 19
I know not what to do, 165
I'll shake the bees, 335
I'm not here, 270
Instead of pearls—a wrought
  clasp—, 15
I said, 215, 322
I saw the first pear, 28
I say, I am quite done, 281
I should have thought, 128
"I tell you it couldn't have
  been," 345
I thought to hear him speak,
  155
It is strange that I should want,
  33
It was easy enough, 118
I was not pure, 369
I will rise, 241
I worship the greatest first—,
  121

Keep love and he wings, 173

Let her who walks in Paphos, 149
Let them not war in me, 291
Lift up your eyes on high, 479
Light takes new attribute, 349
Little scavenger away, 168

Men, fires, feasts, 111
Most holy Satyr, 148
Muse, 93

Nor skin nor hide nor fleece, 190
Not God, 466
Not honey, 131
Now I know, 401
Now that the day is done, 158
Now you are a priest, 419

O be swift—, 5
Only the priest, 190
On the paved parapet, 116
O ruthless, perilous, imperious hate, 172
O take my gift, 336
O the beautiful garment, 577
Other sea-cities have faltered, 359
Over and back, 163

Reed, 14
Re-place me in the firmament, 471
Rose, harsh rose, 5

See, 292
"See, I put them," 346
Shall I let myself be caught, 48
Silver dust, 39
Slay with your eyes, Greek, 175
So I may say, 299
So you have swept me back, 51
Squalor spreads its hideous length, 59

Take from me something, 231
The floor, 244

The golden one is gone from the banquets, 309
The hard sand breaks, 37
The light beats upon me, 10
The light passes, 18
The lonely heart, 480
The night has cut, 33
There is no man can take, 431
There is no sign-post to say, 411
There were sea-horses and mer-men, 461
The sea called—, 21
The serpent does not crouch at Athen's feet, 326
The stratosphere was once where angels were, 502
The white violet, 25
The whole white world is ours, 134
"They cut it in squares," 347
They said, 101
They say there is no hope—, 29
Think, O my soul, 135
This is his gift, 353
Thou art come at length, 58
To climb the intricate heights, 286
To love, one must slay, 378
True, the walls fell, 396

War is a fevered god, 184
Wash of cold river, 147
Was she so chaste?, 138
We can not weather all this gold, 309
We don't have to know, 469
Weed, moss-weed, 36
We flung against their gods, 168
We two are left, 164
What are the islands to me, 124
What do I care, 11
What they did, 179
When everything was over, 341
When I am a cup, 294
"When I grow up," 344

628

Where, Corinth, charm
    incarnate, are your shrines?,
    337
Where is he taking us, 315
Where the slow river, 120
Where you are, 482
Whirl up, sea—, 55
White, O white face—, 141
Whiter, 15
White rose, 284
Why have you sought the
    Greeks, Eros, 133
Why wait for Death to mow?,
    477
Wildly dissimilar, 476
Will you glimmer on the sea?,
    56

Wind of the sea, 237
Who is there, 223

You are as gold, 133
You are clear, 24
You crash over the trees, 36
You have beaten me with
    swords, 330
You may say this is no poem,
    492
Your anger charms me, 201
Your hands, 245
Your stature is modelled, 12
You think a wooden animal,
    470

New Directions Paperbooks—A Partial Listing

Walter Abish, *How German Is It.* NDP508.
Ahmed Ali, *Twilight in Delhi.* NDP782.
John Allman, *Scenarios for a Mixed Landscape.* NDP619.
Alfred Andersch, *Efraim's Book.* NDP779.
Sherwood Anderson, *Poor White.* NDP763.
Wayne Andrews, *The Surrealist Parade.* NDP689.
David Antin, *Tuning.* NDP570.
G. Apollinaire, *Selected Writings.*† NDP310.
Jimmy S. Baca, *Martín & Meditations.* NDP648.
Djuna Barnes, *Nightwood.* NDP98.
J. Barzun, *An Essay on French Verse.* NDP708
H. E. Bates, *A Month by the Lake.* NDP669.
A Party for the Girls. NDP653.
Charles Baudelaire, *Flowers of Evil.* †NDP684.
Paris Spleen. NDP294.
Bei Dao, *Old Snow.* NDP727.
Gottfried Benn, *Primal Vision.* NDP322.
Adolfo Bioy Casares, *A Russian Doll.* NDP745.
Carmel Bird, *The Bluebird Café.* NDP707.
Johannes Bobrowski, *Shadow Lands.* NDP788.
Wolfgang Borchert, *The Man Outside.* NDP319.
Jorge Luis Borges, *Labyrinths.* NDP186.
Seven Nights. NDP576.
Kay Boyle, *The Crazy Hunter.* NDP770.
Fifty Stories. NDP741.
Kamau Brathwaite, *MiddlePassages.* NDP776.
Black + Blues. NDP815.
William Bronk, *Selected Poems.* NDP816.
M. Bulgakov, *Flight & Bliss.* NDP593.
The Life of M. de Moliere. NDP601.
Frederick Busch, *Absent Friends.* NDP721.
Veza Canetti, *Yellow Street.* NDP709.
Ernesto Cardenal, *Zero Hour.* NDP502.
Anne Carson, *Glass, Irony & God.* NDP808.
Joyce Cary, *Mister Johnson.* NDP631.
Hayden Carruth, *Tell Me Again. . . .* NDP677.
Camilo José Cela, *Mazurka for Two Dead Men.* NDP789.
Louis-Ferdinand Céline,
Death on the Installment Plan. NDP330.
Journey to the End of the Night. NDP542.
René Char. *Selected Poems.* †NDP734.
Jean Cocteau, *The Holy Terrors.* NDP212.
M. Collis, *She Was a Queen.* NDP716.
Gregory Corso, *Long Live Man.* NDP127.
Herald of the Autochthonic Spirit. NDP522.
Robert Creeley, *Windows.* NDP687.
Guy Davenport, *7 Greeks.* NDP799.
Margaret Dawe, *Nissequott.* NDP775.
Osamu Dazai, *The Setting Sun.* NDP258.
No Longer Human. NDP357.
Mme. de Lafayette, *The Princess of Cleves.* NDP660.
E. Dujardin, *We'll to the Woods No More.* NDP682.
Robert Duncan, *Selected Poems.* NDP754.
Wm Empson, *7 Types of Ambiguity.* NDP204
Some Versions of Pastoral. NDP92.
S. Endo, *The Sea and the Poison.* NDP737.
Caradoc Evans, *Nothing to Pay.* NDP800.
Wm. Everson, *The Residual Years.* NDP263.
Lawrence Ferlinghetti, *A Coney Island of the Mind.* NDP74.
These Are My Rivers. NDP786.
Ronald Firbank, *Five Novels.* NDP581.
Three More Novels. NDP614.
F. Scott Fitzgerald, *The Crack-up.* NDP757.
Gustave Flaubert, *Dictionary.* NDP230.
J. Gahagan, *Did Gustav Mahler Ski?* NDP711.
Gandhi, *Gandhi on Non-Violence.* NDP197.
Gary, Romain, *Promise at Dawn.* NDP635.
W. Gerhardie, *Futility.* NDP722.
Goethe, *Faust,* Part I. NDP70.
Allen Grossman, *Philosopher's Window.* NDP807.
Martin Grzimek, *Shadowlife.* NDP705.

Guigonnat, Henri, *Daemon in Lithuania.* NDP592.
Lars Gustafsson, *The Death of a Beekeeper.* NDP523.
A Tiler's Afternoon. NDP761.
John Hawkes, *The Beetle Leg.* NDP239.
Second Skin. NDP146.
Samuel Hazo, *To Paris.* NDP512.
H. D. *Collected Poems.* NDP611.
Helen in Egypt. NDP380.
HERmione. NDP526.
Selected Poems. NDP658.
Tribute to Freud. NDP572.
Herman Hesse, *Siddhartha.* NDP65.
Susan Howe, *The Nonconformist's Memorial.* NDP755.
Vicente Huidobro, *Selected Poetry.* NDP520.
C. Isherwood, *All the Conspirators.* NDP480.
The Berlin Stories. NDP134.
Lêdo Ivo, *Snake's Nest.* NDP521.
Fleur Jaeggy, *Sweet Days of Discipline.* NDP758.
Henry James, *The Sacred Fount.* NDP790.
Gustav Janouch. *Conversations with Kafka.* NDP313.
Alfred Jarry, *Ubu Roi.* NDP105.
Robinson Jeffers, *Cawdor and Medea.* NDP293.
B. S. Johnson, *Christie Malry's. . . .* NDP600.
G. Josipovici, *In a Hotel Garden.* NDP801.
James Joyce, *Stephen Hero.* NDP133.
Franz Kafka, *Amerika.* NDP117.
Mary Karr, *The Devil's Tour.* NDP768.
Bob Kaufman, *The Ancient Rain.* NDP514.
John Keene, *Annotations.* NDP809.
H. von Kleist, *Prince Friedrich.* NDP462.
Dezsö Kosztolányi, *Anna Édes.* NDP772.
Rüdiger Kremer, *The Color of Snow.* NDP743.
M. Krleža, *On the Edge of Reason.* NDP810.
Jules Laforgue, *Moral Tales.* NDP594.
P. Lal, *Great Sanskrit Plays.* NDP142.
Tommaso Landolfi, *Gogol's Wife.* NDP155.
D. Larsen, *Stitching Porcelain.* NDP710.
James Laughlin, *Remembering W. C. Williams.* NDP811.
Lautréamont, *Maldoror.* NDP207.
Siegfried Lenz, *The German Lesson.* NDP618.
Denise Levertov, *Breathing the Water.* NDP640.
Collected Earlier Poems 1940–60 NDP475.
A Door in the Hive. NDP685.
Evening Train. NDP750.
New & Selected Essays. NDP749.
Poems 1960–1967. NDP549.
Poems 1968–1972. NDP629.
Harry Levin, *James Joyce.* NDP87.
Li Ch'ing-chao, *Complete Poems.* NDP492.
Enrique Lihn, *The Dark Room.* †NDP542.
C. Lispector, *Soulstorm.* NDP671.
The Hour of the Star. NDP733.
Garciá Lorca, *Five Plays.* NDP232.
The Public & Play Without a Title. NDP561.
Selected Poems. †NDP114.
Three Tragedies. NDP52.
Francisco G. Lorca, *In The Green Morning.* NDP610.
Michael McClure, *Simple Eyes.* NDP780.
Carson McCullers, *The Member of the Wedding.* (Playscript) NDP153.
X. de Maistre, *Voyage Around My Room.* NDP791.
Stéphane Mallarmé,† *Selected Poetry and Prose.* NDP529.
Bernadette Mayer, *A Bernadette Mayer Reader.* NDP739.
Thomas Merton, *Asian Journal.* NDP394.
New Seeds of Contemplation. NDP337.
Selected Poems. NDP85.
Thoughts on the East. NDP802.
The Way of Chuang Tzu. NDP276.
Zen and the Birds of Appetite. NDP261.
Henri Michaux, *A Barbarian in Asia.* NDP622.
Selected Writings. NDP264.
Henry Miller, *The Air-Conditioned Nightmare.* NDP302.
Aller Retour New York. NDP753.
Big Sur & The Oranges. NDP161.

For complete listing request free catalog from
New Directions, 80 Eighth Avenue, New York 10011

†Bilingual

The Colossus of Maroussi. NDP75.
A Devil in Paradise. NDP765.
Into the Heart of Life. NDP728.
The Smile at the Foot of the Ladder. NDP386.
Y. Mishima, Confessions of a Mask. NDP253.
  Death in Midsummer. NDP215.
Frédéric Mistral, The Memoirs. NDP632.
Eugenio Montale, It Depends.† NDP507.
  Selected Poems.† NDP193.
Paul Morand, Fancy Goods/Open All Night. NDP567.
Vladimir Nabokov, Nikolai Gogol. NDP78.
  Laughter in the Dark. NDP729.
  The Real Life of Sebastian Knight. NDP432.
P. Neruda, The Captain's Verses.† NDP345.
  Residence on Earth.† NDP340.
  Fully Empowered. NDP792.
New Directions in Prose & Poetry (Anthology).
  Available from #17 forward to #55.
Robert Nichols, Arrival. NDP437.
J. F. Nims, The Six-Cornered Snowflake. NDP700.
Charles Olson, Selected Writings. NDP231.
Toby Olson, The Life of Jesus. NDP417.
George Oppen, Collected Poems. NDP418.
István Örkeny, The Flower Show/
  The Toth Family. NDP536.
Wilfred Owen, Collected Poems. NDP210.
José Emilio Pacheco, Battles in the Desert. NDP637.
  Selected Poems.† NDP638.
Michael Palmer, At Passages. NDP803.
Nicanor Parra, Antipoems: New & Selected. NDP603.
Boris Pasternak, Safe Conduct. NDP77.
Kenneth Patchen, Because It Is. NDP83.
  Collected Poems. NDP284.
  Selected Poems. NDP160.
Ota Pavel, How I Came to Know Fish. NDP713.
Octavio Paz, Collected Poems. NDP719.
  Configurations.† NDP303.
  A Draft of Shadows.† NDP489.
  Selected Poems. NDP574.
  Sunstone.† NDP735.
  A Tree Within.† NDP661.
St. John Perse, Selected Poems.† NDP545.
Ezra Pound, ABC of Reading. NDP89.
  Confucius. NDP285.
  Confucius to Cummings. (Anth.) NDP126.
  Diptych Rome-London. NDP783.
  A Draft of XXX Cantos. NDP690.
  Elektra. NDP683.
  Guide to Kulchur. NDP257.
  Literary Essays. NDP250.
  Personae. NDP697.
  Selected Cantos. NDP304.
  Selected Poems. NDP66.
  The Spirit of Romance. NDP266.
Eça de Queiroz, Illustrious House of Ramires. NDP785.
Raymond Queneau, The Blue Flowers. NDP595.
  Exercises in Style. NDP513.
Mary de Rachewiltz, Ezra Pound. NDP405.
Raja Rao, Kanthapura. NDP224.
Herbert Read, The Green Child. NDP208.
P. Reverdy, Selected Poems.† NDP346.
Kenneth Rexroth, An Autobiographical Novel. NDP725.
  Classics Revisited. NDP621.
  More Classics Revisited. NDP668.
  Flower Wreath Hill. NDP724.
  100 Poems from the Chinese. NDP192.
  100 Poems from the Japanese.† NDP147.
  Selected Poems. NDP581.
  Women Poets of China. NDP528.
  Women Poets of Japan. NDP527.
Rainer Maria Rilke, Poems from
  The Book of Hours. NDP408.
  Possibility of Being. (Poems). NDP436.
  Where Silence Reigns. (Prose). NDP464.
Arthur Rimbaud. Illuminations.† NDP56.
  Season in Hell & Drunken Boat.† NDP97.
Edouard Roditi, Delights of Turkey. NDP445.

Jerome Rothenberg, Khurbn. NDP679.
  The Lorca Variations. NDP771.
Nayantara Sahgal, Rich Like Us. NDP665.
Ihara Saikaku, The Life of an Amorous Woman.
  NDP270.
St. John of the Cross, Poems.† NDP341.
William Saroyan, Fresno Stories. NDP793.
Jean-Paul Sartre, Nausea. NDP82.
  The Wall (Intimacy). NDP272.
P. D. Scott, Crossing Borders. NDP796.
  Listening to the Candle. NDP747.
Delmore Schwartz, Selected Poems. NDP241.
  In Dreams Begin Responsibilities. NDP454.
Hasan Shah, The Dancing Girl. NDP777.
K. Shiraishi, Seasons of Sacred Lust. NDP453.
Stevie Smith, Collected Poems. NDP562.
  Novel on Yellow Paper. NDP778.
  A Very Pleasant Evening. NDP804.
Gary Snyder, The Back Country. NDP249.
  Turtle Island. NDP381.
Gustaf Sobin, Breaths' Burials. NDP781.
Muriel Spark, The Comforters. NDP796.
  The Driver's Seat. NDP786.
  The Public Image. NDP767.
Enid Starkie, Rimbaud. NDP254.
Stendhal, Three Italian Chronicles. NDP704.
Antonio Tabucchi, Indian Nocturne. NDP666.
Nathaniel Tarn, Lyrics . . . Bride of God. NDP391.
Dylan Thomas, Adventures in Skin Trade. NDP183.
  A Child's Christmas in Wales. NDP812.
  Collected Poems 1934–1952. NDP316.
  Collected Stories. NDP626.
  Portrait of the Artist as a Young Dog. NDP51.
  Quite Early One Morning. NDP90.
  Under Milk Wood. NDP73.
Tian Wen: A Chinese Book of Origins. NDP624.
Uwe Timm, The Snake Tree. NDP686.
Lionel Trilling, E. M. Forster. NDP189.
Tu Fu, Selected Poems. NDP675.
N. Tucci, The Rain Came Last. NDP688.
Paul Valéry, Selected Writings.† NDP184.
Elio Vittorini, A Vittorini Omnibus. NDP366.
Rosmarie Waldrop, A Key into the Language of America.
  NDP798.
Robert Penn Warren, At Heaven's Gate. NDP588.
Eliot Weinberger, Outside Stories. NDP751.
Nathanael West, Miss Lonelyhearts &
  Day of the Locust. NDP125.
J. Wheelwright, Collected Poems. NDP544.
Tennessee Williams, Baby Doll. NDP714.
  Cat on a Hot Tin Roof. NDP398.
  Collected Stories. NDP784.
  The Glass Menagerie. NDP218.
  Hard Candy. NDP225.
  A Lovely Sunday for Creve Coeur. NDP497.
  Red Devil Battery Sign. NDP650.
  The Roman Spring of Mrs. Stone. NDP770.
  A Streetcar Named Desire. NDP501.
  Sweet Bird of Youth. NDP409.
  Twenty-Seven Wagons Full of Cotton. NDP217.
  Vieux Carre. NDP482.
William Carlos Williams, Asphodel. NDP794.
  The Autobiography. NDP223.
  Collected Poems: Vol. I. NDP730.
  Collected Poems: Vol. II. NDP731.
  The Doctor Stories. NDP585.
  Imaginations. NDP329.
  In The American Grain. NDP53.
  In The Money. NDP240.
  Paterson. NDP806.
  Pictures from Brueghel. NDP118.
  Selected Poems (new ed.). NDP602.
  White Mule. NDP226.
Wisdom Books:
  St. Francis. NDP477; Taoists. NDP509;
  Wisdom of the Desert. NDP295; Zen Masters.
  NDP415.

For complete listing request free catalog from
New Directions, 80 Eighth Avenue, New York 10011   †Bilingual